'A stalwart anti-racist and anti-apartheid campaigner.'
Doreen (Baroness) Lawrence

'From fighting for Nelson Mandela's freedom
to exposing his betrayal under Jacob Zuma, a
50 year story of constant campaigning.'
Sir Trevor McDonald, broadcaster

'Peter's gripping story and his passionate activism resonates with
me over our common (African) childhood and exile in Britain.'
Natasha Kaplinsky, broadcaster

'A tour de force over an extraordinary half
century of campaigning for justice.'
*Helen Clark, former New Zealand Prime Minister
and United Nations Development Chief*

'Talk about courage and chutzpah – this
young 'un helped topple apartheid!'
Ronnie Kasrils, former ANC underground chief and Minister

ABOUT THE AUTHOR

Peter Hain was brought up in South Africa. Forced into exile in 1966, he became a British anti-apartheid leader. Labour MP for Neath 1991–2015, he served in Tony Blair and Gordon Brown's governments for twelve years, seven of those in the Cabinet, and was appointed to the House of Lords in 2015.

A PRETORIA BOY

*The Story of South Africa's
'Public Enemy Number One'*

Peter Hain

ICON

Published in the UK and USA in 2021
by Icon Books Ltd, Omnibus Business Centre,
39–41 North Road, London N7 9DP
email: info@iconbooks.com
www.iconbooks.com

Sold in the UK, Europe and Asia
by Faber & Faber Ltd, Bloomsbury House,
74–77 Great Russell Street,
London WC1B 3DA or their agents

Distributed in the UK, Europe and Asia
by Grantham Book Services, Trent Road, Grantham NG31 7XQ

Distributed in the USA
by Publishers Group West,
1700 Fourth Street, Berkeley, CA 94710

Distributed in Canada by Publishers Group Canada,
76 Stafford Street, Unit 300
Toronto, Ontario M6J 2S1

Distributed in Australia and New Zealand
by Allen & Unwin Pty Ltd,
PO Box 8500, 83 Alexander Street, Crows Nest, NSW 2065

Distributed in India by Penguin Books India,
7th Floor, Infinity Tower – C, DLF Cyber City,
Gurgaon 122002, Haryana

ISBN: 978-178578-763-8

All photos courtesy of the author

Design and typesetting by Martine Barker
Set in Futura PT/Baskerville

Printed and bound in Great Britain
by Clays Ltd, Elcograf S.p.A.

In memory of
my inspirational South African-born parents,
Adelaine and Walter Hain

Contents

Acknowledgements

In writing this South African story, I have drawn on my previous books, notably my memoir *Outside In* (2012), published by Biteback, covering my life, including as a British MP and Cabinet minister, up until 2011; *Don't Play With Apartheid: The Background to the Stop The Seventy Tour Campaign* (1971); my parents' story, *Ad & Wal: Values, Duty and Sacrifice in Apartheid South Africa* (2014); *Mandela: His Essential Life* (2018); and *Pitch Battles: Sport, Racism and Resistance* (2021), co-authored with my close friend André Odendaal.

Many thanks to Eugene Ashton and Jeremy Boraine of Jonathan Ball Publishers and Duncan Heath of Icon Books: Eugene, nephew of Terry Ashton, my favourite teacher at Pretoria Boys High School, for his enthusiasm; and Jeremy and Duncan, with editor Alfred LeMaitre, for their skilful editorial advice. Thanks to Martine Barker, Tracey Hawthorne and George Claasen for their help in putting the book together.

My gratitude also to David Preiss and Peter Rogan, classmates at Pretoria Boys High; to Nick Binedell, Rob Davies, Christabel Gurney, Ronnie Kasrils, Martin Kingston, Sam Tate, Helen Tovey and Phil Wyatt for their help, though only I am responsible for the content.

And thanks above all to Elizabeth Haywood for her love and support, and for reading, correcting and commenting on my first draft.

Peter Hain
Cadoxton, Neath
May 2021

Introduction

'SO who do you want to win, Peter? The Springboks or England?'

The land of my childhood or the land of my adoption?

'Wales,' is my invariable reply. Wales is the land that ended up as my home for over three decades, longer than anywhere else in my life, and where, reflecting intense rugby rivalry, a local wag once quipped: 'You may not be Welsh, Peter, but at least you're not bloody English!'

That was in May 1990 when I was, against all predictions, overwhelmingly chosen by the local constituency Labour Party to become Member of Parliament (MP) for the rugby stronghold of Neath, outside Swansea. The Welsh Rugby Union was founded at the town's Castle Hotel in 1881.

The journey from boyhood in Pretoria, South Africa's seat of government, to MP for Neath and on to several of the highest roles in Britain's government, was a long one, with many ups and downs, twists and turns, triumphs and disappointments, and much danger and joy.

A happy childhood became increasingly fraught as my anti-apartheid parents, members of the non-racial Liberal Party of South Africa – Mom the secretary and Dad the chair of the Pretoria branch – were finally forced, with their four children, into exile in 1966.

Arriving in London aged 16, I had no comprehension that a little over three years later I would find myself leading an anti-apartheid campaign using the unprecedented tactic of pitch invasion against the 1969–1970 touring Springbok rugby team.

That campaign also forced the cancellation of the 1970 South African cricket tour, a seismic event that helped propel South Africa into global sporting isolation for more than 20 years, and turned me into a bête noire for white South Africans: 'Public Enemy Number One' they labelled me.

Nearly 50 years later, some even sent bittersweet emails when I used parliamentary privilege in the House of Lords to expose allegations of looting and money laundering by President Jacob Zuma and his business acolytes, the Gupta brothers: 'Congratulations and thank you, though we still hate you for stopping the Springboks,' said one; another, Marius Nieuwoudt, was typical: 'I hated you with a passion.'

'But,' I replied politely, 'the values behind fighting state corruption today are the same as fighting apartheid sports tours 50 years ago.'

❖

FOR the majority of South Africans not aware of my anti-apartheid backstory, a British 'Lord' using parliamentary privilege to suddenly expose evidence of state capture and money laundering in 2017 might have seemed quixotic.

In September 2017 I attacked Bell Pottinger, the British-based global public-relations company, and followed this with further and much more detailed revelations in the House of Lords about corruption. The outraged supporters of Jacob Zuma and the Guptas, along with some in the populist Economic Freedom Fighters (EFF), acidly remarked that I was a 'white', almost caricature 'colonial' figure.

So why *me*? The answer is straightforward. I was asked by prominent members of the ruling African National Congress (ANC) to help them combat the rampant corruption and cronyism that was destroying the country. This corruption was seemingly orchestrated by their own president, whom they were seeking to oust. Their request originated from an informal discussion over dinner organised by a mutual friend, Nick Binedell, the highly respected founder-director of the Gordon Institute of Business Science (GIBS) at the University of Pretoria. This was in late July 2017 when I was in Johannesburg teaching as a visiting professor at Wits Business School.

One of those present at this private meeting was former finance minister Pravin Gordhan. He had bravely spoken out against the cancer that had spread from the Zuma presidency right down through all levels of the government. Others present, members of the ANC's national executive, were then in the middle of a hand-to-hand battle to elect a new leader of the party. The candidacy of Deputy President Cyril Ramaphosa was pitted against the powerful Zuma machine, which had dispensed patronage for more than a decade.

I had met Pravin Gordhan some years before in London, when he was on an official government visit, but the others present were new to me, and I to them. At the start of our meal, under Nick's genial but firm chairing, our exchanges were tentative. They were feeling me out, each of us anxious about the ubiquity of the state intelligence network, which Zuma had commandeered in his own nefarious interests. Mobile phones were switched off and things gradually loosened up.

I had become increasingly aware of the scale of corruption during successive visits to South Africa, especially after I retired as an MP in 2015. But not being intimately involved in South African public life, I hadn't quite realised how deep-seated and prodigious was the reported looting by Zuma's family and the Gupta brothers – Ajay, Atul and Rajesh (Tony) – whose vast multi-billion-rand business empire spanned media, mining and computing, and had grown exponentially under Zuma's patronage.

In his dry, clinical way, Pravin spelt it out. His favoured phrase was 'join the dots': in other words, connect all the diverse components of state capture in the Zuma regime. Every government department had been penetrated by Zuma-appointed ministers and civil servants. Virtually every state agency had been similarly 'captured'. Perhaps the only exception was the Office of the Public Protector (a kind of ombudsman mandated by the Constitution), then under the direction of the formidably independent Advocate Thuli Madonsela. All of the Zuma/Gupta appointees were no doubt placed to do their masters' bidding rather than because they had the ability or expertise to perform the task in hand. And of course to clamber aboard the gravy train.

'Is there anything I can do to help?' I asked, more out of solidarity than expectation.

'Well, actually, there might be,' Pravin mused, thinking aloud. Others chipped in, one or two of them highly placed inside the state system and present because of their integrity and deep sense of betrayal at what was happening to the 'rainbow nation' that had beamed so brightly under Nelson Mandela.

Inside the country, brave journalists with the upstart online newspaper *Daily Maverick* and investigative units such as Scorpio and amaBhungane were increasingly exposing the sheer extent of state capture. But a lot of the looted money had been laundered abroad, Pravin explained, estimating as much as R7 billion (or £350 million). Although the opposition to Zuma inside the ANC was growing, support for Cyril Ramaphosa building, and civil society groups (so important in securing the demise of apartheid) agitating again, the international dimension of state capture was something they hadn't managed to get a grip on. Maybe I could assist with that, Pravin and the others suggested.

During half a century in politics – from stopping whites-only South African sports tours under apartheid to 12 years as a Labour government minister – I had always been forensically focused on trying to make a difference. I was also impatient with big rhetorical flourishes, instead preferring specific practical achievements. Could this be just such an instance?

❖

OVER the years, I had enjoyed returning regularly to South Africa, mostly on holiday. These trips included being driven four hours from East London deep into the rural former Transkei to Hobeni, home of the Donald Woods Foundation (which I chair), not that far from Nelson Mandela's birthplace at Mvezo.

In December 2015, my wife, Elizabeth, and I found ourselves back again. I had unexpectedly been given a national honour, the Grand Companion of OR Tambo in silver, for an 'excellent contribution to the liberation struggle'. It was a privilege to be present at the Presidential Guesthouse in Pretoria for the national awards ceremony – charming, dignified and moving, without any pretentiousness or pageantry, and intended to symbolise 'the new culture that informs a South African rebirth'. Presiding was the Chancellor of Orders, Dr Cassius Lubisi, a former anti-apartheid activist prominent in protests against the 1990 'rebel' English cricket tour led by Mike Gatting. Old veterans of the resistance – some of whom had suffered solitary confinement or torture – walked with difficulty on sticks to receive their awards; several awards were accepted posthumously by surviving relatives.

Like other recipients of the OR Tambo award, I was given a beautiful walking stick carved out of dark indigenous wood as 'a symbol of appreciation for the support and solidarity shown'. Entwined around it is a copper *majola* (mole snake), said in African mythology to visit babies when they are born to prepare them for successful and safe adult lives – as a friend and protector. I was also given a beautiful scroll with my name inscribed, a neck badge and a lapel rosette. Bob Hughes, former chair of the Anti-Apartheid Movement (AAM), had been a recipient in 2004, and others in the international campaign had been similarly honoured.

As the highest honour the country can bestow, the OR Tambo awards were, as always, given by the sitting president. At the time this was Jacob Zuma, and neither of us imagined then that our paths would cross again. 'I'm so pleased, so very pleased it's you,' he whispered to me on stage; at a personal level he could be quite charming. Returning to my seat, I raised my fist in an 'Amandla' salute to cheers from the audience.

And it was after that awards ceremony in Pretoria, during a brief break in Johannesburg, that Elizabeth and I were invited to dinner with the deputy vice-chancellor of the University of the Witwatersrand (Wits). I had expressed an interest in teaching, because I wanted to pass on some of the experience and expertise I had gained in a long political career, especially from being in government. That led to my appointment as a visiting professor at Wits Business School, promoted by its then academic director, Chris van der Hoven, and hence to Nick Binedell's dinner meeting with Pravin Gordhan and others.

❖

SO what exactly was it that I might do to help them? Pravin explained that plenty of the looted billions had left the country through global banks, and since the president, as an alleged direct beneficiary, had absolutely no interest in getting the money back, the only way to do so might be to put pressure on the international banking system from London.

'Okay,' I said, 'I will try to do what I can. But I cannot fire any bullets unless I am given the ammunition.' I explained that although I was still a parliamentarian, members of the House of Lords are allocated no secretarial or research staff, as MPs are. I didn't have the resources or expertise to dig up the information needed.

I still had no idea what exactly was expected of me. But several of those present offered to follow up, and before I flew back home I met privately with someone highly placed, right inside the heart of the Zuma state, who was to become my 'Deep Throat' (an echo of the Watergate scandal, which brought down President Richard Nixon) – a key source of the insider information I needed for an effective exposé.

On the day of my departure, Deep Throat presented me with a wad of material concerning the role of global banks in facilitating the suspected Zuma/Gupta money laundering of billions of rands stolen from South African taxpayers.

All fine, I explained, but I was in no position to analyse this material myself. If I were to use my Lords platform, I needed to have meticulously prepared speeches that, especially if revelatory, had to be impeccably credible and served up to me as the near-finished article. Often, I had found over the years, experts tended to be so engrossed in their own material that they found it difficult to see the wood for the trees. If I had a skill, it was to cut through all the undergrowth and get to the nub of the issue.

Deep Throat seemed to grasp this, and, in the South African vernacular, we agreed to 'make a plan'. A secure system of electronic communication would be established, and drafts of speeches or letters for me, demanding action from the UK, would be sent early enough for me to check, edit and query before time of delivery. I resolved not to tell anybody about Deep Throat, certainly not her or his identity. I still haven't, and won't – unless Deep Throat determines otherwise.

This was in early August 2017, and by then the clock was ticking. A titanic battle for the party presidency was emerging between Cyril Ramaphosa's backers – including all those to whom I had been introduced – and Jacob Zuma's anointed successor, his former wife Nkosazana Dlamini-Zuma. She was a formidable figure in her own right – a former minister of health, foreign affairs and home affairs, and the first woman to head the African

Union Commission, the executive body of the African Union, the successor to the Organization of African Unity (OAU). I had met her when I was Britain's minister for Africa in 1999–2001. And some who had known her during the anti-apartheid struggle as a brave, capable and fiercely independent woman wondered how on earth she had allowed herself to be manipulated into maintaining the evidently corrupt Zuma dynasty.

Zuma had built a political machine that had never lost an internal party fight. Despite the country's systematic economic and administrative decline, he had such an iron grip on the ANC that it was difficult to envisage how he could possibly be defeated five months later at the party's elective 54th National Conference, held in December 2017 at the Nasrec exhibition centre in Johannesburg.

Although the Ramaphosa supporters were growing in confidence, I flew back to London with no illusions that whatever I could do – and it was by no means clear then exactly *what* – would have any effect whatsoever on the outcome upon which South Africa's future rested: a choice between a remorseless collapse into a mire of degeneracy or a fightback to reclaim the high ground upon which the Nelson Mandela presidency had once stood, and for which my parents and I had fought in the anti-apartheid struggle.

As a young teenager in Pretoria in the early 1960s, I'd learnt the critical importance of absolute discretion from my parents as they increasingly became targets of the apartheid state. Once, an escaped prisoner was smuggled into our house to stay overnight before my dad drove him secretly away, evading the eyes of the Special Branch men parked at the bottom of our drive. 'Don't ever tell anybody anything about this,' my mom had exhorted me, explaining that she and Dad could be imprisoned otherwise.

People from all walks of life have trouble keeping a confidence, let alone a secret – something I discovered was a particular disease of the Westminster parliamentary bubble. My dad had a saying: 'If you don't know, you can't tell.'

Boyhood

ENCOUNTERING Pretoria's notorious Special Branch for the first time turned out to be as incongruous as it was threatening.

Very early one morning in 1960, when I was aged ten and my brother, Tom, not yet eight, we awoke to a discomforting rustling of strange figures in our bedroom in the modest house my parents rented at 1127 Arcadia Street, Pretoria. Who were they? What on earth were they doing?

Mom and Dad came in, gave us a hug, explained that they were security policemen and told us not to worry. In a vain search for 'incriminating evidence' the men had my scrapbooks, culled from Dad's weekly car magazines – I was keen on cars and motor sport. Then my sisters Jo-anne, aged five, and Sally, aged three, called out from their bedroom next door that the cupboard drawer where their panties were kept was being searched – embarrassing the officers, who knocked over the cage containing my pet white mouse, which escaped, to be pounced on and killed by the cat.

A year later, in May 1961, I was woken up after midnight. As my eyes adjusted, there was the familiar face of Nan van Reenen, a kindly middle-aged lady, anxious in the gloom: 'Peter, your parents have been jailed,' she said gently, holding my hand.

Although Mom and Dad had warned us a while back this might happen, I immediately wondered, where *were* they? Would they ever come back? What would we do? Then: mustn't panic, mustn't let my parents down, stay calm, carry on.

Nan explained how, along with fellow Liberal Party activists Maritz van den Berg and her son Colyn, they had been preparing to flypost in support of a three-day 'stay-at-home' protest called by Nelson Mandela, who was operating underground and constantly hunted by the police. It was a protest against all racial laws but proved to be the last disciplined, mass, non-violent demonstration of that era. Massive police intimidation and raids led to the detention of some 10 000 activists.

Mom and Dad had enthusiastically decided to distribute stay-at-home leaflets and put up posters in Lady Selborne township, just west of Pretoria city centre. But they had hardly arrived when a car drew up behind theirs. Two Special Branch officers, Viktor and Van Zyl (known to them), stepped out. Although stunned, Mom didn't panic, quickly chewing up and spitting out the draft of the leaflet they'd wanted to discuss with local black comrades. She jumped from the car with the posters and ran off to a nearby shop that she knew had a back entrance. But the shop was locked up for the night: the police cornered her, and Viktor pounded up to grab her and my dad.

After Nan and I checked to see that the others were still sleeping, Nan lay down on our living-room sofa, and I tried to close my eyes, worrying and wondering. Before she left in the morning, Nan and I told the others what had happened – the girls wide-eyed, Tom very quiet, holding back tears. I felt I had to look after them somehow, not thinking of myself as the young boy I was, just that I needed to do what had to be done.

Gran (on my dad's side) soon came over and moved in – though not Grandad, who (I later learnt) objected to his son's 'irresponsibility'. Our domestic worker and close friend, Eva Matjeke, quietly took charge and ensured that everything went as smoothly as possible. We walked to Hatfield Primary School, just around the corner, as usual, and one of my parents' activist friends, Anita Cohen, brought over a large meringue cake to cheer us up.

By then our telephone was tapped, Special Branch cars were constantly parked outside our gate, and Special Branch officers

2

periodically raided and searched the house. Yet somehow Mom and Dad managed to maintain a caring, close-knit family life amid all the trauma of their increasing resistance to apartheid. Life was a blend of the ordinary and the extraordinary, of excitement, stress and shock, and yet lots of family fun and togetherness too.

Dad took time to teach his boys about cricket, to come and watch us play in school teams, and to take us to club football matches and motor races. He made space to help with my home-work and to discuss my emerging interest in what they were doing in politics. Amid all the persistent political pressure and crises she faced, Mom, incredibly, was also always there for us and looked after the family home. She was the fulcrum of both their politi-cal activism and our family life, somehow balancing both. Their activism never seemed to come ahead of their children: we all felt we had the best parents in the world.

Mom and Dad would soon be out of detention, we were reassured. But time dragged and it seemed a very long two weeks before they were released. 'Gran and Eva are looking after us well but we are missing you a lot,' the letter I wrote to Mom said in clear, careful writing. I still have it.

I must have blanked out my worries and emotions – doubt-less a characteristic that was to stand me in good stead later on – because I don't recall it as being a terrible episode. But six-year-old Jo-anne was, in retrospect, reaching for comfort in wanting to feel her mother near her. She modified a petticoat she had always loved Mom wearing. It had layers of stiff net that made her skirts stick out, rather like a crinoline. There was a thin nylon section, from waist to hip before the netting, and Jo-anne cut holes in this so that she could wear the petticoat with her arms through the holes. 'You'll get into big trouble when Mom and Dad get out,' we all chided her – though she didn't.

It turned out they had been the first people to be detained with-out charge under a new '12-day law' – formally, the General Law

Amendment Act 39 of 1961 – aimed at suppressing rising political dissent by allowing for detention without trial. Dad and his two male comrades, Colyn and Maritz, shared a cell in Pretoria Local prison, where conditions were not bad. But he had no contact with Mom until they both were released – his worry about her increasing when he received a letter in prison from his employer, sacking him. What did he expect, Grandad grunted.

Generally, our teachers and friends didn't pick on us, except that a couple of years later Sally, newly at school, found her first teacher hostile, and once she was deliberately prevented from going to the toilet when she needed to, wetting her pants as a result.

Mom was held separately and alone in a large echoing hall in Pretoria Central prison, where white women detainees had been held during the 1960 state of emergency. She could hear the screams of black women prisoners being assaulted reverberating up the stairwell. Wincing in disgust, she witnessed them being deliberately humiliated by being forced to strip, the warders once leering at a pregnant woman. In the days that followed she became increasingly angry at the gratuitous nastiness of prison staff to black prisoners. She also found the wardresses creepy and intimidating, especially when they spied on her having a bath. Instead, she switched to washing in a hand basin – less comfortable, but more private.

Although Mom was reassured that our Gran would be caring for us with Eva, she worried constantly about us – never revealing her true predicament and fears until many years later. Her mood swung between guilt at how she had abandoned us and determination that she would not be cowed. She wondered briefly whether to give up: she had no doubt it had been the right thing to respond to Mandela's stay-at-home call, but her detention sharpened the constant inner tension between her maternal responsibilities and activist duties.

Prior to the new statutory 12 days' detention without charge, she and Dad were held for the maximum two days while the police searched for evidence with which to bring charges. But because Mom had secretly chewed up and spat out the one piece of incriminating evidence – a leaflet urging people to go on strike and stay at home – much as they tried, the Special Branch could not find anything on which to base a prosecution, so had to release them.

We weren't really sure what was going on, so when walking home from school with Tom and Jo-anne, it was really emotional to unexpectedly spot my dad strolling along to meet us with Sally in her favourite perch on his shoulders. Four-year-old Sally had been frightened when she first saw him because he had grown an unfamiliar beard in prison. But Jo-anne, who was especially close to our father, looked up from chatting to a school friend, had a rush of happiness and ran across the road to be scooped up for a huge hug.

It was nice having Dad around the house on weekdays. He'd been fired by the Pretoria municipality, where he'd worked as an architect, because of his anti-apartheid work. But suddenly we were struggling financially, relief only coming via a donation by an anonymous Liberal Party member. Until Dad was offered a temporary post by another party member two months later, we had to survive by living on account. I remember the understanding of shopkeepers as I signed for essential items in the chemist or grocery store – not a comfortable experience and one that made me determined to be both financially prudent and independent in my life. And not to be beaten down by anyone, ever – certainly not by our enemies.

Our life settled back to its abnormal normality as my parents soon sprang into action again.

❖

OUR experience was nothing like that of my white cousins or school friends: like 99 per cent of conventional English-speaking white South Africans, they lived almost in a different world.

Yet we had also come from their white world, and still had a substantial foot in it. My mother was born Adelaine Stocks in the seaside town of Port Alfred, in the Eastern Cape, the descendant of English and Irish 1820 Settlers. My father, Walter, born in Northdene, Durban, was the son of Scottish immigrants who had left Glasgow after the First World War. As a 19-year-old, he had been wounded in action in Italy in 1944 while serving with the Royal Natal Carbineers.[1]

I was actually born a British subject in 1950 in Nairobi, Kenya, where Dad got his first job after graduating from Wits University as an architect. But our stay there didn't last long because in 1951 he was offered a new job back in South Africa.

Showing the kind of courage and daring for which they would become renowned in the anti-apartheid struggle, my parents decided not to make the return journey by Dakota aircraft as they had done coming up to Kenya. Instead, when I was aged about 15 months, they drove their 1936 Lancia Aprilia over 4 000 kilometres through central Africa from Nairobi to Pretoria; they deliberately hadn't informed their parents, expecting disapproval. The trip was eventful, with numerous punctures, engine, steering and suspension breakdowns, and other mishaps in the African bush. But throughout they had friendly help from inquisitive locals amazed at seeing white people out on their own in the heart of Africa, as well as from white settlers in Uganda, the Belgian Congo and Northern and Southern Rhodesia.

They were delighted that I learnt to walk during the trip, though they were occasionally envious as they watched me eagerly munch up my food after they had run out of money to feed themselves. Well into the four-week journey I was apparently reluctant to leave the car, which had become 'home'. I slept on the back seat and Mom and Dad slumped on the front seats.

As I grew up, first in Pietermaritzburg and Ladysmith, and then mainly in Pretoria from 1954, our lifestyle, at least to begin with, was the conventional one of a white family of moderate means. My father worked; my mother ran the home. We were not well off, but we were able to live in a comfortable, rented detached house set in ample grounds. A black domestic worker lived separately in a room with a toilet and shower next to the garage – the usual servant's accommodation on white properties during the 1950s and 1960s.

Until I was about eight, my parents' social circle consisted largely of other middle-class white families. We would visit our white relatives and friends and they would visit us. It was a happy, carefree and secure childhood, with the weather and the space for outdoor activities. Pretoria in those days was an easy-going place, and later on my brother and I were able to roam without restriction with our friends on bicycles and also in soapbox carts we built ourselves.

Every December, the two rear bench seats of our blue Volkswagen minibus were turned into a bed for the 1 100-kilometre overnight trip to my maternal grandparents' home in Port Alfred, on the banks of the Kowie River. There we spent our Christmas holidays fishing off the jetty or enjoying long lazy days on the broad sandy beaches and swimming in the warm waters of the Indian Ocean.

❖

LIKE everyone else in South Africa, apartheid affected every nook and cranny of our daily lives, from sex to sport.

By law I had to go to a whites-only school, travel on a whites-only bus, live in a whites-only area, sit on whites-only park benches and observe my parents voting in whites-only elections. In 1959, when I was nine, I helped them deliver leaflets for a white Liberal Party candidate in a whites-only parliamentary by-election in white suburban Pretoria East.

But, unlike all my school friends and cousins, my parents schooled us in respect for our black fellow citizens. My dad's wartime experience in Italy had broadened his mind, and my mom had had an impishly questioning and rebellious outlook as a teenager. Their eyes had also been opened by the more relaxed race relations they had encountered in Kenya, and by the warm, friendly faces of the Africans they had met on that eventful drive back to Pretoria in 1951.

So, two years later, a South African friend from Kenya was on fertile ground when he recommended that they be invited to join the newly formed non-racial Liberal Party. They were both attracted by the party's policy of one-person-one-vote, regardless of race. But there was no local Liberal branch in Ladysmith, where we were living at the time and where Tom had been born. So the only way they could join was to start their own branch. And the only place to have the inaugural meeting was in our family house, having borrowed chairs from friends (some of whom were not told that blacks might sit on them). The meeting was addressed by party president Alan Paton, author of the seminal novel *Cry, the Beloved Country*.

As he turned up for the meeting, Elliot Mngadi, later the party's national treasurer, remarked, 'This is the first time I've ever come through the front door of a white man's house.' (In those days, black servants or gardeners were only allowed through the back door.) So, from a young age, I became used to blacks being in our home – not only as servants but also as equals and friends.

Years later, well after we had moved to Pretoria, where Jo-anne was born, we would visit party colleagues in the black townships that ringed the towns and cities throughout the country. Because town centres and suburbs were strictly reserved for white residents, it would have been unheard of for any of my white school friends or relatives to do this, just as they would never have considered their black compatriots as friends rather than servants.

BOYHOOD

❖

MY free-spirited parents, having always wanted to visit Britain, decided they had better do so before their three children were old enough to incur substantial travel costs.

Our car was sold to pay for the ocean-liner fare, my Dad arranged for a job in London and we embarked at sunny Cape Town docks in January 1956. Apart from being embarrassingly seasick – once all over a corridor floor while running for a basin – I found it all rather exciting. But I remember how cold and grey London felt in mid-winter. It seemed so strange, so different. No wide-open spaces, no barefoot sunshine. Instead, shoes and socks, thick clothes, coats, huddling in the house to get warm, thick hanging smog, heavy traffic, big city. And so many people: walking, talking, buzzing, thronging the pavements, everywhere and anywhere I looked.

We lived first in the West London suburb of Ealing, where I began school. Then, because the rent was much less, we moved to a tiny cowman's cottage on a farm in Ruckinge overlooking Romney Marsh, in Kent. My sister Sally was born there that Christmas of 1956, and I recall playing happily on the farm and helping with the haymaking. During one spell of very hot summer weather, we all took our bedding and slept out on the front lawn. That seemed a real adventure – especially when the milkwoman surprised us in the early morning.

Soon after they arrived in Britain, my parents discovered the liberal newspapers *The Guardian* (then still called the *Manchester Guardian*) and *The Observer*, through which they gained a much better understanding of world affairs than was possible from the parochial and conservative South African media. Great events occurred in 1956: the Suez Crisis, when the British, French and Israelis attacked Egypt, and the Soviet invasion of Hungary. These and other developments made a big impact upon them, and they joined progressive British opinion in strongly opposing both.

But they also read of the tumult in their home country. In August 1956 more than 10 000 women of all races gathered at the seat of government, the Union Buildings in Pretoria, in protest against the extension to women of the hated pass laws, which controlled the movement of blacks, who were required to carry an identity document (or 'pass') at all times. That December, 156 people – including Nelson Mandela and the entire leadership of the ANC – were arrested for high treason, the subsequent 'Treason Trial' lasting more than four years before they were acquitted. Meanwhile apartheid laws such as the Immorality Act (outlawing sexual intercourse between whites and members of any other racial group) were introduced, provoking increasing protests and boycotts.

Mom and Dad followed all these events avidly, and became concerned and restive. Late in 1957, when Dad's old architectural firm in Pretoria telephoned and asked him to return, they decided to do so, and he flew out alone in early December. We had no car, so Mom was left to pack up and travel with four small children (aged between one and seven), first by bus and train up to London, and then down to Southampton to board an ocean liner. I remember helping her shepherd the younger children, though, in retrospect how she managed I have no idea.

A fortnight later there was a hum of excited anticipation as the ship pulled into Port Elizabeth docks in the hot summer sunshine. For a seven-year-old boy it seemed an enormous drop from the deck to the quay below, where my Dad, whom we had not seen for six long weeks, waited with both sets of grandparents. Holding on to the railings, three-year-old Jo-anne sang over and over again a little song, 'Hello, My Daddy'. But I distinctly remember glimpsing the shivering sight of ugly hammerhead sharks circling the hull.

❖

WITH wide streets lined with jacaranda trees, majestically purple in flower, Pretoria in the late 1950s and 1960s was a place of white suburbs with detached homes and large gardens nicely manicured by black gardeners.

The old capital of Afrikanerdom was a bastion of apartheid, with few progressive instincts, quite unlike cosmopolitan, big-city Johannesburg. Yet a branch of the Liberal Party had become active by the time we returned to Pretoria early in 1958, and my parents explained to me that they intended to rejoin.

Their introduction was dramatic. A peaceful women's demonstration against the pass laws in Lady Selborne was broken up by baton-wielding police. Many women were injured, and feelings ran high, especially when their menfolk returned from work. The township was soon in an uproar, and the local Liberal Party chairman, John Brink, drove in to try to restrain the police.

But he failed to return. I remember feeling worried as my Dad drove out in our Volkswagen minibus to look for him. He came back soon, to our relief, but only because he had met John returning from the township, bloodied, in a windowless car that had been stoned by residents venting their fury at a white intruder, not knowing he was on their side. Brink only managed to escape when the local ANC leader, Peter Magano, recognised him and jumped onto the car bonnet to protect him.

I was just eight years old. I looked at his car, wide-eyed at the sight of blood and shattered glass. He could easily have been killed, I thought – and Dad too, trying to rescue him. What on earth was happening to us?

I recalled another recent frightening and shocking image. It was the bloodied face and clothes of a black teenager called Tatius, who had arrived at our house one day. Some white youths had taken exception to his walking along a nearby pavement playing his

11

penny whistle – even though he had stepped into the road to make way for them – and had beaten him up 'to teach him a lesson'. He arrived in tears, with billowing, bloody bruises on his face, his legs and arms raw. Tatius had been allowed to stay with his mother in our servant's quarters, but only as a special favour. Under apartheid rules, black workers in white suburbs could not bring their families with them.

Mom and Dad explained that what had happened to Tatius was all too typical of the random, savage cruelty faced by blacks. Protests made by my dad at the local police station were greeted with barely hidden contempt, and he angrily wrote a letter to the *Pretoria News*. On publication, his name was duly noted by Special Branch as somebody new to keep an eye on.

Lady Selborne township was named after the wife of Lord Selborne, a former British high commissioner for southern Africa. It was unusual in being a mixed-race township with an old British colonial heritage. It was cheek by jowl on one side with a white suburb, without the normal restrictions on whites visiting. During the day, Mom would visit regularly, accompanied by Sally, who would usually be left at the local Tumelong English Mission in a black crèche (unthinkable for a white child) while Mom went about her political business. The English women who ran the mission, Hannah Stanton and Cecily Paget, were Liberal Party members. I occasionally went along too at weekends, sometimes with my siblings, as we were too young to be left alone at home.

The more we did so, the less novel it became to drive along the dusty or muddy tracks and peer at the houses, some ramshackle, others more solid, but all so starkly different from the comfortable white communities in which we, our relatives and our school mates lived. I remember staring in wonderment then – as I have ever since – at black women hanging out clothing to dry, pristine despite the primitive conditions for washing and the dust swirling around.

Soon, Mom and Dad were both on the Pretoria Liberals' committee, and she became the branch secretary. Our rented houses, first in Hilda Street and then in Arcadia Street, were regularly filled with Liberal members and activists, both black and white.

But my parents were also at pains to ensure that we had in other respects a 'normal' childhood. Our friends came around to play, and we went to their houses. At 1127 Arcadia Street, Tom and I later organised bicycle races through our yard and out via the garage entrance onto the pavement, then back in through the front gate; these sometimes went on for several hours, with school friends teaming up in pairs and sharing the cycling as Mom and Dad acted as race controllers and my small sisters cheered us on. During a night bike race Jo-anne and Sally held torches to light up particularly dangerous spots. One time, Mom invited spectators from our school and charged an entrance fee to raise money for the school's black caretaker when he retired (I had discovered that he had no pension). My best school friend was Dave Geffen, and his mother, Gladys, helped Mom provide refreshments for sale towards the collection.

I caught the motor-sport bug from Dad, and we were taken regularly to watch races at the Kyalami circuit, some 50 kilometres away on the road to Johannesburg. The nine-hour, all-night race was a special treat, and I watched my favourite, the British driver David Piper, win every time in his green Ferrari.

Tom and I also built box-carts, as did Dave, using pram wheels with rope steering to veer downhill, sometimes on winding streets from the Union Buildings, once on a very steep *kopje* (hill) near the Voortrekker Monument with competitors from across Pretoria. In our early teens, Dave and I organised bike rallies. We built streamlined wooden platforms over our handlebars. These contained pre-prepared sheets that enabled us, in those pre-calculator days, to work out times manually for reaching the endpoints of each rally stage from average speeds and mileages provided by the organisers (usually one of us taking it in turns). Mom and Dad acted as timekeeping marshals along the route.

Cricket was also a passion, and Tom and I went to see England (touring as the Marylebone Cricket Club, or MCC) playing North Eastern Transvaal at Pretoria's Berea Park in December 1964. Near where we sat, the rising young stars Mike Brearley and Robin Hobbs walked around the edge of the field; six years later, Brearley was to figure courageously in the sport's apartheid story.

My boyhood was focused on schoolwork, sport and playing with friends, though I did have a secret crush at Hatfield Primary School on Jennifer Gee – not that I ever told her. She was a popular girl in our year, with a cheerful demeanour and short, curly blonde hair. A special treat in 1963 was getting permission from my parents to see, in the main Pretoria cinema, the James Bond film *From Russia With Love*. The scenes of his Casanova-like behaviour seemed very daring, because sex was a pretty taboo subject in our culture at the time.

Not all was innocent, however. When I was about ten, Tom and I stole a tin of condensed milk from boxes in our house intended for a black township and hid it in our tree house for illicit sips. We occasionally went around at night throwing small stones on the mostly corrugated-iron roofs of nearby homes and then scampering away. We got old clothes, winding them up to look like snakes, then crouched behind our garden hedge and pulled them through the gloom across the pavement so that passing pedestrians jumped in fear as we screeched in delight.

But one of these pranks rebounded terribly, as I remember to this day with shame. Some friends and I would put a balloon in a plastic bag and leave it lying on the road for unwary cyclists to ride over. From our vantage point on the garage roof, we would enjoy how startled they were when the balloon burst. Then one day we placed a large stone inside an empty-looking bag, and I watched mortified as an old black man crashed against it, all his precious shopping – food and provisions – spewing out over the street. I rushed out of my hiding place to help him gather it up, seeing him weeping and feeling awful, not least because I knew he was poor. I never did anything like that again.

❖

IN August 1958 Mom and Dad excitedly told us that they had met and talked to Nelson Mandela, his close comrade Walter Sisulu and other defendants in the Treason Trial, explaining who they were.

The trial was held in the Old Synagogue in Pretoria, and many of the accused would go outside during the lunch break for food provided in turn by the local Indian community, Liberals and other sympathisers. The charismatic Mandela, my parents told me, was 'a large, imposing, smiling man'. Increasingly, their activities overlapped with those of the ANC, whose Pretoria leader, Peter Magano, had become a friend and key contact.

Also in 1958 the Liberal Party launched a weekly news and comment magazine, *Contact*, covering the anti-apartheid struggle. My parents subscribed and Mom later became its Pretoria correspondent. Telling us to 'keep quiet and go and play', she would clatter away on her small Olivetti typewriter, covering Nelson Mandela's trial and other trials until she was eventually banned from doing so.

Mom was a self-trained journalist. Unlike my dad, she was not university-educated, having gone to work as an office clerk straight from school. By now she was in her early thirties, small, dark-haired and pretty in an unaffected way, and she cut quite a dash as she scurried about organising people and harrying the authorities, especially in courts and police stations, where blacks were treated the worst.

The Liberal Party's appeal was based on membership open

to all racial groups on an equal basis. Committed to a universal franchise, the party contained a range of political opinion, from socialists to free-market liberals, but both its unity and its radicalism sprang from an uncompromising support for human rights and a fierce anti-racism, the principles that above all inspired my parents and were increasingly imbibed by their children.

But most whites in Pretoria remained bitterly opposed to the very existence of the Liberal Party, seeing it as in some respects even worse than the ANC because it contained whites like them. Students at the University of Pretoria, then an Afrikaans-language white institution, were militantly pro-apartheid and would line up outside Liberal Party meetings, shouting slogans and abuse. I remember vividly their noisy, intimidating barracking outside a party colleague's home as we sat inside, fearfully wondering if they might burst in at any moment, until they finally went away.

Among my parents' close friends was David Rathswaffo, a particular family favourite who would call at our house and take the time to swap greetings and stories with me. He had some great one-liners where syntax and grammar got horribly jumbled, to hilarity all round: he would always say 'Can I see you *in camera?*' if he had some confidential information. He also never quite came to terms with telephone tapping. One day, needing to give my mother an urgent message about helping a black comrade who had escaped from the court, David lowered his voice and whispered, 'Please come, Jimmy has escaped' – as if the whisper might fool those listening in.

David was a clerk at the Supreme Court in Pretoria, where all the major political trials took place. That was until 1959, when the government decided that such 'responsible tasks' should be strictly reserved for whites. David was made redundant and then replaced by a white man – whom he had to train for the job.

It was incidents and events like these, part of the staple diet of our daily lives, that led to my becoming politically conscious without being politically involved. Dad used to spend time with me explaining some of the absurdities of apartheid, such as reserving better jobs for whites: that black decorators could paint the undercoat but not the final coat, that they could pass bricks to white builders but not lay bricks themselves.

By this time the new Nationalist prime minister, Hendrik Verwoerd, was well into his stride. A more intellectual leader than his predecessors, DF Malan and JG Strijdom, Verwoerd was seen as the 'architect' of the ideology of apartheid. He had earlier complained that the pre-apartheid system of schooling had misled blacks by showing them 'the green pastures of white society in which they are not allowed to graze'. As minister of native affairs, he would introduce the baleful policy of Bantu education, intended to ensure that blacks received a substandard education. In 1959 the ironically named Extension of University Attendance Act was introduced to end the attendance of what had been a handful of blacks (such as Nelson Mandela) at white universities.

In 1959 a prominent Pretoria Liberal and local doctor, Colin Lang, contested the Pretoria East by-election to the Transvaal Provincial Council as the ruling National Party's only opponent. He turned in a creditable performance, with 24 per cent of the vote, saving his deposit. Our home was the campaign headquarters – my parents' first experience of electioneering and canvassing for a non-racial party among the overwhelmingly racist white electorate.

I remember, aged nine, helping to leaflet in the tree-lined white suburbs, and finding it fun. Party members travelled from Johannesburg to help. One of them, Ernie Wentzel, a young white lawyer who subsequently became a great family friend, addressed open-air public meetings from the back of a flatbed lorry, silencing the bitterly hostile audience's shouts of 'Would you like your sister to marry a black?' with the response (in a heavy Afrikaans accent), 'Christ man, you should see my sister!' I thought this hilarious and used to enjoy my dad's recounting it to friends.

The by-election raised the profile of the Pretoria branch and brought my parents and other key activists to the attention of the authorities. Mom and Dad were soon helping to produce a monthly newsletter called *Libertas*. It was typed by Mom and printed on a noisy old Gestetner duplicating machine that stood in a corner of our dining room, its black ink frequently dripping where it shouldn't, and its wax stencils hung up for reuse if needed. I would be roped in to collate the sheets for stapling and help with pushing them through doors, as the leaflets were distributed by a team transported in our minibus – all rather exciting, I felt.

❖

MOM buzzed about the city helping and advising people, and cajoling the stubborn authorities. She was a hive of energy and determination.

In March 1960 she illicitly signed scores of passes for men fearing arrest in Lady Selborne after the ANC called for an economic boycott in protest against the pass laws. She explained to me how these identity documents were designed to restrict and control the movement of blacks about the country, and if a black person was outside a designated rural area, their pass had to be in order and signed by a white employer.

Then came a peaceful pass-laws protest organised by an ANC breakaway, the Pan Africanist Congress (PAC), in Sharpeville township, south of Johannesburg, on 21 March 1960. Policemen sitting in armoured vehicles suddenly opened fire on the crowd, using over 700 rounds and killing 69 men, women and children and wounding over 180 others. Most were shot in the back while running away.

For days afterwards, the police laid siege to Sharpeville. Food was running short. Mom explained the horror of the massacre, and told us she had to go and help. I was worried – maybe the police would open fire on her too? So it was a relief when she returned, buoyed up, explaining that after filling up our minibus with provisions donated through the Liberals, she had stopped for petrol at a service station and asked for the tyre pressures to be checked because 'we are heavily loaded with food for Sharpeville'. The vehicle was instantly surrounded by the black attendants, checking the tyres, cleaning the windscreen and then escorting it onto the highway with encouraging shouts and whistles.

Chief Albert Luthuli, the president of the ANC, publicly burnt his pass on 26 March 1960 and called on others to follow suit. A state of emergency was declared. Riots swept the country and the Sharpeville killings reverberated around the world. Luthuli was staying at the house of John Brink while giving evidence in the Treason Trial, and was arrested. Mom was asked to pay the fine and transport him back to the Brinks' home, where I remember meeting him. With his silver-grey hair he seemed a grandfatherly figure, austere but friendly towards a boy who knew little of the details except that his treatment by the police was plain wrong. Although still only ten, I was by now very conscious that the police were our enemies.

In the aftermath of Sharpeville, there was talk of apartheid teetering. My parents were excited by the prospect, though Dad, always a hard-nosed realist, told me that it was a mistake to raise expectations. He was proved right.

On 8 April the ANC and the PAC were banned as unlawful organisations. It was a heavy blow, particularly for the ANC, which for nearly half a century had struggled non-violently against harsh and discriminatory laws. Mandela and his colleagues decided they had no alternative but to reorganise the ANC to enable it to function underground, and the PAC adopted the same course.

The government had imposed a state of emergency, granting itself even more draconian powers. Along with some 2 000 anti-apartheid activists, many prominent Liberals were detained, including many whom I knew on first-name terms and who had visited our home. It seemed that a bright light was shining on everything we did as a family. Our phone was tapped, our mail intercepted and our house regularly observed by the security police. I got used to knowing that harmless phone calls to friends were no longer private. But, with Special Branch cars parked outside the house, for my brother Tom and me there was also a sense of 'cops and robbers', eerie yet exhilarating.

Harassment

IN June 1960 Mom was advised that her name was on a list of people to be arrested, that she should leave Pretoria immediately and go to friends unconnected with the Liberal Party. We arrived back from school to be told by Dad that we were going on holiday right away. It was a nice surprise, until I (as the oldest) was told the real reason. In Mom's absence (she had slipped away earlier), I had to ensure that clothes and toys were properly packed.

Dad came home early from work and we loaded the vehicle, checking there were no Special Branch people around, before we drove across the city to collect Mom. Dad peered anxiously for a tailing Special Branch car and asked me to do the same. Then Mom took the wheel and we waved goodbye to Dad for the 14-hour overnight drive to our grandparents' home in Port Alfred. Constantly looking back at the road behind, I was mightily relieved to spot no one following us.

But an hour or so out of Pretoria, nearing a bridge, I was terrified to see police ahead stopping and searching vehicles. Before Mom had time to think, we were on the bridge and then across: the police were clearly on the lookout for someone or something else, not a white mother driving her children.

Normally, on the long overnight journey to the seashore, Mom and Dad would share the driving. Now I fell asleep next to her and awoke to find we had pulled off under a tree by the side of the open road. Mom was slumped over the wheel. She had nearly fallen asleep, managing just in time to pull off the road and lock the doors for a snooze.

Granny and Grampa were stunned but delighted to see us, because Mom had not been able to risk phoning ahead to alert them. We children quickly settled into the routine of a break by the seaside, albeit in the middle of the South African winter.

Dad later joined us. We were thrilled to see him, but he explained his real purpose to me. It was a criminal offence under the emergency regulations to divulge information on detainees, and there was difficulty communicating between areas, so he had been asked to check on the state of the Liberal Party in the eastern Cape and Natal (today's KwaZulu-Natal) provinces. We set off again, later reaching Alan Paton's house overlooking the hills north of Durban. He was kindly, though a little gruff, to a ten-year-old barely aware of his growing international reputation.

Something he told me made a big impact: 'I'm not an all-or-nothing person, Peter. I'm an all-or-something person.' These became words to live by for my subsequent political activity, in which strong principles had not so much to be compromised as to be blended with hard-edged practicalities: the aim was to achieve concrete goals, not to bask in the luxury of ideological purism.

Eventually, we returned to Pretoria, eagerly peering at our house: it was still there. Things seemed okay, I thought. There were not even any Special Branch officers parked outside.

But soon they raided again, seizing statements made by people wounded at Sharpeville. These had been taken secretly the day after the shootings, Mom explained bitterly when I returned home from school. The precious statements were never seen again.

From then on, every night, Eva would take a suitcase to her quarters with any sensitive papers my parents had in the house. But on one occasion, she came back late and was shocked to find security policemen in the house. Realising that Mom had hidden the case in a slot between a kitchen cupboard and the cooker, she opened the cupboard door and searched the cupboard for an inordinate time, deliberately screening the case from the prying officers.

I also remember how once Eva called from a phone box to say she couldn't come to work. The reason: the roof was being ripped off her house in Lady Selborne. She and all the other Africans living in the township were being forced to move out to make space for whites. Eva was distraught: she had three children and nowhere else to live. As the workers moved in to kick her out, she was officiously informed she had to go on a list to find a house in Atteridgeville, another township several kilometres away. Mom and Dad's campaign against forced removals had suddenly become personal. Eva had to retrieve her furniture and search for somewhere to live, staying temporarily with friends.

❖

I SOMETIMES went with my parents in our minibus to help deliver food parcels contributed by white Liberal Party members for the black families of ANC or PAC detainees in Lady Selborne, Atteridgeville and Eastwood.

By then Mom had become known in Pretoria as the person to contact whenever anyone fell afoul of the police. She once helped to find bail for a group of women from Soweto, including the mother of Walter Sisulu. With the ANC and PAC now banned, many blacks joined the Pretoria branch of the Liberal Party – by this time the only legal anti-apartheid group in the city. There seemed a constant flow of people in and out of the house. Branch meetings were held in our living room, with Dad and others collecting black and Asian members from their segregated townships and taking them home afterwards.

Amid the increasing political turmoil surrounding us, I was enjoying school life at Hatfield Primary School, where to my surprise I became head prefect. It didn't feel like it at the time, but I suppose I must have been seen as a bit of an organiser, perhaps because of our bicycle races.

Up to that point, music hadn't played much of a part in my life. Dad's favourite was Beethoven, especially the Piano Concerto no 5 in E major. While still at primary school I bought my first 78 rpm single, Elvis Presley's 'GI Blues', but I did not follow pop music like my classmates, and later on had never heard of the Beatles when someone excitedly mentioned the group.

Strict discipline, doing homework conscientiously and on time, and playing sport virtually every afternoon were my watchwords. We were fortunate that certain teachers, aware of the Hains' growing notoriety, were quietly supportive, as were some of my friends and their parents.

In March 1961 the Treason Trial ended with the acquittal of all defendants. The ANC president, Oliver Tambo, immediately left the country to ensure that the organisation survived outside South Africa. Nelson Mandela went underground before he could be rearrested, and became leader of the ANC's armed wing, Umkhonto we Sizwe (Spear of the Nation), which he said would carry out acts of sabotage, with strict instructions to avoid civilian casualties.

I recall having intense discussions with my father, who was totally opposed to violence. But he did not criticise Mandela's decision, arguing that he had been left with no alternative, and ac-knowledging to me that the longer apartheid continued, the more violence there would inevitably be. That was why the Liberal Party had to persuade apartheid's rulers to change before it was too late.

❖

DESPITE her hyper-activism, Mom was devoted to her chil-dren and her husband. Looking back, I don't know how on earth she managed to keep it all together, nor how any of the mother-activists of that South African generation did. Winnie Mandela and Albertina Sisulu, among many others, lost their husbands in the prime of their lives, had to face constant police harassment – in Winnie's case, banning, beating and banishing – and had to bring up their children on their own.

Mom was much more fortunate. Dad was always beside her, the two inseparable in politics, love and family. Affectionate and close, they also became renowned for selflessly looking after others. Unwilling to give up on a challenge until all avenues were exhausted, they were always practical and impatient with the petty personality tensions or starry-eyed idealism present in left-wing politics. I was proud of them, and these values and attitudes would later become important guides for me in my own political life.

Moustached and fit, Dad was informal and friendly, though strict and severe with any of his children if we ever strayed. Self-discipline and hard work were the ethics he instilled in me. 'The things that are really worth achieving are usually difficult to do,' was one of his sayings. He always seemed something of a renaissance man. From motor racing, rugby, football and cricket to art, science, literature, history and politics, he seemed to know enough about most things to give an opinion or at least some guidance. However, Dad also encouraged us to enjoy ourselves, and both my parents were gregarious and popular among my school friends. Dave Geffen remembered Dad with great fondness, impressed that 'he was practical, could adjust a bike's wheel bearings, for instance'. And Mom? 'She baked the best rock cakes. I felt like another son.'

❖

ALTHOUGH our wider family was quite close, none of our relatives, with the exception of Aunt Jo, Mom's younger sister, was at all politically involved. Her eldest brother, Hugh, the millionaire founder-owner of Stocks & Stocks construction company, did not want his business affected.

When we were holidaying in Port Alfred, we would be invited out on Uncle Hugh's speedboats and I attempted water-skiing. We also regularly visited his Pretoria house to play with our five cousins, who were of similar ages, and to swim in their pool. But these invitations suddenly stopped.

Mom and Dad tried to explain why, concealing from us how upset they were. Jo-anne and Sally (aged six and four, respectively) were far too young to understand why they would no longer be seeing their close cousins Annie and Liz. My mother, who had been brought up as a Christian Scientist, now felt estranged from her relatives: what was Christianity about if not to give support and understanding in times of difficulty? Hugh and his wife were devout Christian Scientists, as were most of her wider family. How could the principles of Christianity be reconciled with apartheid? And how could the conservative Dutch Reformed Church, which provided the spiritual backbone for National Party rule, possibly justify the human misery deliberately inflicted by apartheid?

At the nearby Christian Science Sunday school that we attended, my crunch moment came while my parents were in prison. Realising that our Sunday-school teacher was a police officer, I decided that we were not going to attend any more. And after Dad came out of prison, I started to discuss religion with him. He had always been an atheist, and I gradually came to the conclusion that I was possibly an atheist too, but probably more of an agnostic.

Aunt Marie Hain, meanwhile, ran a travel agency in Pretoria and felt obliged by the owner to place an advert in the *Pretoria News* saying that her company had no relationship with the Mrs Hain of the Liberal Party – who just happened to be her sister-in-law. There was no personal hostility between us, but a barrier grew as we moved in different worlds.

When Dad was sacked, our well-off relatives could have helped, but chose not to. They remained in all other respects friendly and (within the white community) decent, caring family folk. It was simply that they were not 'political', we were a gross embarrassment and they feared it would be risky to be too closely associated with us. This was upsetting and difficult to understand, especially for my siblings.

Then, in December 1961, Umkhonto began a campaign of placing incendiary bombs in government offices, post offices and electrical substations, carrying out 200 attacks in the following 18 months. When I asked my parents about the attacks, they were amazed that the ANC had managed to place some of these bombs in Pretoria offices, where all government workers, down to the cleaners, were white – until Peter Magano said: 'Don't forget the messenger boys are still black!'

The term 'boy' was patronisingly applied by whites to all black men. From an early age, I remember castigating friends when they called out to their black gardeners in this way. The spectacle of bumptious white kids casually talking down to greying black grandfathers tending their gardens epitomised for me the daily indignity of apartheid. On one occasion Dave Geffen knocked off the hat of an elderly black man and I remember having a real go at him and insisting that he pick it up and give it back – which he sheepishly did.

❖

BY 1962 Dad was working in a private architectural practice, and had taken over as chair of the Pretoria Liberals. He and Mom occupied what were effectively the two top positions in the city's only legal anti-apartheid organisation, and so they became even more prominent targets. They seemed to be permanently in the *Pretoria News*, and late in 1962 Dad began to write frequent leader-page articles for the *Rand Daily Mail*, the country's main liberal newspaper.

He also helped me with my essays on current affairs when, in 1963, I moved to Pretoria Boys High School, which he had attended, as had my Uncle Bill, cricket captain in 1937. 'Boys High', as it is known, stands on a shallow *kopje* with sports fields spread out below. Considered one of the grandest examples of school architecture of its era, it was officially opened by Jan Smuts in 1909.

When I arrived, the headmaster was Desmond Abernethy, who had emigrated from Ireland with his family in 1919. He epitomised the role of headmaster – stern, strong values, someone to be obeyed. My favourite teacher, Terence Ashton, always erudite and rather mysterious, remarked that my writing 'seemed remarkably similar to that of WV Hain in the *Rand Daily Mail*'. Terry (though he was always strictly 'Mr Ashton' to us) taught English; in trying to explain the phrase *persona non grata* to our class, he said: 'Hain's parents are *persona non grata* with the government because they *think*.'

Terry could draw a perfect circle on the blackboard. He'd apparently perfected that little bit of trickery while training, simply by using his elbow as a pivot, and could instantly silence a class by doing this. Terry was also an avid reader of *The Times* of London, and was extremely put out when, in 1965, *The Times* finally succumbed to modernity and printed a photo on its front page for the first time.

As one of my classmates David Preiss recalled: 'Terry was a brilliant man, idiosyncratic and unique. He knew how to handle people and how to hold their attention. He once began writing on the blackboard, seemingly became manic and in a frenzy, kept writing off the blackboard, onto the wall and, because of a corner of the room, continued to write on the adjoining wall. Another time, he was baited by one of our classmates and tolerated it beyond what seemed reasonable. Finally, he appeared to snap, hauled the miscreant out and announced that he was going to beat him with the large blackboard ruler that lay nearby, a six-foot monstrosity. He instructed the victim to bend over and in order to prevent him from squirming away, insisted that he set his head just under Terry's desk. If he jerked up when caned, he would suffer a double discomfort of a painful rear and a bruise on the back of his head. Terry then took the ruler, marched back five paces and raced in swinging. He stopped an inch from the quaking pupil's behind and sent him back to his place. That student never uttered a peep in Terry's class again. It was the most brilliant form of discipline I ever saw.'

In 2000, after he had retired and I had become a minister of state in Britain's Foreign and Commonwealth Office, Terry came to see me for a cup of tea. We had not met for 40 years; he was entranced by the sense of history and grandness in my office, and we chatted happily for a while. Around that period I had done an interview as part of a series with public figures on 'My favourite teacher' – for me it had been Terry, of course.

Fortunately for me, Boys High had some liberal-minded teachers who were increasingly aware of my parents' growing role. While they never referred to it, some were quietly sympathetic, with my reputation as a hard worker and enthusiastic sportsman perhaps standing me in good stead. The only time I was picked on was when some boys started calling me 'a communist'; despite being upset, I was determined to ignore them, and stared fixedly ahead as if I hadn't heard.

Boys High has always had an unusually open-minded ethos. In August 1988, at a time when apartheid was crumbling, though still the law of the land, the school held a referendum on whether to admit black pupils: 70 per cent of staff and 69 per cent of parents voted for an open admission policy. And in May 1994 a large contingent of its boys acted as waiters during Nelson Mandela's inauguration as president. I still maintain it's the best school in South Africa, if not the world.

❖

HAVING been 17 months on the run, Nelson Mandela was finally captured on 5 August 1962, near Howick Falls in Natal, after an informer tipped off the police. Mostly disguised as a chauffeur, Mandela had evaded the authorities and travelled throughout the country organising the ANC underground, with the media dubbing him the 'Black Pimpernel'.

His trial opened at the Old Synagogue in Pretoria on 22 October and Mom covered it for the Liberal magazine *Contact*. Often, she was the only one in the white section of the public gallery. When Mandela entered each day, he would first raise his fist in the ANC's traditional 'Amandla' salute to the packed black section, and then do the same to Mom, she raising her own fist in acknowledgement. Nearly 30 years later, when she and I met him in the House of Commons in May 1991, she said: 'I don't suppose you remember me.' To which he replied, giving her a great hug: 'How could I forget!'

It was during this trial that I first became properly aware of Nelson Mandela's importance. His beautiful wife, Winnie, attended the sessions each day, often magnificent in her traditional dress. Once, when my sisters went with Mom, Winnie bent down and kissed the two little blonde girls in their light-turquoise school uniforms, to the evident outrage of a white policeman looking on. But, although Mandela's magnetic personality dominated the courtroom, it did not prevent his being sentenced to five years' hard labour on Robben Island.

By now the world was beginning to mobilise against apartheid. On 6 November 1962 the General Assembly of the United Nations (UN) voted to impose sanctions against South Africa. My parents had become friendly with two sympathetic officials from the Netherlands and West German embassies, Koen Stork and Rudie Ernst. We children got to know them too, as our families mixed. Both mentioned the difficulty of meeting blacks socially, and suggested that the Liberal Party host gatherings to remedy this. Held in our house, these 'diplomatic parties' were exciting occasions, as I took to spotting the different models among the dozens of limousines pulled up on our front drive.

But our lives were about to take a dramatic turn for the worse. In January 1963 Mom was summoned before the chief magistrate of Pretoria and warned to desist from activities 'calculated to further the aims of communism'. When she asked, he was unable to specify which of her activities fell within this definition and advised her to write to John Vorster, the minister of justice, for clarification. The reply from Vorster's office merely repeated the phrase and then stated: 'Should you so wish, you are of course at liberty to ignore the warning and, if as a result thereof, it is found necessary to take further action against you, you will only have yourself to blame.'

When I was 13, I remember clearly a cartoon, 'The Strange Case of Adelaine Hain', in the South African *Sunday Times* from 27 January 1963. It had Vorster instructing his police chief: 'Go directly, and see what she is doing, and tell her she mustn't.'

Mom was by now spending hours haunting the courts – sometimes dashing from building to building when 'grapevine' information told of yet another group of black detainees. She would find out their names, inform their parents and get them legal representation if necessary. Many had been assaulted and tortured. I remember being distressed when she told me how one young man had been tortured using electric shock and had gone completely out of his mind, staring vacantly into space.

Another young man whom Mom helped at his trial in Pretoria later came to symbolise the remarkable story of South Africa's transformation. Nervous in his khaki shorts and without any legal representation or support, 15-year-old Dikgang Moseneke was sentenced to ten years on Robben Island in mid-1963. She took him food every day during his trial, including (she discovered) his favourite, a bar of chocolate.

He had been charged with 15 other young PAC activists, all either teachers or students from Atteridgeville. They were accused of a variety of non-violent activities – holding meetings and stating that apartheid should be overthrown – tantamount to 'conspiracy to overthrow the state' on the charge sheet.

But both the young defendant and Mom only discovered each other's identities and careers 50 years later, when he told me: 'At first we couldn't understand why as a white person she was supporting us. We had never experienced that before: whites were always either the oppressors or couldn't care about us, yet she was there every day. It was also difficult to understand why a white lady of such a tiny frame would want to invite the wrath of that hideous system on herself and family. She was an inspiration to all of us. She was amazing, and I am eternally grateful, and she did much to form my own notions of a non-racial South Africa because suddenly she criss-crossed, she cut across lines that we thought were eternal.'

Mom was thrilled, all those decades later, to discover that Dikgang Moseneke had risen to become the revered Deputy Chief Justice of the post-apartheid South Africa they had both helped create.

❖

AT this time, my parents were excited by the rise of the American civil-rights movement, led by the charismatic black minister Martin Luther King, Jnr. '*There's* the answer to white South African prejudice,' Dad used to say; 'how can anybody deny King is a highly intelligent man?' He said the same about world champion boxer Muhammad Ali (then still known as Cassius Clay). Yet when confronted with this question, whites invariably replied,

'Yes, but he is not like *our* blacks: they really are inferior.'

With Liberal activists like my parents proving increasingly troublesome to both the security police and ministers, the government set about the systematic destruction of the party. In Parliament, John Vorster (who had been detained during the Second World War for his pro-Nazi activities) accused Liberals of being communists in disguise and tantamount to terrorists. Government ministers spoke of the need to restrict the Liberal Party. A cartoon in the *Pretoria News* of 11 March 1963, titled 'The Scapegoat', had a goat marked 'Liberal Party' being dragged by a knife-wielding Vorster up a hill towards a sacrificial pyre at the summit, with Prime Minister Verwoerd and other government luminaries forming an applauding procession behind him.

During 1963 many prominent Liberals throughout the country were banned and the fear of repression increased almost daily. The government introduced a notorious law that increased the period under which people could be held without charge from 12 days to 90 days. My parents warned me that life was going to get much more difficult, but it never occurred to me that they should give up their ideals for a more comfortable life.

Instead I remember clearly the front pages of the main newspapers luridly headlining the 'Rivonia plot', with pictures of all those arrested on 12 July. This was the day that Mandela's close comrades Walter Sisulu, Ahmed Kathrada and seven others, secretly based at Liliesleaf Farm in the Rivonia district just outside Johannesburg, were arrested and charged with sabotage. A mood of retribution swept through white communities.

The trial that followed, from 9 October 1963 to 12 June 1964, was known as the Rivonia Trial. Nelson Mandela was brought back to Pretoria from Robben Island and labelled as Accused No 1. Perhaps the most electric moment of the trial came when Mandela concluded his statement from the dock with these now famous words: 'During my lifetime I have dedicated myself to this struggle of the African people. I have fought against white domination, and I have fought against black domination. I have cherished the ideal of a democratic and free society in which all persons live together in harmony and with equal opportunities. It is an ideal which I hope to live for and to achieve. But if needs be, it is an ideal for which I am prepared to die.'

I was 14 when I read these powerful words, trying to take in their full significance, and aware they were a great inspiration to my parents and to everyone involved in the struggle. If found guilty, the men in the dock faced the death penalty. In fact, after worldwide pleas for clemency, the defendants were all sentenced to life imprisonment, and in July 1964 Mandela returned to Robben Island, not to be seen or heard in public again for nearly 26 long years.

Suppression

IN July 1963 we moved from Hatfield out to a smallholding at The Willows, to the east of Pretoria, in what is now known as Lynnwood East. The rented house consisted of two large thatched rondavels (African-style round houses) on a terrace set well back from the road and at the foot of a *kopje*.

With a small, leaky swimming pool and plenty of space to play, it was wonderful for children. I laid a makeshift cricket pitch that I used to water every evening, and Tom and I used to play football until it was too dark to see the ball.

Our move to The Willows took the security police by surprise, and it was some weeks before they traced us, during which we escaped their attention for the first time in years. Our telephone had not yet been connected, so they were unable to trace us that way either. Then one day Eva answered the door to a man who asked her the name of her *baas* (employer). Eva had adopted a routine with white strangers of pretending to know nothing and understanding less, and the man was turning away when Mom went to see what was happening. He saw her, turned back and said that he was looking for a house that he'd heard was for sale.

Eva was furious with Mom. 'He is Special Branch,' she hissed. 'Now they'll know where we live.' She was right. Thereafter we had the usual security-police cars parked on the road outside, our phone was speedily connected and tapping resumed.

In September 1963 there was a knock at the door, which I answered, quickly joined by Mom. We were confronted by the same two large security-police officers who had arrested my parents in 1961 – sergeants Viktor and Van Zyl (the latter referred to as 'banana fingers' because of his huge hands). I distinctly remember their burly figures in the doorway and trying to seem calm and not intimidated, even though I felt anything but.

They handed Mom an envelope containing a five-year banning order, which limited her to being in the company of not more than one person at a time. The 3000-word document had a whole list of restrictions, including confining her movements to the Pretoria magisterial district and prohibiting her from entering certain specified places, such as factories, black communities, schools or university areas. It also required her to report to a police station eight kilometres away every Wednesday.

The ban effectively ended her work as secretary of the Pretoria Liberal Party and stopped any overt political activity whatsoever. She was also prohibited entrance to the courts, the first time such a measure was used in a banning order. Clearly, her practice of haunting the courts to provide representation for political prisoners was the main reason for her ban.

Mom and Dad had discussed the possibility for months. It was a weird existence, and left her feeling angry and frustrated. She effectively ceased to be a public person and could not be quoted by the media. The restriction on meeting more than one person at a time was near-fatal politically, and I was dismayed that she could no longer continue with all her good work helping so many stricken people.

She was not even allowed to come into our schools and discuss our progress with our teachers. That could only be done standing outside on the pavement, which was just about feasible for the primary school, but not for my high school, which stood in the middle of large grounds. It was a blow because she had always taken a very close and active interest in our progress and was well known by our teachers. We had become used to my parents' being targeted, but why should *our* schooling be so affected, why did *we* have to be picked on this way? It made me feel even angrier about the growing state restrictions on our freedom as a family.

Gradually, however, she adjusted and worked out ways of acting as a contact for political prisoners, whose relatives continued to approach her for assistance when they had problems. She seemed to me to be just as active. Although she could no longer participate openly in the life of the Liberal Party, she was kept in touch daily with events by David Rathswaffo, who took over as secretary. He would make a coded telephone call from a call box near the party office and she would then drive to a prearranged rendezvous.

The Hain 'diplomatic parties' continued nevertheless, with the security police taking down the registration numbers of the cars parked outside. Party luminaries such as Alan Paton and national chairman Peter Brown attended, in addition to Pretoria members. But Mom's ban meant that she had to sit in the kitchen and be visited by ambassadors one at a time; I was deputed to escort them through to her. One-to-one in the kitchen was legal. But if she stepped into the living room, thronged with diplomats, she could be arrested. Tom and I also had fun serving drinks under the guidance of the coloured activist Alban Thumbran, who had worked as a waiter, while Jo-anne and Sally helped with the snacks.

On one occasion I heard a noise just outside. Peering through the window into the dark, I was startled to catch a glimpse of someone lurking there, and called out to Dad, 'Special Branch, Special Branch.' As we ran out there was a commotion and a figure began charging noisily up through the bushes and rocks of the dark *kopje*. Dad, running after his quarry, shouted, 'Peter, bring the gun!' Although this was a ruse, as we had no gun, the man ahead must have panicked. Before making off into the night, he threw a stone that glanced off a tree right in front of Dad's face. By now the partygoers had spilled outside and it all seemed like a bit of a thrill. But the next morning we went up to have a look and found a large gash on the tree branch, forcibly bringing home to me that what had seemed like an exciting incident could have ended in a terrible family tragedy.

❖

THE pressure was rising remorselessly and soon Dad's work opportunities were curbed by the limited number of employers who would take him on. He and Mom found increasing difficulty in making ends meet. Very reluctantly, they had to let Eva Matjeke go. It was a blow to her as well as to us because she had become one of the family and needed the job.

The only positive was that her room was vacant when Mom received a frantic telephone call from David Rathswaffo. Jimmy Makoejane, a PAC activist comrade from Lady Selborne, had escaped from court and needed help. Conscious that our phone was tapped, she cut David short and promised to come into town right away, asking me to look after the other children.

Jimmy had participated in the 1963 campaign by Poqo, the armed wing of the PAC, and had managed to flee. But he had been kidnapped from a train on the Rhodesian border by the security police and returned to Pretoria for trial. He had managed to escape again during a lunch recess; astonishingly, he had just walked out undetected. Jimmy was dropped off late that night near our house, its semi-rural location ideal for the task at hand.

Carefully walking through the surrounding bush, Dad collected Jimmy, away from the prying eyes of the Special Branch parked at the front gate, and installed him in Eva's empty room. Although I was intrigued to glimpse Mom giving dinner to a black stranger in our kitchen, wondering how he had got there, I had learnt not to ask too many questions (and only heard the full story long afterwards, when I was in exile in London).

The next day, with Jimmy lying down on the back seat of a friend's car and covered by a rug, Dad drove him to a nearby railway station, attracting no interest from the security police who were watching at the gate for our cars. Jimmy got clean away, eventually ending up in Tanzania. But when the security police played back their surveillance tapes, they arrested David, who maintained that Jimmy had told him he'd been acquitted, had 'borrowed ten bob' and disappeared. They held David for a few days, taking away his epilepsy medication. Fortunately, he told them nothing about my parents' involvement or they would have faced immediate arrest and imprisonment.

❖

IN one respect I was a typical South African boy: I was mad about sport, and my only rebellion at Pretoria Boys High was over my *choice* of sport.

In those days Boys High was very much a rugby-playing school, and despite my Dad's rugby enthusiasm, I wanted to continue playing football, both because I had enjoyed it at primary school and because I didn't like the apartheid symbolism of the Springboks. Dad insisted I try rugby for a year, which I did, playing unconvincingly as a second-row forward. Then I was ominously summoned to Desmond Abernethy's study. He'd heard I was insisting on playing football – for a *private* club (the word said with some distaste). In vain he tried to dissuade me, eventually accepting my polite insistence. I first joined Berea Park because its football calendar did not clash with my school rugby. Then I switched to Arcadia, helping its Under-14 team win the Challenge and League cups in 1964.

Meanwhile, I experienced first-hand the extent to which apartheid both regulated and infected sport – uniquely in the world – with both oppressive and bizarre consequences.

We used to swim regularly at Hillcrest, Pretoria's international-standard swimming pool for whites. In 1962 South Africa was involved in lucrative trade deals with Japan, and visiting Japanese businessmen were granted 'honorary white' status, allowing them to stay in hotels and enjoy privileges usually reserved for whites alone. But this caused consternation when a Japanese visitor was mistaken for a local Chinese and ejected from a bus reserved for whites.

An important part of the trade-deal fanfare was the arrival of a Japanese water-polo team. After initially refusing the team access to the pool, the Pretoria City Council relented: business before racism. But there was such a public uproar that the pool was drained after the team departed so that white customers could have 'fresh' water.

Because I attended the white state schools of Hatfield Primary and Pretoria Boys High (and it would have been illegal to do otherwise), I had to play in whites-only school or club sports teams, and could not play against black teams. Sport was legally segregated from school right through provincial up to national-representative level. We also used to watch our home football team, Arcadia, at the Caledonian Stadium, and partitioned off on the other side of the stadium from the whites were the black spectators, some of them personal friends. We used to mingle in advance of the match before being forced to separate. As with all other sports events, we could not stand together or use the same entrances, toilets or facilities.

But although Arcadia was an all-white team playing in an all-white league, black spectators were among the noisiest and most partisan supporters. Then the government introduced proclamations banning blacks (including our friends) from such major sports events. In their absence, the carnival atmosphere – sometimes raucous – at Arcadia's home matches evaporated. But crowds of black fans still gathered outside, listening to the match. Some of the keenest shinned up to watch from trees, causing apoplexy to white neighbours. I watched in horror and anger as police dogs were used to drive them from these vantage points, pulling them down bloodied and screaming.

Football remained an important part of my boyhood. At Boys High, I got my mates together during the midmorning break for what became a daily football match, kicking a tennis ball around a terrace above the swimming pool, just below the main forecourt of the school. These matches gained in popularity and dozens took part, spectators cheering us on. There was also a ready response when I initiated a full-scale match on the school hockey pitch, near the main entrance on Roper Street. We hadn't asked for, or been given, permission to stage the match and it therefore happened amid a frisson of disapproval from the school. But it went off smoothly and I even scored a goal, dribbling around the keeper to slot the ball between the small hockey goalposts.

Arrest

WITHOUT any warning, five days in July 1964 were to prove the beginning of the end of my Pretoria boyhood.

That was when many members of the African Resistance Movement (ARM) were arrested, some of them close friends in the Liberal Party. They felt that non-violent means had reached the end of the road and that the sabotage of installations such as power pylons was the only way forward. Others were mostly young white radicals frustrated by the denial of legal and peaceful channels for change. Still others were from the ANC Youth League.

ARM's first act of sabotage had taken place nearly three years earlier, and my parents had themselves been confidentially sounded out to join the movement by Hugh Lewin and John Harris, friends from the Liberal Party. But, quite apart from the serious moral questions raised by violence, Mom and Dad considered such action naive and counterproductive, believing it would simply invite even greater state repression without achieving anything tangible. Those who did undertake the sabotage did not resign from the Liberal Party, as its rules obliged them to do, provoking considerable acrimony when they were eventually exposed.

Dad often talked to me about this when I joined him driving around on political business. He had witnessed the horror of the Second World War – a German shell had wounded him and killed his close friend 'Lanky' Brasler right next to him in their Apennine trench. The trouble with violence, he insisted vehemently, was that it tended to develop a life of its own. Whatever the intention, once started, it spread automatically. Also, there was no way of containing it: even blowing up a remote pylon risked killing an innocent person who might be passing by.

The police had discovered a goldmine of incriminating documents at the Cape Town flat of the national ARM organiser, Adrian Leftwich, also a prominent Liberal. Incredibly, he had kept a record of the entire cell structure of the ARM. Turning state witness, he was later paraded around the country giving evidence against his former comrades, among them Hugh Lewin at whose wedding he had been best man.

Mom and Dad felt their attempts to live something akin to a normal life were now being thwarted in every way. Then, on 24 July 1964, everything changed for us when a bomb exploded on the whites-only concourse of Johannesburg's Park Station, mortally injuring an elderly woman and severely wounding her young granddaughter. I remember hearing the news on my bedroom radio and rushing to seek reassurance from my parents, not imagining for a moment that they would be involved, but needing to hear them say so. Both were very upset, my father sounding off against the 'idiots who did that sort of mindless thing'. Whoever was responsible had better not come to him for help, he told me grimly.

A few days later, Ann Harris, with her six-week-old son, David, turned up unexpectedly from Johannesburg at our home in The Willows, telling us that John had been arrested and was being held in Pretoria Local prison. Both were teachers, and John shared Dad's interest in sport, cars and motor racing (rather uncommon interests among the politically involved). So they got on especially well, as did Ann and Mom. They had visited us in Pretoria, we had been to their home and John had gone with us to several motor races. At Kyalami, we would park our minibus at Clubhouse Corner and the whole family would watch from the roof.

Dad later told me of a fierce argument between them on a lengthy drive back after a party meeting in the Cape. John was insistent that although an act of violence might cause casualties in the short term, in the long term it could save lives if it hastened the end of the violence of apartheid. Like Mandela's ANC had already become, he was deeply frustrated by the inability of young white radicals like him to accomplish anything against a police state that remorselessly crushed all peaceful opposition. He and other Liberal friends were attracted to the ARM, and he was very upset that Dad – ten years older and something of a mentor – would have none of it.

When she arrived suddenly at our home, Ann was distraught, explaining how she had been refused permission to see John in Pretoria Local. But she had been told that she could bring food for him each day and collect his laundry. Could my parents put him on their list for regular food parcels to political detainees? Of course, they replied.

However, as Ann could not drive and was dependent upon others to bring her from Johannesburg – almost 65 kilometres away – Mom and Dad, with typical generosity, suggested that she stay with us until his release. They assumed that John, who had been under police surveillance after his banning in January that year, could not possibly have been involved in the station bombing and would be released in a week or so.

Jo-anne and Sally gave up their bedroom for the adjoining playroom, and Ann and baby David moved in. But, instead of a short stay, they were with us for nearly 18 months and became part of the family. Helping look after and play with David as he grew from baby to toddler, including changing his nappies, was a formative experience for a teenage boy, and was to help me as a father more than a decade later.

Life revolved around a daily visit to the prison by Mom and Ann, taking food to John, Hugh and others who were all held incommunicado under the 90-day law. The extra housework involved with a tiny baby, the daily 40-kilometre round trip to the prison, transporting children to and from school and Dad to and from work – it all meant that it became difficult for Mom to cope without help. Eva, still without a job, eagerly took up residence again as we welcomed her back into our family.

❖

THE station bomb triggered a frenzy. Never before had whites been attacked in this way. As Dad had prophesied, the security services were quick to exploit the resulting panic, including by giving us extra attention.

I was sure John would be out soon. But, after a while, when all the other ARM detainees had been visited by relatives, and Ann still had heard nothing, we began to realise that there was something seriously amiss. Then, in John's laundry, Mom noticed a bloodstain on a shirt. After his lawyer made inquiries, a menacing member of the security police turned up with a letter for Ann – frightening nine-year-old Jo-anne, who worried that Mom was going to be arrested again and came running in, saying through her tears, 'I didn't cry in front of him.'

It was the first direct communication that Ann or the lawyers had received from John. He wanted to reassure her that he had cut himself shaving – and he joked that he was unused to wet shaving as he'd had to hand in his electric shaver. In reality, he was still bleeding from horrendous beatings, including a broken jaw and damaged testicles. The letter somehow did not ring true for Ann, who suspected, rightly, that he had been forced to write it, and she was dreadfully stressed.

Mom meanwhile – covertly, because we kids never knew at the time – was ingeniously engaged in receiving and passing messages to her comrades in detention. She regularly washed their clothes and one day noticed a dirty handkerchief with a large 'C' in ink on it. Racking her brains, she recalled that lemon juice could be used as invisible ink. So she ironed it and found a message. Thereafter she developed other methods: taking the pith out of an orange and gluing it back after inserting a message inside, or after cooking a whole onion sliding a note between the leaves to be covered as it cooled. These were never discovered and formed an invaluable communications route.

However, as John's detention continued, Mom – who had an uncanny intuition – began to suspect that he must have had some connection with the station bomb. Even by the standards of the security constraints we operated under (phone tapping and not knowing whether rooms in our home were bugged), it was a particularly awkward period for my parents to communicate with one another, and they regularly walked outside into the garden to do so. I was worried about John being in jail, especially when it became evident he had been badly beaten, but I remained unaware of the extent of his complicity.

Then, a month after the explosion, the elderly woman, Ethel Rhys, died (her 12-year-old granddaughter, Glynnis Burleigh, was maimed for life). John was charged with murder. Ruth Hayman, a Liberal Party friend and John's lawyer, was then able to see him for the first time, finding him in a terrible state; he had only been charged after his broken jaw, which had been wired up, had mended enough for him to be presentable in court.

By now, Ann had admitted to my parents what she had known all along: that John was indeed responsible for the bombing. Once he was charged, on 14 September, Mom and Dad told us. I could not believe it. How had he done this? It was shocking, and I felt numb – not so much betrayed as confused, discussing it over and over again with Dad.

He and Mom were equally upset, and I could sense their torn feelings. Although they condemned without qualification what John had done, they remained convinced that he never intended to harm anybody. He had meant it as a spectacular demonstration of resistance to tightening state oppression. Indeed, he had telephoned a 15-minute warning to both the railway police and two newspapers, urging that the station concourse be cleared. But the warning was ignored and the result was devastation. This gave the government the pretext to enforce an even more oppressive regime, with Mom and Dad telling me at the time that they strongly suspected this was deliberate. Indeed, two decades later, the former security-police informer Gordon Winter stated in his book, *Inside BOSS*, that the decision not to use the station loudspeaker system to clear travellers from the concourse had gone up through the notorious head of the Bureau for State Security (BOSS), Hendrik van den Bergh, to the justice minister, John Vorster.[1] Winter's testimony was never disputed.

For my parents it was less a dilemma about where their duty lay – despite their vehement disagreement, they supported John and his family – than a sombre realisation of the likely serious consequences for our family. 'We have to stand by Ann and give what help we can to John in prison,' they insisted. At 14, I did not fully comprehend just how grave it would be for us. To me, it seemed like another dark twist in a pattern of life that had got steadily tougher over the years.

Having long been targets of the local security forces, my parents were now the principal targets of the whole state and its compliant media. Instead of being one of many enemies, it was almost as if we were *the* enemy, and I became only too aware that the white community had now completely turned on us. The harassment became vitriolic. Our house was under constant surveillance. Security police cars were parked on the road outside 24 hours a day. As we left we would be tailed – on one occasion even when Tom and I rode down to the shops on our bikes. If I had thought too much about it, I would have been terrified, but I was determined to follow Mom and Dad in carrying on as normally as we could, trying not to be cowed.

Raids on our home also became more regular. Once I cycled the eight kilometres home from school to find security police turning over the house and searching through my school books and papers. Mom looked understandably upset and I glared at them, determined not to be intimidated and to stand up for her. But then their menacing presence took a comic turn. A young officer had discovered a list of star names that constituted my own chosen two 'World XI' cricket teams. It included West Indies stars Gary Sobers and Wes Hall, Australia's Richie Benaud and even South Africa's Graeme Pollock – like me, a left-handed batsman, and my idol. But the names were listed at random and I had attached numbers indicating positions in the batting order. The officer thought he'd found a coded list and rushed excitedly to show it to his captain, who, after a quick glance, told him not to be a damned fool. One up to us. It was the kind of small victory that kept up spirits then and whenever we recounted the story.

Meanwhile another Liberal friend, Maritz van den Berg, had been detained under the 90-day law on 29 July and held in Pretoria Local prison for a month before being unconditionally released. It was soon obvious that he had spoken freely, because others were immediately pulled in for questioning. One of them, Alban Thumbran, was released again almost at once and telephoned a warning: 'Maritz is singing like a bird.' This was to be the signal for messages to be relayed, by various clandestine means, to as many people as my parents thought might need to know.

One party colleague, Derek Cohen, was only contacted after Mom had thrown off pursuing security-police vehicles in an exciting manoeuvre with all of us children in the car providing cover for her, as if on a routine family outing. She pulled up at some traffic lights in the lane indicating left, then suddenly jumped the lights and tore rightward, leaving the tailing vehicle blocked by oncoming traffic. We drove straight to Derek's house, and he immediately left on the next plane for London. Shortly afterwards, the security police called round looking in vain for him.

Then, in September 1964, Dad was visited at the office where he had set up on his own and handed a banning order with a special clause inserted. On the same day I opened our front door to a burly security policeman, who handed Mom an addendum to her ban, also personally signed by John Vorster. It contained a similar new clause to Dad's, giving her special permission to communicate with him. This was exceptional: as a married couple, they had to be given an Orwellian exemption from the normal stipulation that banned persons were not allowed to communicate in any way.

Dad's banning was clearly a reprisal for his having provided support to the hated John Harris and his family. It meant that my parents had no more flexibility for their political activity. Mom could not act behind the scenes for Dad because he too was now barred from doing anything. So they co-opted me as a sort of surrogate. From the ages of 14 to 16, I became increasingly active in a liaison role, taking and passing messages to individuals with whom my parents were prevented from communicating, such as journalists and other banned people, and so helping them to continue much of their political work behind the scenes.

This I enjoyed because I was helping them, and because I believed in their cause, even if I was not up to speed on all the detail. It was also quite exciting – and sometimes scary, as I worried that, if my subterfuge were to be discovered, they might be arrested for breaking their bans. I idolised my parents. Although they never once pressured me to assist them, I felt it the natural thing to do so. Stereotypical adolescence – resentment of and rebellion against parents apparent in friends and school mates – somehow passed me by.

Another consequence of his banning order was that Dad, who would often come to see me playing cricket on school fields on his way home from work, was now barred from doing so, except when a game was near enough to the school fence and he could pull up on the road and look over. Seeing him there always gave me a boost, although I had trouble trying to explain to my uncomprehending team-mates why he couldn't come in, as they didn't have the faintest idea of what a banning order was.

Hanging

JOHN Harris's trial opened on 21 September 1964 in the same Pretoria Supreme Court chamber as, a year before, Nelson Mandela and his underground leadership comrades captured at Rivonia had been sentenced to life imprisonment.

Mom and Dad's banning orders prevented them from attending, so instead they gave as much support as they could from the outside – sometimes literally on the courthouse steps, though careful to meet only one other person at a time.

At the outset came a terrible blow: Harris's co-conspirator, John Lloyd – another friend and Liberal Party member – was to be the main prosecution witness. Mom, who knew Lloyd's girlfriend, was able to smuggle a message to him and establish from her that he had received it: if he gave evidence, John Harris would be sentenced to death.

To their horror, Lloyd ignored this warning, and the emotional stress on Ann Harris and my parents grew. At the trial Lloyd did not merely give evidence in corroboration of John's own confession (which would have carried a life sentence for manslaughter), but, damningly, went much further, insisting that John's act was *premeditated* murder. It was devastating, because John had consistently denied this, and police testimony in court confirmed that he had indeed telephoned the warning to the railway police urging them to clear the concourse so that nobody would be injured, and repeated this to newspapers. The consequences were to be fatal, for the judge accepted Lloyd's version.

I arrived back after school to find Mom and Dad distraught as they described the savage turn of events, with Ann increasingly tearful and Mom trying to console her while herself feeling much the same. All were desperate and I did not know what to do; nothing at all, it seemed, could be done.

Lloyd had been kept away from all the ARM and other political prisoners. When they were transferred to Pretoria Local prison at the end of July, he was housed on his own at a Pretoria police station, allowed frequent visits from his mother and given proper bedding with sheets. Evidence at the trial showed that Harris and Lloyd had been the only ones in their ARM cell still at liberty after the main arrests. The two had discussed a number of projects to 'make a big splash' to show that the organisation had not been destroyed, as Vorster had boasted on the radio. Among these were the bomb at Park Station, a bomb in an underground car park and bombs in private post boxes at Pretoria Post Office, all to be carried out on 24 July. John Harris was to carry out the first and Lloyd the other two.

However, Lloyd (the flatmate of fellow ARM member Hugh Lewin, who had been arrested on 9 July) was detained on 23 July, the day before John carried out his part of their project. It was not established whether the security services thereby had advance notice of the station bomb, but Lloyd's initial statement to the police mentioning John Harris, and his plan to plant a bomb at a station, was made at 12.45 pm on 24 July, nearly four hours before the explosion. It may therefore have been that the security services had even greater forewarning than John himself gave by telephone. If so, like the decision to ignore that warning, it suited their purposes to allow the bomb to explode as an excuse for the clampdown that followed.

The judge concluded by stating that Lloyd's evidence proved incontrovertibly that John indeed had 'an intention to kill' and so was guilty of murder. Although there was no other supporting evidence, there was now a hideous inevitability that John would face the gallows.

Although she had been brave, Ann was inconsolable at home that night, as we all waited for sentence to be passed. My younger brother and sisters had been shielded from just how desperate John's predicament was, but I had been kept fully apprised throughout. I felt numb, trying all the time to imagine some escape route for John. Tormented, I couldn't think of one.

❖

IN December 2012 I visited the wood-panelled chamber of the Supreme Court where John faced his fate sitting directly in front of the judge on a long crimson-covered bench previously occupied by Nelson Mandela and his Rivonia comrades (and subsequently by Hugh Lewin).

That day, 6 November 1964, Mom waited for Ann outside the court. As usual, she parked on her own at the bottom of the wide steps so that she would not break the terms of her banning order by mixing with more than one other person, and so that Ann could climb straight into the car and get away. Party supporters, black and white, chatted anxiously. Inside, the large marbled waiting area with a first-floor gallery was packed. White office workers had poured in to witness the spectacle, staring morbidly at John's anxious parents, who were sitting on a wooden bench outside the courtroom.

In the waiting crowd was the hangman, there to bear witness as he sized up his promised victim. The executioner, who, quite extraordinarily, had brought his young son with him, was not disappointed. John was formally sentenced to death by hanging – the first and only white to be so adjudged during the struggle – an outcome cheered by the government-controlled media.

Ernie Wentzel came straight out to Mom with the shocking

news. As soon as Ann appeared, walking down the courthouse steps, Mom opened the car door for her and they sped away.

I remember Mom, deeply upset and shaking, arriving home to speak to us. Ann, staring ahead blankly, went straight to her bedroom. Twelve-year-old Tom (who like me was a great fan of John's) went completely white with shock; Jo-anne and Sally (nine and seven) could hardly take it in. I was stunned: although I had been conditioned to expect the worst, the dreadful reality now sank in. But, surely, somehow, we could do something, I worried frantically.

In the final year of our stay in our rondavel home, an activist friend gave us a new album, *Judy Collins #3*, and the American folk singer's beautifully lilting voice soon regularly rang out of our living room. The album was very evocative for us as a family, with one track, 'Anathea', especially so: 'Anathea, Anathea, don't go out into the forest. There among the green pines standing, You will find your brother hanging.'

For the next five months, Mom and Dad tried everything they could in a desperate effort to save John's life, as the shadow of the noose hovered over him. And all this time they kept their children together for school exams, sports, friends and family. When John's legal appeal failed on 1 March 1965 – because no additional evidence was forthcoming – they rushed about helping to organise appeals for clemency. Ann and John's father flew down to Cape Town for an interview with John Vorster, which proved predictably pointless: he was aggressive and dismissive, even trying to get Ann to incriminate herself. Petitions from a range of public figures were presented and the matter was even raised in the British Parliament.

A week after John's sentencing, four more ARM members stood trial in Pretoria, including Hugh, who was jailed for seven years. Mom stood behind the court building each day to catch a glimpse of Hugh being driven in, and they would exchange waves. Again – and although he had promised not to give evidence – the main prosecution witness in Hugh's case was his flatmate and fellow conspirator, John Lloyd. Another state witness was his former best man, Adrian Leftwich. Both were allowed to leave for safety in England, with Lloyd never recanting (indeed, claiming to having been a leading anti-apartheid activist) and Leftwich never concealing his role.

Lloyd was released as part of an immunity deal, by which he avoided being charged as an accomplice, and flew to London with his mother. A new job awaited him there. A friend, Jill Chisholm, travelled to the UK to ask him to assist in John Harris's appeal by retracting his 'intention to kill' evidence. But he refused and instead threatened to tell the security police that she was 'trying to get him to perjure himself'. Then Ruth Hayman, also well known to Lloyd as a fellow Liberal, flew over: Lloyd initially agreed to a draft affidavit retracting his evidence, promising to return in the morning to sign it. But he failed to do so.

After a third similar encounter, with Randolph Vigne, another ARM member who had escaped to Britain, Lloyd eventually signed a watered-down, anodyne statement that was forwarded to the state president, CR Swart – but it was too little and too late. Lloyd even ignored Ann's final desperate cable: 'I plead for John's life with the conviction that he and your friends would have done it for you.'

❖

A GRIM cloud of foreboding enveloped us all as the date for the execution was set for 1 April 1965. I found myself daydreaming about acquiring a helicopter, or summoning up a James Bond, to get John out somehow. I went to sleep the night before the execution still trying to think of something fresh to change what, deep down, I knew was unchangeable.

The grisly, medieval ritual of being hanged by the neck until dead weighed heavily. I recalled vivid discussions with Dad about his total opposition to capital punishment, and descriptions of the brutal violence of the act: a trapdoor opening underneath, the sudden jerk of the body, jack-knifing as the neck bore all the weight and broke, the blood spouting. This was all about to happen to our friend – my friend.

Dad and Ernie Wentzel had previously asked permission from the prison commander for the body to be released for cremation. It was not normal procedure, but to everyone's surprise, permission was granted, and a service was arranged at the Rebecca Street Crematorium for a few hours after the execution. (Ernie thought that the permission was given so that the security police could monitor those attending.) As banned persons, my parents required permission to attend, and this was duly given – again surprisingly.

But no sooner were their spirits raised than they were dashed again. Dad's request to read the main address was refused the evening before. It was too late to ask anyone else, and there would not have been many people willing or able to undertake a task that invited notoriety in the eyes of the febrile white public and the media, who were baying for blood.

I remember coming across my parents in the garden as the sun set. They were attempting to console Ann, who was crying. I didn't know what to do. When I saw her, I felt frustrated and deeply sorry. So I said somewhat lamely, 'Can I help?' I wasn't quite sure how, but Ann turned, her face lighting up.

I was quickly shown a copy of the typed two-page funeral address Dad had prepared according to Ann's wishes, and reflecting John's strong atheist convictions. Dignified yet uplifting, it began with a Shakespearean sonnet, and continued with these lines from John Donne's 'Meditation XVII':

No man is an island, entire of itself;
Every man is a piece of the continent, a part of the main.
...

56

Any man's death diminishes me, because I am involved in man-
kind,
And therefore send not to know for whom the bell tolls; it tolls
for thee.

From the Bible was Matthew's 'Blessed are they which are
persecuted for righteousness' sake', and from Ecclesiastes, 'To
everything there is a season' – sung so beautifully by Judy Collins
on our album. The songs were 'Battle Hymn of the Republic' and
'We Shall Overcome', the latter immortalised by Joan Baez at so
many American civil-rights and peace demonstrations.

❖

JUST before 5 am on 1 April 1965 John Harris ascended the
52 concrete steps to the pre-execution room next to the gallows
at Pretoria Central prison. A Catholic priest, Father McGuiness,
walked up the steps talking with John. (He had originally agreed
to see a priest because it got him an extra visitor, and they became good friends, though John's atheism never wavered.) Inside
the execution chamber, which had barred frosted-glass windows
along the top, waited the hangman. So did a medical doctor, to
certify John's death, and a policeman, to take a set of fingerprints
to ensure he was the person stipulated; his face was also checked
by an official against a photograph to confirm his identity. The
death warrant was read to him and he was given the opportunity
to say his last words.

When he was ready, he was led forward by a warder into the
large and brightly lit execution room, some 13 metres long, with
white-painted walls. The gallows beam ran the length of the room
(seven black prisoners could be – and often were – hanged simultaneously). It had a low ceiling with barred windows in the top of
the wall. In the corner there was a table with a telephone, in case

a last-minute clemency was ever granted. There is no recorded instance of the phone ever having rung – and it certainly did not ring for John.

In the middle, the cruel hole was hidden by rectangular trapdoors hinged along each edge, with a waist-high railing alongside to ensure that the warder holding John's arms did not fall down the hole when the trapdoors opened. Above this was the machinery of the gallows. The ropes and fittings had been adjusted to match his height and weight.

The hangman began his grisly routine, tying John's wrists behind his back and attaching a rope around his neck with the knot next to an ear. Then he fastened a hood over John's face, with a flap at the front left up until the last moment.

John was singing 'We Shall Overcome' when the hangman turned down the hood flaps, checked all was ready and pulled the lever, plummeting him through the huge trapdoors. The rope jerked with such force that it not only broke John's neck but left a severe rope burn. Chris Barnard, South Africa's pioneer heart surgeon, wrote years later about the physiology of death by hanging: 'The man's spinal cord will rupture at the point where it enters the skull, electrochemical discharges will send his limbs flailing in a grotesque dance, eyes and tongue will start from the facial apertures under the assault of the rope and his bowels and bladder may simultaneously void themselves to soil the legs and drip onto the floor.'

As to whether John would have felt any pain, Barnard added: 'It may be quick. We do not know as none has survived to vouch for it. We make the assumption that the *danse macabre* is but a reflection of a disconnected nervous system … and the massive trauma of the neck tissues and spinal column does not register in that area of the human psyche where horror dwells.'

In keeping with the custom of the Pretoria gallows, John was left to hang for 15 minutes. In the corner of the gallows chamber was a concrete staircase leading to a high-ceilinged room below. Set into the floor was a 'blood pit' about half a metre deep, lined with coloured tiles, with a plug hole in the middle. To one side was a large low wooden trolley, which could be wheeled over the whole pit. The doctor stood on the trolley after John had been stripped to certify his death. Then his body was lowered onto the trolley and washed off with a hose, the water draining into the pit. A warder put a rope around John's body, which, by means of a pulley, was then lifted to allow the rope to be taken off. He was then lowered onto a metal stretcher and placed directly into his coffin.

John was later described as 'very brave' by the hangman, also named Chris Barnard. As South Africa's longest-serving executioner, he was alone responsible for 1 500 hangings between 1964 and 1986.

I woke unusually early that morning, finding Ann and my parents already up, as still and silent as the darkness outside. Then the phone rang and the caller asked to speak to Ann. Mom refused, recognising the familiar voice of a security-police officer, who went on to say mockingly, 'Your John is dead.'

I was overwhelmed by a sort of blank hopelessness and deep anger. Like my parents, I condemned what John had done. But under any civilised system, he would have continued to devote his life to teaching children and would never have been involved in the act that ended his life so grotesquely.

❖

SET in green spacious grounds, Pretoria's Rebecca Street Crematorium is a serene, peaceful building, and its chapel has a simple charm.

Aged 15, dressed in my Pretoria Boys High School blazer, tie and grey trousers, I found myself ushered up to the raised lectern before the assembled congregation, waiting as the coffin was carried in. I spotted Tom, in his khaki school shorts, inserting himself among the pallbearers, who had grabbed hold of the coffin from the prison warders and police.

The chapel was packed and the gathering included black comrades, who were not usually permitted to attend a white funeral. But the event was something of a blur. I glimpsed many friends – Liberal Party members from both Pretoria and Johannesburg, people from the townships and even members of the diplomatic corps. Everyone knew that their names would be diligently recorded by the Special Branch officers outside.

Although the ceremony had been carefully prepared, and I had only to read out the address distributed to those present, I had never spoken from any platform before and had always avoided school plays or performances, being regarded as a private, undemonstrative and rather shy boy.

The occasion made me even more nervous. Grown white men were crying and Eva was sobbing heart-wrenchingly out loud. As I readied to begin, I trembled, my voice seeming not to want to come out. But fortunately it did as I started to speak the words written before me.

The proximity of the coffin, a metre to my left, containing the body of a friend hanged just two hours earlier, made the ordeal especially unnerving. It had been explained to me how I needed to press a button to take the coffin away. But in the middle of the service I almost panicked, realising that I hadn't been told when exactly to do it. The last thing I wanted was to get that wrong. But then, while singing 'We Shall Overcome', I thought it must be the appropriate time. It seemed like a totally irrevocable step as the coffin moved eerily away out of sight, as John's body was lifted on a trolley into the oven. It took half an hour to burn, with only the ashes of his bones remaining.

(When I returned to film for the BBC in 2012, the white

crematorium operator – earthily descriptive and hyper-talkative but with no idea who I was – spared no gory detail as he gave me chapter and verse on what happens to the body and coffin. He'd been doing the job for many years and complained that there were far too many 'fat people these days' and that the oven found it difficult to cope. He was particularly caustic about pacemakers because they sometimes exploded, and metal hips or knees were even more of a problem.)

I stepped awkwardly down from the lectern, to be surrounded by a tearful Ann and my family huddled together. Embarrassingly, people kept coming up and thanking me. I thought I was just doing what anybody would have done, and it all seemed over almost before it had begun.

An hour later, I was back at school. Having missed the first lesson, I tried to slip into the classroom. Terry Ashton gave me a sympathetic but unobtrusive welcome. Although the school had been warned I would be late, none of my classmates knew the reason until a report with my photograph in Boys High uniform appeared in the papers the following day. However, my school friend David Preiss later recalled how another teacher, Keith Gibbs, had 'made a very brief but poignant speech to our class in anticipation of your return from the funeral of John Harris. We knew very little about what was happening to you, but Keith guided us in the art of quiet, kindness and empathy.'

When Sally arrived in her classroom, her teacher, Mrs Parry, played 'Battle Hymn of the Republic' on the piano, not saying anything but giving the eight-year-old a comforting smile.

Fourteen hundred kilometres to the south, on Robben Island, the political prisoners were already out in the morning digging limestone from the quarry, a gruelling daily process – especially in bright sunshine, which damaged their eyes. During their lunch break, John's ARM colleague Eddie Daniels called on all the prisoners to stand and observe a minute's silence 'to a great freedom fighter'. Nelson Mandela and all members of the ANC, PAC, Communist Party and other political groups readily obeyed the call.

❖

PECULIARLY – and this only emerged in 1998 after a persistent search by Ann's sister Meg – the authorities kept John's ashes for years, apparently in an urn in the office of the Pretoria Central prison commander. The urn was handed over to the prison chaplain, who arranged for a burial in a simple grave in the public cemetery 100 metres from the crematorium, the prison authorities marking the spot with a stone bearing John's name and dates. Meg arranged for the words 'A True Patriot' to be added (as he had wanted) to John's gravestone. His family travelled from the UK in 2005 to mark the 40th anniversary of John's death.

This was followed by a 'Symbolic Cleansing and Wreath Laying Ceremony' at the Isivivane – a Garden of Remembrance – at Freedom Park at Salvokop, on a hill outside Pretoria. The park, deliberately situated to the north of the Voortrekker Monument, is a beautiful, tranquil shrine to the fallen, from the colonial and Boer wars through the world wars to the freedom struggle. Thousands of names are etched onto the light-brown stone Freedom Wall. Under the heading 'Executions' is 'John Harris 1937–1965'. John's family members were also invited to the opening in December 2011 of Pretoria's Gallows Museum.

❖

THE 1964 station bomb was a pivotal event for our family and the country. As Dad had predicted when refusing to join his friends in the ARM, the bombing was exploited both to increase repression and systematically to discredit and destroy the Liberal Party.

John Vorster, the justice minister, made a bellicose attack on Mom and Dad, fulminating (totally inaccurately) that John Harris had been recruited into the ARM 'at the house of Hain'. If he had been, 'the house of Hain' would certainly have joined ARM comrades in the dock.

After John's execution, the period for which people could be held without charge was extended from 90 to 180 days; two years later it would become indefinite. The Liberals' magazine, *Contact*, closed after its fifth editor was banned. Alban Thumbran was also banned. Ruth Hayman, John Harris's lawyer and my parents' friend and legal mainstay, was banned and placed under house arrest. Our battered old Volkswagen minibus, for years effectively the Pretoria Liberals' main transportation, was stolen by the security police; it was eventually found months later in Hartbeespoort Dam, west of Pretoria, after the water level had fallen drastically in a drought. The engine was recovered and lifted into our garage, where I tried to clean it up to establish if we could get it working again. My interest in cars and engines was strong if rather amateurish, and I never managed it.

Other leading Liberals were also targeted. Randolph Vigne's house was petrol-bombed after he escaped abroad. Peter Hjul's infant son narrowly missed being killed by a bullet fired through the house's front window. Alan Paton's car windows were smashed and iron filings inserted into the oil sump of the engine. Other Liberals were subjected to extreme harassment and intimidation by the security forces, designed to terrify them into inaction. Party members were also fed disinformation leaflets and forged letters encouraging them to give up before they too were targeted.

But at the July 1965 Liberal Party Congress the party fought back defiantly, refusing to be cowed. A motion was unanimously carried condemning 'savage, systematic and … unconstitutional persecution' by the government. It also urged members: 'Now is the time to hold fast to our conviction and our faith.'

On the other hand, the reputation of the party among the wider movement resisting apartheid had been badly damaged when John Lloyd and Adrian Leftwich turned state witness. This was in stark contrast to the heroic stance of Nelson Mandela and his ANC comrades at the Rivonia Trial, who openly defied the judge and risked the death sentence.

Activist Magnus Gunther argued bluntly: 'Sadly, not much pride, defiance or heroism was shown at the trials. It was not just police torture that broke ARM members. They seemed morally stricken ... The fact that one of their members had killed someone and maimed several others seemed to drain all resistance from many, though ... others [including Hugh Lewin and Eddie Daniels] refused to turn state witness ... but it was the spectacle of Leftwich betraying his friends, himself and his ideals that personified the defeat of the organisation and led to others making statements. There were no stirring challenges to the regime from the dock, no expressions of pride about their considerable contributions to the struggle, as had been the case during the Rivonia Trial.'

❖

THE bell was tolling for our life in South Africa, as Dad's continued employment as an architect specialising in hospital-laboratory design was threatened. He had been out of work for two months after being fired during his imprisonment in 1961. Then he had found a temporary job in Johannesburg before being taken on by a Pretoria firm that, among other commissions, designed hospitals for the Transvaal provincial administration. But soon after his ban, the firm was told that if they continued to employ him, they would no longer receive any government work. So he had to resign, and Dad opened his own office. Then local work dried up: although he had a few commissions of his own for projects outside the Pretoria magisterial district (to which his ban confined him), the minister of justice refused him permission to leave Pretoria to inspect and survey the sites. Then the word went out from the security police to the profession in Pretoria that private architectural firms would get no work if they employed him – even indirectly, through work contracted out.

The police state was taking its revenge on our family by depriving Dad of the ability to earn a living. It was traumatising. They had found our vulnerable spot, and it seemed there was nothing we could do. Mom and Dad were torn. They were desperate not to desert their close comrades, but they had no private means and were being remorselessly propelled towards the only remaining option: to leave the country. So Dad wrote to the firm in London that had employed him in 1956 and was immediately offered a job. He then accepted a generous offer from Harold Smith, a friend, of rented accommodation in a flat above his home in Putney, southwest London.

Dad was 41, and his already badly disrupted architectural career was being further undermined. He and Mom were leaving the country of their birth, which they loved and for which they had sacrificed many of the comforts and privileges of white life. They were also leaving their parents, relatives and close friends. My siblings and I were similarly leaving our friends for a future unknown: we hated the idea and resisted until we were told it was inevitable.

One small consolation for Tom and I was that, on inspecting a map of London, we discovered that Chelsea Football Club's home ground, Stamford Bridge, was near our new home; the team was doing well at the time, with stars such as Terry Venables, George Graham and the young Peter Osgood, and we became fans. I was able to book cheap tourist tickets for the 1966 FIFA World Cup finals, which were being held in England that year, so there was something exciting to look forward to. We also talked of seeing cricket at Lord's and motor races at Silverstone and Brands Hatch – places of awe to a young 'colonial' boy like me.

Liberal Party friends raised the finance for our passages on a Union-Castle liner from Cape Town – by far the cheapest way for a family to travel at that time. Dad was eligible for a British passport because his father had been born in Glasgow, and Mom was eligible as she had married him before 1951. I was British, having been born in Kenya, but, unaccountably, my birth certificate was missing – probably stolen by the Special Branch in one of their raids on our house. And Kenya did not recognise apartheid South Africa, so a copy of my birth certificate had to be obtained indirectly via a friend in London. Sally had been born in Britain. That left Tom and Jo-anne, and the British Embassy helpfully registered them, so that we all had British documents. That was a relief. Although a fog of resigned depression hung over us, Mom and Dad were characteristically phlegmatic, prompting a 'make the best of it' attitude in us all.

The security police were caught on the hop until they were alerted, as the banning orders required Mom and Dad to apply for permission to leave the Pretoria area. They immediately became obstructive, until it was pointed out that we had British passports and had already been issued with departure permits. But these were withdrawn and replaced with one-way exit permits, which prohibited my parents from returning to South Africa and withdrew their citizenship. In the typically bloody-minded manner of the local bureaucracy, permission to leave Pretoria was then delayed until the last moment; at one point it looked as though we would have to postpone our departure.

A farewell party was held in the Liberal Party offices. Mom and Dad dropped us children off, because their bans prevented them from attending. Everyone present treated us as surrogates for the absent parents they held in such high and affectionate regard.

Mom and Dad were emotionally torn apart. There was no

glory to going into exile: they felt intensely guilty at deserting those closest to them, though they were simultaneously relieved that the all-consuming pressure under which our family had been living for the preceding three years might now be eased.

They drafted a press release, which had to be issued in my name, and which I wrote out by hand (because their bans still prevented them from saying anything publicly themselves). Over the decades that followed, I was to issue many press statements, but this was my first. Dated March 1966, it read:

> My parents have reluctantly taken the decision to leave South Africa.
>
> Both are South African born and bred, and had hoped to live their lives working, as in the past, towards the attainment of a just society in South Africa; a society of which all South Africans could be proud, whatever the colour of their skins, whatever their religious beliefs, whatever their political convictions.
>
> But the Nationalists have made it virtually impossible for them to remain, for by direct pressure upon employers the Government has made it extremely difficult for my father to obtain employment and by refusing him permission to inspect clients' buildings outside the Pretoria magisterial district it has ensured the failure of his architectural practice. The stage has now been reached where he is no longer able to make a living in his own country but must seek work elsewhere to support his family.
>
> This is the sole reason for my parents' decision to leave.
>
> They do not subscribe to the view that nothing more can be done within South Africa by radical opponents of Apartheid and that there is consequently no point in South African Liberals remaining here to continue the struggle for justice and equality. On the contrary, they believe that the very scarcity of genuine opponents of racialism amongst white South Africans greatly

magnifies the relative importance of white non-racialists here, and they point to the banning of nearly forty Liberals as evidence that the Nationalists share this belief.

The decision to leave has therefore been a painful one for them, especially as it means leaving behind not only their parents and friends – both white and non-white – but also the many Liberals who are also banned and so cannot communicate with them without risking prosecution.

We hope to return when South Africa is governed, not by narrow sectional government as at present, but by one that truly represents all South Africans; without the injustice of the Pass Laws, the Group Areas Act; and [when] detention without trial laws are no more than a bad memory; when there is a decent, dignified life for all.

Edmund Burke once said: 'All that is necessary for the triumph of evil is that good men do nothing'; we believe that the evil of Apartheid is temporarily triumphant in South Africa today because so few good men will become committed. And in Alan Paton's *Cry, the Beloved Country*, the African priest, Msimangu, says, 'I have one great fear in my heart, that one day when they are turned to loving, they will find we are turned to hating.' I and my parents share this great fear, and I urge my fellow whites to 'turn to loving' before it is too late.

On 14 March 1966, the tears flowed as many party stalwarts, together with Grandad and Granny, came to Pretoria railway station to see us off to Cape Town; the banned Alban Thumbran stood waving alone at the end of the platform. We would never see Alban – or Grandad – again.

Mom gave Eva Matjeke a hug and kiss goodbye. Eva stood there as if turned to stone, knowing that if she let go of her emotions she would simply break down, as she had done at John Harris's funeral. Gladys Geffen, Dave's mother, found Eva a job at a Pretoria clinic and she was offered all our remaining household goods and furniture. As the steam train chugged out, the waving figures became smaller and smaller, then disappeared. Mom was tearful, Dad stoic.

Waiting on the platform at Johannesburg station as the train passed through were more party members to say farewell and shower us with parting gifts. Although our departure was deeply upsetting, I also found it exciting: the train journey was novel and so was the waiting ship.

We were just making the best of it, as we always had through the years of increasing adversity. Looking back, I must have been toughened by the various experiences thrust upon me. By then I was 16; I had learnt to cope, and also perhaps to blank out the inevitable emotion of those experiences, to 'move on', telling myself that nobody and no group would get the better of me. Although I was deeply angry about what had happened to us, I knew that far, far worse had happened to black activists in the freedom struggle.

But I didn't feel a 'victim', and I didn't feel damaged. Angry, yes, but not bitter. I despised the ministers and security policemen, but I never hated them. 'Haters', I learnt, become consumed with their hatred, and that hands victory to their opponents.

Nevertheless, Mom and Dad later freely admitted to being more worried about me than their other children, because I had been more exposed and was at a critical moment in the final years of my high-school career. In retrospect, Tom, Jo-anne and Sally found it much more difficult to adjust to their new life in England than I did. And there was soon to be a shocking reminder of the psychological pressures people like us had been through: a school friend, Alan Lazar, the same age as me, and whom I looked up to as an extremely bright student and a very talented young crick-eter to boot, abruptly committed suicide a year after coming into exile in London at the same time as us. Nobody who knew him could find an explanation except in the turmoil of his parents' involvement in the struggle and the family's enforced departure from their homeland.

❖

WHEN our train arrived at Cape Town docks, Special Branch officers beadily watched to ensure my parents complied strictly with the terms of their permission to leave by going straight onto the ship. We all trooped along the quayside, settled into our economy family cabin on a lower deck, and went up to wave a last goodbye to a small group of relatives and party friends down below.

By the time we steamed out, Mom had fled down to our cabin, trying to shield from us how bereft and ill she was feeling. I remember looking out over the deck railings, feeling queasy as the ship heaved heavily in the Cape rollers, and glimpsing Robben Island, grim behind the cold spray, imagining how Nelson Mandela was surviving in his cold, bleak cell, where he was then into the third of his long 27 years in prison.

We were leaving behind a South Africa with the powers of darkness totally in the ascendant. The principal liberation movement, the ANC, was outlawed and in disarray: its leaders were in prison and its military wing, Umkhonto, seemingly crushed. Other resistance groups had similarly been banned or paralysed. The Liberal Party had been badly damaged by the banning of its main activists (and two years later new legislation banning multiracial parties would force it to disband).

Since 1994, there has been a tendency to airbrush out the role of Liberal Party activists in the anti-apartheid resistance, but a balanced perspective would recognise their important if subsidiary influence, which was clearly regarded as a serious threat by the apartheid government or it would not have smashed them and closed down the party.

Although the ANC and its partners were overwhelmingly the dominant force in the eventual overthrow of apartheid and the transition to the new South Africa, the Liberal Party, during its short but eventful life between 1953 and 1968, was a catalyst for change, especially but by no means exclusively for whites. In 1960, the banning of the ANC, PAC and Congress of Democrats meant that the Liberal Party was the only publicly active and – until its forced dissolution in 1968 – legal anti-apartheid force. When Mom and Dad were most prominent, and under greatest attack from the security forces and the state, in the period between 1960 and 1965, there was no other visible and permitted political party committed to a truly non-racial society with equal rights for all. The Progressive Party of Helen Suzman, despite her courage and importance, did not stand for universal suffrage, and played nothing like the heroic role of the Liberals.

Although the new post-apartheid constitution was the brainchild of the ANC's President Oliver Tambo, was drafted by Albie Sachs and then meticulously negotiated under Nelson Mandela by Cyril Ramaphosa, the 'liberal beliefs and ideals the [Liberal] Party had championed against all comers were to arise phoenix-like and prevail at last in the first constitution of a new non-racial South Africa,' Randolph Vigne later claimed in his history of the party.[1]

❖

WHEN asked later why they had – so unusually for whites – sacrificed a wonderful (if increasingly stressful) life for their beliefs, my parents always played down their role: 'We only did what we felt we had to do.' Others might say they were an ordinary couple who did extraordinary things.[2] I have always been immensely proud of their record, and, had fate placed me at that time in their position, I hope I would have had the courage to follow in their footsteps.

71

As the Cape coast disappeared into the mist, my Pretoria boyhood did too. Despite talk that we would be back one day to savour the freedom of a new South Africa, these seemed only the ritual exchanges of close comradeship. We had no illusions: the apartheid state seemed immortal.

We were going for good, Dad always made clear: we must make a new life for ourselves in Britain. As it transpired, however, we were destined to join others in exile in what was to become a decisive era of international struggle against apartheid. But I had not the faintest idea that within three years I would be catapulted into playing a significant role in that struggle.

Exile

'WOULD you like to write an essay, boy?'

The question came from the head teacher, Charles Kuper, a lugubrious and ruddy-faced man with whiskers – and a whiff of alcohol.

'No, thank you very much, sir,' I replied, putting a literal interpretation on the very English phrase 'would you like', and not recognising it for the instruction it actually was.

Tom and I had arrived with Dad for an interview at what turned out to be a boys' state grammar school, Emanuel, in Battersea, near Putney. Curiously, it had been recommended by our friend and landlord Harold Smith, an ex-member of the British Communist Party. A letter of reference from Desmond Abernethy at Boys High had listed my exam results and recommended me as 'a most promising pupil. He is of excellent character and of a most pleasing personality.'

The culture at Emanuel seemed to me a world away from Pretoria Boys High. There appeared to be plenty of wasted time, with the school day extending from nine in the morning until nearly four o'clock in the afternoon, with too many free periods and an over-long lunch break. When Mom and Dad later understood the system of secondary schools in Britain, they were horrified: their strong preference was for comprehensive schooling – without any academic selection, like in South Africa (albeit for whites).

I was used to starting school by eight, working hard and then finishing by 1.30, either to travel home for lunch or to eat my sandwiches, leaving plenty of time for afternoon sport and then homework. But I managed to escape joining the Combined Cadet Force by claiming (falsely, I confess) that I had not done that sort of thing before. (The truth was I had been part of a Boys High full of squeaky clean polished shiny shoes, glinting leather belts, drilling and marching in step.)

I had left Boys High a year before 'matric' (matriculation), the top school qualification in South Africa, normally taken at age 17. The matric standard was between Britain's O-level and A-level exams, which students typically took aged 16 and 18, respectively. But I was placed into Emanuel School's 'Lower 5 General' – the bottom-performing class of that year. The recommendation was that I spend an additional year there catching up with the curriculum for the O levels, which the other boys my age were due to sit in six weeks' time.

That rankled with me: I didn't want to lose a whole year treading water. Against official school advice, I resolved to sit the exams anyway. Mom and Dad agreed to pay a special fee from their meagre resources to cover late entrance. But my pass grades awarded in all ten O levels I entered – which, ironically, included Afrikaans – were creditable, though not anything like as high as I was used to. But at least I had passed the threshold to begin two years of A-level studies.

❖

SOUTHAMPTON docks had loomed, chilly and misty in the morning as our ship was piloted to its berth in April 1966. The weather was a stark contrast to the heat that had accompanied us for most of the journey and that we had left behind in our sunny homeland.

By coincidence a fellow Liberal activist, Ann Tobias, was also on board the ship. But because she had been banned too, Mom and Dad couldn't speak to her until the ship had left South

African waters. I was deputed to contact her and arrange for her to eat at our table in the dining room.

Another unexpected delight was to discover the presence on board of our friends Fabian and Florence Ribeiro. Fabian was a prosperous black doctor from Mamelodi township, outside Pretoria, and his wife was a sister-in-law of the PAC leader, Robert Sobukwe. Both were Catholics, and they were going on a pilgrimage to Lourdes, the only way as Africans they could get a passport and permission to go overseas on holiday. Their presence was a source of astonishment to the overwhelming number of white South African passengers: after all, holidays were something that only whites did.

Dad asked two strangers on our table if they could switch places with the Ribeiros. But the two wouldn't move; instead, they sat pointedly and refused to acknowledge us throughout the two-week voyage; Mom and Dad wondered if they were Special Branch eavesdroppers.

Unusually for black South Africans, the Ribeiros were financially well off, but apartheid drastically restricted the way they could spend their money. They could not own a house in their township, send their children to the school of their choice or take their family on holiday, since there were no resorts set aside for blacks. So they drove a Mercedes – way above Dad's pay level – and dressed very well, Florence in the height of fashion. But because blacks were not permitted to try on clothes before purchasing, absurd special arrangements had to be made for Florence to go in to Hamiltons, Pretoria's top clothes shop, which wanted her custom. The shop was kept open for her after hours, so that she could try on her choices without upsetting white customers.

At a fancy-dress evening on the ship, Dad and Florence went jauntily dressed in their pyjamas labelled 'The Immorality Act' (the apartheid law banning both mixed-race marriages and mixed-race sex) – to incredulity and some disapproval. Fabian and Ann Tobias – who though 'white' had an Asian complexion – went as the first black president of Ghana, Kwame Nkrumah, and his Egyptian wife. Mom had Elastoplast over her mouth and wore a sash across her dress labelled 'The Perfect Woman'.

❖

WE arrived at our flat, 21A Gwendolen Avenue, Putney, the day after Labour's huge victory in the general election, and Labour Party election posters were still displayed on Harold Smith's downstairs front windows. But I was more struck by watching television for the very first time: *Champion the Wonder Horse* became a favourite of us kids.

A few days later Tom and I went to see our chosen football club, Chelsea, at Stamford Bridge, where the crowds seemed enormous. (Mom and Dad opted to join Harold on a nuclear-disarmament march.) I played cricket on weekday afternoons at Emanuel and joined a local club to play at weekends. Later on I was recruited to my Dad's office cricket team, playing mostly in Regent's Park. I also found every opportunity I could to play football.

My other pastime was restoring a 1937 Lancia Aprilia, the same model that my parents had driven from Nairobi to Pretoria in 1951. I bought it for £10 from a Buckinghamshire farm, where it had been stored under bales of hay, and had it towed back to Putney. I joined the Lancia Club, rewired the car and eventually got it going after extensive renovation. But by that time I was so involved in politics that it had to be sold – for £15.

As we were to discover, many South African exiles in Britain lived a kind of limbo existence – waiting to return. That was their choice and their dream. But my parents were determined to put down roots, to get involved in the community and to make a new future. We must not be outsiders: Britain was now our home, they made clear to me.

Although my parents became active in the Anti-Apartheid Movement (AAM) almost immediately, regularly meeting other exiles, including old friends, it took a while before we were thrust into hyper-activism again.

Meanwhile the teacher who squeezed in careers advice between teaching history and supervising the Combined Cadet Force asked me: 'What do you want to do, boy?'

'Don't really know, sir,' I replied.

'In that case you will be an engineer,' he decided. My grandad had been a civil engineer and Dad encouraged me, so my school future was planned: A levels in physics, applied maths and pure maths, and catching up on curriculum gaps.

That summer proved exciting. Tom and I went to see the visiting West Indies cricket team play England in three Test matches. It was awesome going to Lord's, the venerable home of English cricket, and then to the Oval and Trent Bridge, and to watch English legends such as Colin Cowdrey and Tom Graveney. These had been figures of distant wonderment back in South Africa, where I had been a keen but second-rate left-handed batsman and spin bowler, noted for catches close up to batsmen.

We were especially excited by West Indies players such as Gary Sobers, Wes Hall, Rohan Kanhai and Lance Gibbs, never having seen these black legends perform before. Then there was the extraordinary sight of Basil D'Oliveira, a Cape coloured, who was selected that year as an English Test player, having been barred from playing for South Africa because he wasn't white.

We were also able to go to Wembley with our bargain World Cup football tickets purchased in Pretoria. I was lucky enough to win a ticket in the draw for the final between West Germany and England. Standing next to a Tottenham Hotspur fan at what became the Geoff Hurst end of Wembley, I cheered on my new country to an exciting and historic 4–2 victory.

I settled phlegmatically into my new existence in grey, wet

London. But Tom found adjustment much more difficult, escaping from home and school until he was eventually discovered experimenting with cannabis. My parents later freely admitted that it was painful coping with the free-spirited behaviour and changing sexual mores of 1960s London youth, especially when it came to teenage Jo-anne and Sally. It was a far cry indeed from the Calvinism of South African family life.

I had also brought with me a naive colonial image of England – all royals, pomp and ceremony, with cricket on the village green. So it was startling to discover the extent of poverty and shabbiness that still pervaded so many parts of London. I read my Dad's *Guardian* for the sport and, increasingly, the politics. It was an eye-opener watching leading politicians being questioned on television, and seeing top-quality current-affairs programmes such as *World in Action* and *Panorama* – quite a contrast to the state-controlled propaganda of South African radio and the deference paid to the select group of favoured white apartheid politicians who were allowed on it.

❖

ABOUT a year after arriving in Britain, I decided to join the Anti-Apartheid Movement. Formed in 1959 in response to a call from ANC president Albert Luthuli for an international boycott movement, the AAM had gathered momentum after the Sharpeville massacre in 1960.

By late 1967 and early 1968, when I was 17 going on 18 (and in my final year of A levels), I gradually became more politically involved, following the current debates and avidly discussing with Dad topical issues such as the Vietnam War. I joined him in becoming hostile to American intervention in South East Asia.

In October 1968 Tom and I went on the big anti-Vietnam War demonstration in Grosvenor Square, witnessing violent clashes between police and protesters determined to storm the US Embassy. Mom and Dad had been worried before we went, after media reports about possible crowd trouble. They had taken great risks under apartheid, but what if their young sons got caught up in conflict in Britain? Watching on television, they became even more worried by the scenes of repeated confrontations between demonstrators and police – some on horseback.

Central London was eerily boarded up as we marched from Victoria Embankment to Mayfair. The excitement of the time resonated in our chants: 'London, Paris and Berlin – we shall fight, we shall win!' And 'Hey, hey, LBJ, how many kids have you killed today?' (LBJ being US President Lyndon Baines Johnson, who massively escalated US involvement in Vietnam and later refused to seek a second term, a towering politician broken by the war.)

Then, amid the noise and fervour, I lost Tom. We had separated in all the melee and violence in Grosvenor Square, despite having been on the periphery of the trouble. I arrived home, looking for him, thinking that he must have got there first and aghast to find he hadn't. Mom was frantic with worry. She didn't know what to do. There had been lots of arrests but there was nobody they could check with. Hours later, Tom turned up, exhilarated, still chanting slogans and cheerfully brandishing a red banner given to him by a Marxist group. He was to use it as a bedspread.

Although everyone on that march felt that Harold Wilson's Labour government had not taken a tough enough stand against the war, in retrospect at least he did keep Britain out of it by refusing to send troops. (This was in stark contrast to Tony Blair's stance on the Iraq war more than 30 years later.) But at the time we didn't see it that way.

Many of us also felt that Wilson was not dealing firmly enough with the illegal rebellion by the white minority in Rhodesia. Their leader, Ian Smith, had made a Unilateral Declaration of Independence (UDI) to maintain racist rule in that country. The campaign against UDI was being organised by the AAM and I began to attend more of its meetings.

I was 17 when I decided to join the Young Liberals (YLs), the youth wing of the British Liberal Party. My choice arose partly because of what I felt was the Labour government's abject timidity on Rhodesia, partly because of our connection to the South African Liberal Party, and partly because the YLs were then a vibrant, irreverent force for radicalism.

But that choice was far from straightforward. Although my parents had joined the local Liberals in Putney where we lived, there was no youth branch. So in order to join, I had to form a branch, rather as my parents had had to do in Ladysmith in 1954. It was daunting, but I warmed to the notion of setting up something myself rather than joining an established body as an outsider.

Two others joined me: Miranda Timaeus, a girl my age, and Mike Wallace, an older trainee accountant. We divided up the officer posts between us. I ended up as chairman, discovering a zest for organisation probably instilled by observing my parents.

❖

YL radical politics quickly took over my life, and led me into an exciting culture of left-wing ideas. YL leaders, expert at attention grabbing, had appropriated for themselves the term 'Red Guards' from Mao Zedong's Cultural Revolution, which was then convulsing China, and called for a 'cultural revolution' in their senior party and in Britain as a whole.

The YL movement's energy and flair for publicity, together with its continual pamphleteering and campaigning, provided an ideal crash course in political education. I started reading left-wing books and pamphlets voraciously, and was taught how to draft press releases, deal with the media and organise.

We supported militant, though non-violent, direct action

where necessary, emulating the wave of protest and civil-rights demonstrations in America and university student sit-ins. I was almost 19, and politics was in my DNA from my Pretoria boyhood. But my belief in socialism really crystallised around 1968–1969 – the years of the Paris uprising, of student agitation throughout Europe and the US, of the Soviet invasion of Czechoslovakia and of anti-Vietnam War protests. A 'new left' had emerged, iconoclastic and just as opposed to capitalism as to Stalinism: 'Neither Washington nor Moscow' was our slogan. We favoured a 'bottom-up' socialism rather than a 'top-down' one, popular participation not state bureaucracy, workers' control not nationalisation: these were the watchwords, and the more radical YLs like me described ourselves as 'libertarian socialists', distinguishing ourselves from both Soviet-style state socialism and free-market classical liberalism.

I was immersed in a ferment of new and radical ideas, shaped by the passionate debates in teach-ins, conferences, demonstrations and sit-ins. But when it came to the 'sex, drugs and rock and roll' folklore of the late 1960s, I must have cut a rather boring figure. Girls interested me, but short-term relationships didn't. I was deeply anti-drugs and never touched the stuff; in total frustration, a fellow YL once tried to stuff a cannabis spliff into my mouth. I wasn't attracted to drink and barely followed the pop charts, in contrast to Tom, who got caught up in the bohemian youth culture of the late 1960s; Jimi Hendrix was his icon.

Despite my busy activism, however, I had been instilled with an ethic of hard work, both by my parents and by Boys High, and so managed to get three good A levels. On the strength of these, I was accepted for a year's engineering student apprenticeship, consisting of both technical education and factory experience. That was to precede a mechanical-engineering degree course at the University of London's prestigious Imperial College, starting in October 1969. I turned down an opportunity to apply to

Oxford, having frustratingly travelled there and searched for what I had been told was 'Maudlin' College; how could that pronunciation possibly apply to the actual Magdalen College? I did not take to the upper-class snobbery of Oxford, though in later years I became a regular speaker at student meetings there.

As apartheid moved up the political agenda, early in 1968 a number of leading YLs had formed a Southern Africa Commission (SAC). This brought together members with an interest in the area, and although I had only joined the YLs in Putney a few months before, through the SAC I quickly came into contact with national YL leaders. As the only ex-South African involved, I found myself propelled to modest prominence, which was also to bring me into close touch with AAM leaders such as Ethel de Keyser, Alan Brooks and Abdul Minty. That October I was encouraged to stand for office, and, at the age of 18, was elected, to its national executive committee.

One of my first activities with the SAC was setting up a 'Medical Aid for Southern Africa' appeal in 1968 to assist the ANC and other liberation movements. Many people sympathetic to, or actually involved in, anti-apartheid organisations would not associate themselves with guerrilla activity but would back medical aid. I visited the ANC's London office and held discussions with, among others, Thabo Mbeki, recently a student at the University of Sussex.

With Mom's help, we typed up and printed on a second-hand Gestetner machine (similar to her old one in Pretoria) copies of a pamphlet supporting the medical aid appeal. Dad, who was an excellent artist, did the artwork for the cover. Miranda Timaeus, the Putney YL secretary, and I hitch-hiked 400 kilometres to our first national YL conference, in Scarborough, in April 1968. We booked into cheap rooms and I later wondered wistfully about pretending not to notice her romantic overtures. Instead I immersed myself in the conference excitement, meeting the leadership stars and soaking up the politics, being called to the rostrum

82

to make a brief speech in favour of a resolution supporting the ANC's liberation struggle – the first time I had spoken to a large gathering. But, despite the radicalism of the YLs, the resolution was narrowly defeated after strong appeals by pacifists.

For me, violence was no academic matter: I had seen too much of it in South Africa, and my Dad was vehement about it. But the predicament of those resisting apartheid convinced me that the ANC was justified in adopting guerrilla tactics. With all democratic and legal channels blocked, I was persuaded by those such as Nelson Mandela who argued there was no alternative to an armed struggle, and started advocating the cause of the ANC and its sister liberation groups fighting racist regimes in southern Africa.

However, my support for the ANC's guerrilla struggle was never to be confused with support for 'terrorism'. The vital distinction is that the violence of guerrilla movements such as the ANC was directed against an oppressive state, whereas the violence of terrorist groups such as al-Qaeda or Islamic State, the Irish Republican Army (IRA) or ultra-right American bombers is directed indiscriminately against innocent bystanders. Although the distinction did sometimes become blurred, as on the few occasions when sabotage carried out by the ANC unintentionally caught bystanders, I believed that it nevertheless remained valid and important – and a foundation for building political solidarity.

A violent strategy by resistance movements can only be justified when, as was the case with European countries invaded by Hitler during the Second World War, or with a more recent tyranny such as apartheid, all other means have been exhausted with no viable alternative. In the debates that raged around the radical politics of that era, I argued that to deny people the right to resist such tyrannies violently was to deny them their humanity and to acquiesce in their oppression, adding that, when the crunch came, all the pacifist could do was to bear moral witness, dying bravely as the tanks rolled in.

AS a sports fanatic, I instinctively saw the importance of anti-apartheid campaigning in sport, which some activists saw as at best peripheral, at worst eccentric. I was from the white South African psyche – pretty well all sports-mad, with Afrikaners especially fanatical about rugby. I knew that international sport, whether the Springboks, the Olympics or a cricket tour, gripped the white nation as nothing else. Importantly, sport granted whites the international respectability and legitimacy they increasingly craved as the evil reality of apartheid began to be exposed by horrors such as the Sharpeville massacre. Moreover, it was easier to achieve success through practical protest against sports links than it was to secure sanctions by taking on the might of international capital or military alliances, although I also fervently advocated this course. Victories in sport were crucial during a period when internal resistance was being smashed and it was extremely hard to impose international economic and arms boycotts.

Apartheid politics was inserted into the very core of South African sport, beginning with schools. A multitude of statements by top white rugby, cricket, sports or government figures justified racism in sport on the most spurious and blatant basis. And any doubt that sports apartheid was absolutely central to the ideology of white domination was demonstrated with devastating clarity by an editorial in the pro-National Party newspaper *Die Transvaler*, on 7 September 1965. Arguing that 'the white race has hitherto maintained itself in the southern part of Africa' because 'there has been no miscegenation', it continued:

> The absence of miscegenation was because there was no social mixing between White and non-White ... If they mix on the sports field then the road to other forms of social mixing is

wide open … With an eye to upholding the white race and its civilisation, not one single compromise can be entered into – not even when it comes to a visiting rugby team.

But the real game-changer came in the case of Basil D'Oliveira, who unwittingly found himself at the centre of a major storm in 1968. A highly talented coloured South African, he had been unable to play first-class cricket in his own country, let alone for it. So in 1960 he had travelled to England with the assistance of legendary BBC cricket commentator John Arlott. He became a British citizen and rose meteorically to become an automatic choice for England from 1966. The question became: should he be selected for that year's cricket tour to South Africa? On merit, there was no question that, as a free-scoring middle-order batsman and medium-pace bowler, he should be selected. But following weeks of seedy manoeuvring and high drama, D'Oliveira was offered £40 000 by a South African-based representative of the cigarette company Rothmans to declare himself unavailable for selection. When he was omitted from the touring party, John Arlott epitomised the public reaction: 'No one of open mind will believe that he was left out for valid cricketing reasons.' And, as it transpired decades later, Doug Insole, the chairman of the selectors, had been in touch with the South Africans beforehand, to be told that D'Oliveira would not be welcome.

However, after weeks of raging controversy, D'Oliveira was reluctantly included when the Warwickshire all-rounder Tom Cartwright withdrew, apparently with a shoulder injury. (Ironically, Tom, who married a Neath woman, was one of my constituents when I was elected MP for Neath in 1991, and my teenage son Jake was coached under his supervision. We became friends and he told me in 1995 that he had always been unhappy about the idea of going on tour to South Africa, that pressure had been put on him to accept despite the fact that it was known to Lord's that he was injured, and that he withdrew out of conviction – not simply for the publicly quoted explanation.)

Then came a dramatic new twist. Pretoria refused to accept D'Oliveira's selection. 'It's not the England team. It's the team of the anti-apartheid movement,' Prime Minister John Vorster preposterously thundered at a gathering of the ruling party, to fervent cheers. He cancelled the tour: so much for 'keeping politics out of sport' – the line ritually levelled at anti-apartheid campaigners. There was universal outrage from centrist opinion in Britain, which until then had not really engaged with the arguments the AAM had been making for a decade.

What became known as 'the D'Oliveira affair' marked a turning point, and D'Oliveira himself became an enigmatic servant of the anti-apartheid struggle. Enigmatic because, although he never personally committed himself to the cause, it was strengthened by the searing injustice of his predicament. A breakthrough was achieved partly *because* of Basil D'Oliveira, but it also occurred *without* him. Unlike, for instance, Mike Brearley, D'Oliveira never openly backed the AAM, though he privately enjoyed the hospitality of leading activist Chris de Broglio's Portman Court Hotel in West London. At the time, many campaigners felt let down, yet because D'Oliveira retained all along the quiet dignity of a cricketer first and last, he reached and touched parts of public opinion that anti-apartheid activists could never do.

D'Oliveira inadvertently triggered what became the British anti-apartheid campaign's finest hour in sport. For, despite the unprecedented veto of their tour, a few months later, in January 1969, the English cricket establishment, as usual hunkered down from the world at its Lord's headquarters, brazenly announced that they would proceed with the scheduled 1970 cricket tour to Britain by a white South African team – cricket as usual, as if the D'Oliveira affair had never happened.

❖

I WAS outraged at the news of the tour, and immediately got backing for a YL motion pledging ourselves 'to take direct action to prevent scheduled matches from taking place unless the 1970 tour is cancelled'. It got a small mention in *The Times* and was sent to the cricket authorities.

The previous year I had been introduced to those in exile in London running the South African Non-Racial Olympic Committee (SANROC), which John Harris had chaired before he was banned (his passport had earlier been withdrawn as he tried to board a plane to argue internationally for South Africa to be expelled from the Olympic movement).[1] SANROC had been successful in getting white South Africa suspended from the Olympics for the first time in 1964, and in May 1969 it held a public meeting in London where I raised from the floor the question of direct action to stop the cricket tour. The former Robben Island prisoner Dennis Brutus was in the chair and was very supportive, as was his colleague Chris de Broglio.

Since the 1950s, AAM sports protests in Britain had been largely symbolic: holding up banners outside stadiums. These had been vital in the process of mobilising awareness – and indeed still had an important role to play. But direct action to physically disrupt sports tours could not be ignored by the sports elites who had been impervious to moral appeals and symbolic protests.

The idea was the product of that unique late-1960s era in which I had been caught up. My inspiration came from student sit-ins such as that at London's Hornsey College of Art in 1968, worker occupations and the squatting of empty houses by the homeless. It was no longer enough simply to bear witness, I felt, and a new, more militant movement gathered momentum alongside the AAM, which maintained a discreet, sometimes uneasy, distance that I respected as necessary to its more conventional role.

Militancy

A PRIVATE tour by an all-white South African club side spon-sored by a wealthy businessman, Wilf Isaacs, experienced the first-ever taste of direct action against cricket anywhere, when, in the Essex town of Basildon in July 1969, I led a group of YLs onto the pitch. I had contacted a dozen or so beforehand and planned our intervention, gathering as spectators at the small club ground, having tipped off journalists. Play was interrupted for over ten minutes until police dragged us, limp, off the field, with photo-graphs and stories in the media gaining attention for this novel tactic.

Subsequent tour matches in Oxford and at the Oval saw even greater and more successful disruptions, organised by local AAM branches. That July, a Davis Cup tennis match was due to take place in Bristol between white South Africa and Britain. On the opening day I drove my parents' VW Beetle to Bristol with two Putney YLs, Helen Tovey and Maree Pocklington, like me in their late teens. We planned our protest on the drive down, not know-ing quite what to expect. We were tense and worried as we arrived and purchased tickets. Taking our seats separately, we waited until I signalled and then ran onto the court, disrupting play for the first time in an international event in front of live television cov-erage and causing consternation, which was widely reported in the media.

We were carried off and taken to the local police station before being released after perfunctory questioning. It was my first taste of a police cell – ironically, my parents later remarked, a British rather than a South African one. Later in the three-day tournament, play was further disrupted by an invasion, and flour bombs were thrown onto the court in protests organised by the Bristol Anti-Apartheid group.

Because sport was being targeted by direct action, the protests were highly newsworthy, as I had anticipated, with publicity for each encouraging others. Crucially, these events were taking place across the country and action could be initiated locally, instead of converging on London. This meant that the emerging movement was characterised by considerable local autonomy and spontaneity. A network soon fell into place and, with active encouragement by Dennis Brutus and Chris de Broglio of SANROC, we decided to launch the Stop The Seventy Tour (STST) committee at a press conference in September 1969. It had broad support, from the AAM and United Nations Youth to the National Union of Students, Christian groups and young communists, Trotskyists and Liberals. A Reading University student, Hugh Geach, became the secretary.

Although I was only 19, I was pressed by Dennis Brutus, Chris de Broglio and others into a leadership role, and found myself acting as press officer and convenor of the committee (later encouraged to assume the chair). It was daunting, because I had anticipated being a foot soldier supporting more experienced and illustrious figures. Joined by Dennis Brutus, I pledged, at the press conference in Fleet Street's White Swan pub, that there would be 'mass demonstrations and disruptions throughout the 1970 cricket tour' – confident that a national organisation would emerge, just as local activity had begun to gather pace in the previous few months. My very public threat was deliberately pitched to be newsworthy and therefore to capture the sense of interest needed to galvanise a big movement.

We needed to be quick, because I also promised demonstrations against the Springbok rugby tour, which, we had realised rather belatedly, was due to start in six weeks' time. We aimed to use it as a dummy run to build a campaign capable of stopping the following summer's cricket tour. Looking back, I recall a fearless innocence, part exhilarating and part just getting on with what I felt had to be done: determined to win a decisive battle against the evil of apartheid and convinced, perhaps more than anybody else, that we could achieve this through non-violent direct action.

Also that September, I spoke for the first time at the Liberal Party's annual conference in Brighton, urging support for direct action. I wasn't a natural or experienced orator and it was rather nerve-racking. My photograph appeared in national newspapers and I was invited to do television interviews, also for the first time. I found myself taking it one step at a time, unsure whether I could manage the next one, but then finding indeed that I could – and quite successfully. It did not change me much as a person; I was still seen as quite shy and modest, living at the family home, though gaining experience and with a growing public profile, while my South African roots and still-strong accent enabled me to speak authoritatively for the anti-apartheid cause.

Throughout all this I had been spending the 1968–1969 year as a student mechanical-engineering apprentice, and was ready to begin my London university course. But London-based South African journalists had begun to take an increasing interest in me, and I formed good relationships with several, including David Beresford and Ian Hobbs. Their regular reports rapidly elevated me to the status of a 'hate' figure in my old homeland. I was la-belled 'Public Enemy Number One', which caught on. Outraged at the threats to their sport, white newspaper commentators first awarded me the label. It was soon taken up by white politicians and in news reports, where it became a familiar adornment. I was routinely vilified and turned into an ogre. The fact that 'one of their own' had turned against them provoked stories about my 'taking revenge' for the treatment of my parents. Among white

South Africans a Pretoria boy had suddenly gone rogue, and I received a registered letter dated October 1969 from the minister for the interior. It informed me that my right as a British citizen to enter the country without an 'alien's temporary permit' or visa had been withdrawn. (I had no intention of returning nor had I indicated any desire to do so.)

Around the same time, Desmond Abernethy, the head of Pretoria Boys High School, arrived in London and sought me out, courteously pressing me to stop my activities. When I was at Boys High he had been quietly, albeit distantly, sympathetic as my parents' notoriety grew. He had also given me a fulsome letter of reference. But the London encounter was rather strange. I had been used to obeying his dictates – head teachers in those days were both revered and feared – but now he found himself unable to persuade his formerly well-behaved pupil, as I politely declined his request. The sense that he was doing his duty was confirmed by a newspaper story reporting his mission back in South Africa.

On the back of growing excitement and publicity, the campaign took off and our modest Putney flat became the headquarters address and office. Volunteers turned up to help, sitting all over the living room, and Mom quickly assumed the crucial role of office secretary, fielding phone calls, coordinating information, helping with correspondence and banking donations. The experience she had gained in Pretoria in running an organisation, though in this case a national one, stood her in good stead as organisers across the country got used to dealing with her. Dad came home from work to write leaflets and background briefs. Suddenly, in a reversal of roles from our life in South Africa, I had become the front person, but I could not have done this without my parents' constant support in the background.

My public threats of direct action against the rugby tour and confident predictions that we could stop the cricket tour generated widespread attention. I found myself being regularly interviewed on television and radio, using the guidance and experience I had gained through the YLs to deal with the press on a daily basis, while cycling daily to my mechanical-engineering lectures at Imperial College. I spent my lunch breaks with homemade sandwiches in a call box taking phone calls from journalists and local organisers through messages relayed from my mother at home, where the phone rang incessantly (she complained, only half-jokingly, that she hardly had time to go to the toilet). As I entered my twenties, my life was both that of the everyday student wrestling with the mysteries of thermodynamics and the exhilarated national protest leader.

❖

MEANWHILE, a mass movement was snowballing. It was locally based, largely spontaneous, and usually focused around student unions, though involving local branches of the AAM, socialists, radicals, liberals, independents, trade unionists, vicars, priests and bishops.[1] It was predominantly young, though by no means exclusively so, and soon took the Springbok rugby tour by storm.

The venue for the opening match, against Oxford University in October 1969, was switched after strong opposition from both the college authorities and the students, who sprayed weed killer on the ground and threatened to wreck the match. The new venue was kept secret to avoid demonstrations, but Bob Trevor, a friendly Welsh sports journalist (and Labour Party member) with the London *Evening News*, had promised to phone us immediately the press were informed. At 9.30 pm the night before, our phone rang and his familiar voice said: 'Twickenham, 3 pm.'

I immediately phoned the Oxford Committee Against Apartheid and scores of organisers around the country. Coaches full of demonstrators were waiting: more than 1000 rushed to the ground and we all purchased tickets, gathering together in the main stand. The match took place under siege, with pitch invasions and constant hostile chanting. Midway through the match, I spotted an opening in the police cordon and tried to jump over the spectator fence, but was immediately grabbed, carted out and dumped on the pavement. Sensationally, the mighty Springboks lost, clearly unnerved by the atmosphere.

This played right into our hands. Switching the first fixture from Oxford at the last minute had attracted front-page stories on the morning of the match and set the scene for the remaining games of the 25-match tour. Local organisers realised that they were part of a mass national movement, and each of the matches saw demonstrations of varying sizes. Several of the biggest set-piece confrontations took place at the home of the Rugby Football Union, Twickenham, within easy reach of central London. We were able to get 2000 inside for the first scheduled match in late November – some 'disguised' by cutting their hair or wearing Springbok rosettes – and a similar number outside. I was one of over a hundred demonstrators who managed to climb over the fence surrounding the pitch and outwit the police, though I was grabbed immediately. Play was stopped for over ten minutes until we were carried off and summarily ejected from the stadium.

The week before, in Swansea, the most brutal confrontation of the entire tour had taken place. A Wales Rejects Apartheid Committee had been formed, with widespread support from all walks of life. But in South Wales – a socialist stronghold with an honourable tradition of international solidarity going back at least to the Spanish Civil War, much of it coordinated through the miners' union – rugby fanaticism came first. At Swansea, there were ugly scenes as police threw 100 peacefully invading demonstrators back from the pitch and deliberately into the clutches of 'stewards', who promptly handed out beatings. One demonstrator's jaw was broken and he nearly lost an eye. Others, including women, were badly assaulted. Journalists from papers such as *The Times* not supportive of the demonstrations condemned the 'viciousness' of the police and stewards.

Looking back more than 50 years later, we were possessed of a fearless idealism. I was never deterred by possibilities of violence against me, threats of prosecution or the very personal fury and threats I increasingly attracted. Morality was on our side, our cause was just, our militancy necessary. I was determined to win.

The police and rugby authorities increasingly got wise to our tactics, and we were heavily infiltrated. In 2020, after being invited to give evidence at the official Undercover Policing Inquiry, I was shown scores of old confidential police documents proving that I had been targeted for close surveillance for over a quarter of a century. An undercover British police or security service officer was in almost every political meeting I attended, private or public, innocuous or routine, or serious and strategic like the STST.

Why were they not targeting the criminal and oppressive actions of the apartheid state? BOSS was responsible for, among other crimes, fire-bombing the ANC's London office in Penton Street in March 1982, and for the 1970 murder of South African journalist Keith Wallace, who had threatened to expose BOSS's operations in the UK. A large South African spy ring had operated in Britain since 1965, regularly bugging phones, and facilitated by the British security services. In December 1971 documents about church-sponsored exchange visits between South Africans and Britons were stolen from Friends House, the London headquarters of the Quakers. The AAM headquarters in Charlotte Street, London, was periodically burgled. Its senior officials were kept under surveillance, including its chairman, Bob Hughes MP, secretary Abdul Minty and executive secretary Mike Terry. Also targeted were Albie Sachs and Ruth First, both prominent in the AAM and the ANC while in London, and both the target of bomb attacks in Maputo by apartheid agents.[2]

The British police and security services were on the wrong side of justice, on the wrong side of the law and on the wrong side of history. There was also a systematic pattern of malevolence, deceit and exaggeration by undercover officers (UCOs). One, known as Mike Ferguson (not his real name), claimed to have been my 'number two' in the STST campaign – a straight lie. I had no number two, and if he is the person I vaguely recollect, he was on the periphery of those around me.

Ferguson and other UCOs claimed that our campaign intended to attack the police at Twickenham when England played the Springboks. A lie: we did not. They claimed we planned to sprinkle drawing pins on the pitch. Another lie: we did not, and indeed were at pains to avoid personal injury to players as we ran onto pitches in acts of non-violent direct action, sometimes being beaten up ourselves by rugby stewards or police. They reported that we planned to put oil on Lord's cricket pitch and dig it up. Again a lie: we never did. UCOs also played agents provocateurs on occasion, daring militant but non-violent protesters into violent or criminal activity.

It was clear from the voluminous secret police documents that the authors had never expected these to be revealed or publicly dissected, for they were packed with self-serving, self-promoting, entirely false allegations about the STST's intentions, with phrases like 'spreading panic', 'attacking' and 'subversive'.

Shortly before appearing before the inquiry on 30 April 2021, I was made aware of a previously undisclosed police record that described me as a 'South African terrorist', a description given by undercover officer Mark Kennedy, who formed an intimate relationship with environmental activist Kate Wilson – who had been at primary school with my children in Putney. It was documented by the National Police Order Intelligence Unit and dated November 2003 when I was a member of the British Cabinet, Secretary of State for Wales, Leader of the House of Commons, Lord Privy Seal, and a member of her Majesty's Privy Council. What was it in the DNA of British undercover policing that allowed its officers to imbibe such a biased and reactionary view of the world that they could make that kind of false and defamatory statement about me in this instance and no doubt about others?

Another secret document stated that my mother and father had been members of the South African Communist Party (SACP) in the 1950s and that as a young teenager I had attended its meetings. It presented my mom as a Svengali, manipulating me during the STST campaign. None of that was true. My parents were South African Liberals. But the information had clearly been supplied from Pretoria, further proof of British intelligence service collaboration with apartheid's security forces.

These exercises involved a massive waste of limited police resources – for example, infiltrating a North London women's liberation group with three or four members, missions described to the inquiry as a 'complete waste of time' by UCO 'Sandra'. Or meetings in 1969–1971 of Putney YLs in my parents' living room, attended by Jo-anne, Sally, myself and the UCO, where we discussed, among other obviously subversive topics, homelessness, old-age pensions and threats to the environment. Surely those officers could have better spent their time catching criminals, drug traffickers and terrorists?

❖

IN Northern Ireland (itself in turmoil following civil-rights protests, and sliding into barbaric violence), the Springbok match was cancelled for security reasons. Elsewhere, matches were made all-ticket and security inside was massively increased, with police standing shoulder to shoulder around the pitch facing the spectators. In Cardiff all pretence at a normal rugby match was abandoned as barbed wire was put up around the field. In blue-rinse-conservative Bournemouth, the match had to be abandoned because the open ground there could not be defended.

Our tactics changed as well. We knew that the STST campaign had by now been infiltrated (including at a national level). My home telephone number was tapped – a familiar though uncomfortable experience we thought had been left behind in Pretoria. So we established an 'inner group' of some of my most trusted and experienced activists, several older than me, who had years before participated in direct-action demonstrations through the Committee of 100, the militant offshoot of the Campaign for Nuclear Disarmament. It was called the Special Action Group and worked on clandestine projects under the leadership of London dentist Mike Craft and radical activist Ernest Rodker.

The Special Action Group booked Rosemary Chester, a vivacious young woman, into the Springbok team's London hotel in Park Lane. (Decades later, she became Lady Kirkwood, wife of the former Liberal MP Lord Kirkwood; she died in 2019.) Rosemary slipped through the hotel in the early hours gumming up the players' door locks with solidifying agent, forcing them to break down the doors to get out on the morning of the pre-Christmas international match at Twickenham. Michael Deeny, an STST activist who worked in the City of London, turned up most undemo-like in a smart suit, politely told the driver of the team's coach waiting outside their London hotel that he was wanted inside, slipped into his seat, chained himself to the steering wheel and drove the coach off to crash it nearby as he was grappled by some of the Springbok players who had already boarded.

Springbok vice-captain Tommy Bedford later recalled what he saw from his seat as 'chaos … The guy had tried to hijack the Springbok rugby team. And all this only four hours before kick-off.' Deeny, meanwhile, was subjected to a mauling.

At the match, protesters evaded the heavy police cordon. Two of my Putney YL friends, Mike Findlay and Peter Twyman, had rehearsed their plans in our back garden, running and quickly attaching themselves to a broomstick with handcuffs we had purchased. Unlike other protesters, they were also deliberately dressed in jacket and tie. My South-African-accented aunt Jo had purchased special ringside seats in front of the security cordon and, at a pre-arranged moment, Mike and Peter suddenly burst out, dodging to evade furious pursuers, one just managing to chain himself to the goalposts. Play was interrupted until he was cut free. Orange smoke pellets were also thrown among the players, which, as well as disrupting play, produced dramatic television and newspaper pictures.

An attractive student involved in the campaign became a 'Mata Hari', deputed to chat up the players. She struck up a friendship with one Springbok in Bristol, and they met again in London. He and some colleagues agreed to go with her to a 'reception party' we had organised – its purpose to talk, not to intimidate. But when she went to collect them after the post-match festivities, she discovered that her man was completely drunk and interested only in groping her.

At the last Twickenham match in late January 1970, we distributed packets of powdered dye to selected protesters (including me). The powder turned black on contact with dampness. These were thrown onto the pitch so that the Springboks, rolling on the wet grass, were smeared with black stains, to chants from protesters on the terraces of 'Paint them black and send them back.' Wherever the team went – resting, training or playing – it was under siege.

Over the Christmas break, an STST activist ingeniously managed to attach an ANC flag to fly from the team's hotel flagpole, and it was reported that the players had taken a step inconceivable in the annals of Springbok history and voted to abort their tour and go home. But the management, under political pressure, ordered them to stay, and the tour finally staggered to an end with the players bitter and unsettled. For Tommy Bedford, it proved a cathartic experience; within a year, he publicly stated that I should be listened to, not vilified, and praised our objectives. Although his response was a relatively isolated one in South Africa, it signalled the huge and destabilising impact of our campaign.

For the first time, the Springboks – accustomed to being lionised as perhaps the leading national rugby team in the world – had been treated as pariahs. They were no longer faced merely with what they habitually dismissed as the spluttering of 'misguided liberals and leftists' while they retreated to the warm hospitality of their rugby hosts. This was something of quite a different order. Anti-apartheid opponents had now shown a physical capacity to disrupt or stop the Springboks' ability to tour in the old way.

The white minority was apoplectic. The Afrikaans progovernment paper *Die Beeld* stated in an editorial: 'We have become accustomed to Britain becoming a haven for all sorts of undesirables from other countries. Nevertheless, it is degrading to see how a nation can allow itself to be dictated to by this bunch of left-wing, workshy, refugee long-hairs who in a society of any other country would be rejects.'

The reaction among the black majority in South Africa was, however, diametrically different. After their release from prison many years later, both Nelson Mandela and Govan Mbeki told me that on Robben Island, news of the demonstrations transmitted to them by infuriated warders had been an enormous morale boost; Mbeki said it had also brought a smile to their faces when they learnt that 'the son of the Hains' was leading the campaign.

Hugh Lewin was then in the fifth of his seven years in Pretoria Central and, like the Robben Islanders, had a news blackout imposed. He described how reports leaked through his warders, Afrikaner rugby fanatics to a man. First they started swearing to each other about the 'betogers' (demonstrators). Initially confused, Hugh began to piece it together and realised that something big was riling them. Gradually, the truth seeped out. He and his fellow 'politicals' were thrilled. For him, the *coup de grâce* came when the warders began moaning about 'that bastard Peter Hain', though he found it difficult to match his recollection of a well-behaved boy in his early teens with the monster apparently responsible for these dreadful events. Hugh claimed to have detected in the quality of the soup served up on a Saturday evening how successful the demonstrators had been in disrupting that afternoon's game: the poorer the soup, the more successful the demonstration …

Jonathan Steele of *The Guardian* reported on 5 March 1970: 'It is not hard to find South Africans who are delighted by the demonstrations against the Springboks. Go into Soweto … or into any other African township … and if you are not accompanied by a white South African, the masks fall. Eagerly they want the news confirmed. "Is it true that they are having to use a thousand police to hold back the demonstrators today?" … Their views on the Springbok tour were straightforward. They were against it. And so were their neighbours, and anyone else you talked to.'

The saturation coverage given to the campaign in the South African media reached parts of South African life that no other boycott campaign was able to, because most white South African men cared about sport first and foremost. The huge psychological and political impact was well illustrated by banner newspaper headlines – 'NO DEMONSTRATIONS!' – welcoming home a Springbok canoeing team in February 1970. The members of the team had arrived in Britain, canoed and left in virtual secrecy – we certainly never got to hear of it. But the team's captain was very clear about the reasons for such 'success' at an ecstatic homecoming reception when he exclaimed: 'Most demonstrators are hippies and hippies don't like water – that's why we weren't worried by them.'

❖

ALTHOUGH dutifully attending university lectures and tutorials, my academic engineering studies seemed a world away from my enjoyable apprenticeship year in an engineering company and at technical college. I was also changing fast as a person and becoming clearer about what I did and did not want to do. I quietly applied to switch degrees and was accepted elsewhere within the University of London, at Queen Mary College, to study economics and political science. It was only afterwards that I informed my worried parents. Decades later, the head of the department, Maurice (later Lord) Peston, told me that the university authorities had unsuccessfully tried to pressure him to block my admission as an undesirable subversive.

The rugby tour had provided the movement with a perfect springboard from which to plan direct action to stop the cricket tour, due to start at the beginning of May 1970. But opposition, coordinated by the AAM, went much wider. The churches, led by the former England cricket captain and Bishop of Woolwich, David Sheppard, urged cancellation. The Commonwealth Games, due to take place in Edinburgh that summer, also became an important lever. SANROC's international expertise and contacts were put to good use as it was privately pointed out to African and Asian countries that they would be in an intolerable position if they participated in the Games at the same time as an apartheid cricket tour was under siege elsewhere in Britain.

Then, late in the night on 19 January 1970, demonstrators simultaneously raided 14 of the 17 county cricket club grounds. All were daubed with paint slogans. In addition, a small patch in the outfield of Glamorgan's Cardiff ground was dug up, and weed killer was sprayed on Warwickshire's Birmingham ground. Pre-planned telephone reports from each small, tight group poured in throughout the night to the Press Association news agency and to my home. In the morning the coordinated protest dominated the radio bulletins and television programmes, and there were screaming headlines with photos in the evening papers and the following day's national newspapers.

It was a devastating shock to the cricket authorities. The wide-spread strength of the movement had been starkly revealed in an operation seemingly carried out with military precision. More than this, the spectre of a cricket tour collapsing amid damaged pitches and weed killer was conjured up and began to crystallise.

Speculation was rife about who was responsible. The AAM denied all knowledge. People inevitably accused the STST, as it alone had the organisational capacity necessary to mount the raids. But I said (entirely accurately) that the STST national committee had not authorised or approved the action, thereby distancing us from it. The only national figure to give the raids full backing was the YL chairman, Louis Eaks, who attracted head-lines and dominated the airwaves when he said that 'some Young Liberals had been involved' (which was accurate as far as it went, though his intervention provoked irritation among those involved who considered it opportunistic – especially since most were not YLs). It was in fact a covert operation by key STST activists in the clandestine Special Action Group, executed with meticulous planning, efficiency and impact.

Within weeks, 300 reels of barbed wire arrived at Lord's, and most county grounds introduced guard dogs and security. Then pressure on the cricket authorities intensified. West Indies crick-et leaders angrily denounced the tour, and African, Asian and Caribbean countries talked of withdrawing from the Edinburgh Commonwealth Games. One by one, a range of public bodies came out against the tour and there was talk of trade unions taking industrial action. Some Labour MPs, including the AAM's vice-chair, Peter Jackson, said they would join sit-down pitch invasions. The chairman of the government-sponsored Community Relations Commission, Frank Cousins, told the home secretary that the tour would do 'untold damage' to race relations.

On 12 February the Cricket Council called a press conference at Lord's, which I managed to infiltrate until spotted by officials, who stiffly ushered me out. But not before I glimpsed an extraordinary sight: the pitch eerily surrounded by barbed wire, silhouetted in the snowy night. Lord's, the magisterial home of international cricket, looked for all the world like a concentration camp, symbolising the torment that had torn asunder this most dignified and graceful of games.

The Cricket Council issued a sombre statement explaining that the tour had been cut drastically to just 12 matches from its original schedule of 28. And it was to be played on just eight grounds instead of the original 22, with artificial all-weather pitches to be installed as an additional security precaution. It was a striking decision, on the one hand indicative of bunker-like obstinacy, on the other testimony to the growing power of the campaign. I denounced the decision, quipping that we might rename ourselves 'The Stop The Seventy *Half*-Tour campaign'.

However, the Conservative shadow attorney general, Sir Peter Rawlinson, attacked the Labour home secretary, James Callaghan, for remaining 'neutral' and 'acknowledging the licence to riot'. Rawlinson also called for an injunction to be taken out against me, insisting that my public statements threatening to stop the tour constituted a direct incitement to illegal action. After Cabinet documents were made public 30 years later (and, ironically, when I was a serving Labour government minister), it was also revealed that ministers had discussed whether or not to prosecute me, with James Callaghan in favour and Tony Benn against.

I was also privately warned by a friendly solicitor that my open advocacy of disruptive protests made me extremely vulnerable to a charge of conspiring unlawfully and a likely prison sentence, because British conspiracy laws then were a catch-all device for curbing radical political action.

But our whole strategy was predicated upon being open about our disruptive plans; it was public knowledge of our planned direct action that constituted our prime tactical weapon. That threat held the key to our strategy to get the tour stopped in advance. As its author, I was determined to carry it through regardless, believing we would succeed. It never occurred to me to stop under threat of possible prosecution.

Victory

'IT would be a mercy for humanity if this unpleasant little creep were to be dropped into a sewerage tank. Up to his ankles. Head first.'

The celebrated right-wing editor of the *Sunday Express*, Sir John Junor, was cheered to the rafters by the outraged conservative-minded for denouncing me. He was joined by my former Emanuel School head teacher, Charles Kuper, who roundly denounced me in a school assembly, and by the editor of *The Spectator*, George Gale, who labelled me a 'Demo Mobster'.

Three years later, in July 1973, when I obtained a first-class honours degree in political science and economics, the Liberal peer Lord Avebury sent a tongue-in-cheek letter to the *Daily Telegraph* suggesting that its readers would be relieved to hear the news, for the paper's letters column had, during the STST days, been filled with denunciations of me as 'a student layabout' who was 'protesting at taxpayer expense'. His letter provoked a torrent of fulminations about how the standard of degrees had self-evidently collapsed.

A sizeable slice of the British public might well therefore have identified with white South Africa's label, 'Public Enemy Number One', not least because our campaign was snowballing. Action groups to complement those established during the rugby tour sprang up throughout the country. By now the nickname 'Hain the Pain' was in familiar usage by British journalists – and white South African ones too – with the STST campaign regularly in the headlines.

Meanwhile, the AAM was deluged with offers of help and its membership shot up. About a hundred inquiries a day by phone and letter poured into our home, which remained the STST headquarters – with Mom almost tied to the phone and our flat filled with volunteers and callers.

Labour Prime Minister Harold Wilson publicly opposed the tour for the first time. The West Indian Campaign Against Apartheid Cricket was launched by leading black activist Jeff Crawford, whom I actively encouraged, because linking the campaign to racism in Britain added an important extra dimension. SANROC, through the Supreme Council for Sport in Africa, an agency of the OAU, consolidated the basis for a Commonwealth Games boycott. Trade unions came out against the tour. Television workers and journalists threatened a media blackout, and radio's 'voice of cricket', John Arlott, announced he would not do the ball-by-ball commentary for which he was internationally renowned. Mike Brearley (later to be one of England's most successful cricket captains) took the courageous step of speaking at STST's national conference on 7 March 1970.

Opposition was by now reaching right into the establishment. Leading public figures, including David Sheppard, formed the Fair Cricket Campaign (FCC), whose vice-chairman was the senior Conservative Sir Edward Boyle. Though explicitly committed to lawful, respectable methods and publicly opposed to the STST's tactics, the FCC was privately friendly. Through a mutual contact I was invited for a meeting with its leaders that I undertook not to disclose, arriving to an atmosphere that was courteous if edgy. However, we quickly found cordial common ground when I said I was relaxed if they felt it necessary to criticise our militancy, but it would be best if we both refrained from arguing publicly with each other since we had a common objective (to stop the tour) and a common enemy (apartheid). David Sheppard in particular saw the sense of this immediately, and we agreed to stay in touch and keep our contacts confidential.

As the radical, by now notorious, outsider, dressed in my habitual jeans and anorak, here I was in a posh Kensington drawing room of suits and plummy accents. Perhaps because I had not been brought up in Britain's deeply stratified and class-ridden society, I did not feel at all awkward about this – instead, I was rather intrigued, which also seemed to be the case for those to whom I was introduced. They all seemed decent, well-meaning people, though I thought it naive to believe that letters to *The Times* and words in well-placed ears might stop the tour.

I saw the power in having a 'spectrum of protest': the STST's militancy; the AAM's conventional pressure-group role and its very effective links with the labour movement; SANROC's expert international diplomacy; and the FCC's impeccable respectability. There was now a very broadly based opposition to the tour, which I knew was essential for victory. It also reflected my antipathy to the debilitating sectarianism I had witnessed over the previous couple of years of radical activism.

Although the STST's direct action powered the whole campaign, it could have been isolated without a great hinterland of broad public support, and I was at pains to stake out a non-sectarian position, refusing to criticise the more moderate groups and understanding their concerns about our militancy. This also enabled STST activists under my leadership to include Liberals as well as Trotskyists and communists, who normally wouldn't be seen under the same political umbrella. We could all sink our differences under the banner of action to stop the tour.

My casual dress was by now a personal badge. I did not possess a suit and never wore a tie; smart for me was what in modern parlance would be called 'smart casual'. So in major television studio interviews I would typically wear a trademark polo-neck shirt or white polo-neck jersey – with jacket and trousers. Anything smarter would have been 'selling out' my radicalism.

However, I was clean-cut, my hair longish and curly, compared with the scruffiness, shoulder-length hair and beards then the norm among radical males. Indeed, by the radical, student, hippie standards of the late 1960s and early 1970s I was awkwardly unfashionable, only struggling into flared trousers a couple of years after everyone else had been wearing them and they were about to go out of fashion. I didn't do trendy.

However, some could not cope with my polite but firm informality. In February 1970 I travelled to Oxford for a set-piece televised debate at the Oxford Union. I arrived mid-afternoon in my anorak, neat jacket and clean white polo-neck shirt. Waiting for me on the station platform was the Union's secretary, in a preposterous dinner jacket and bow tie. Then, at the end of a heated and excellent debate, our opponents fiddled the voting, requiring a recount the next day, when it transpired our side had won. The media, meanwhile, delightedly reported that we had lost. (Thank God I hadn't chosen Oxford for my degree, I thought.)

At Durham University – a sort of aspiring Oxford for upper-class debutantes where the Union Society officers were even more pretentious – my informal dress caused palpitations. I arrived in the early evening after several days touring North East England, dressed in standard anorak and polo-neck shirt, grip bag in hand. 'We will show you to your room, sir,' a Jeeves-like older man said, taking an inscrutable look at me. 'Thank you,' I replied, surprised at having a room to myself at all. A little weary, I lay down on my back for a doze. Half an hour later there was a knock on the door and Jeeves squinted in. 'Oh, you are not changed yet, I'll be back in a few minutes.' Before I could respond he closed the door and scurried away. It was getting towards the time of the debate, in which I was due to lead the case for stopping apartheid sports tours. When he returned he looked in, aghast.

'You *still* haven't changed?'

'No, *these* are the only clothes I have!'

It was clear I was inadvertently breaking all the rules. But the debate was about to start and I was the star guest, albeit the sole speaker not in the dinner jacket nobody had warned me about and which I didn't possess. Fortunately, the debate went well, with a majority of the audience clearly on my side. But the *pièce de résistance* was a silver-service dinner afterwards, clearly the evening's highlight for the Union officers, as they pretentiously pulled out cigars. To my bewilderment, a silver mechanism on wheels came chuntering around the long table towards me, passing by each dinner guest in turn. What on earth *was* it? Apparently, I was being offered a glass of port: good training for the upper classes.

By April, the campaign's momentum was still increasing. Prime Minister Harold Wilson went further, saying people 'should feel free to demonstrate against the tour', drawing fierce criticism from right-wing MPs and media, even though he was careful to criticise disruptive protests. The British Council of Churches also called for peaceful demonstrations. The Queen announced that neither she nor any member of the Royal Family would make the traditional visit to the Lord's Test match, and the South Africans would not receive the traditional invitation to Buckingham Palace.

Then, with the tour just six weeks away, all SANROC's patient lobbying paid off when the Supreme Council for Sport in Africa announced that 13 African countries would definitely boycott the Commonwealth Games if the tour went ahead. Asian and Caribbean countries soon followed, raising the prospect of a whites-only Games in Edinburgh running alongside a whites-only cricket tour. Sparked off by local direct action, the campaign had provoked an international diplomatic and political furore.

The AAM played a crucial organisational role, both as a participant in the STST and in its own right. Its indefatigable and formidable executive secretary, South African-born Ethel de Keyser, worked herself into the ground. An AAM poster caught the public's imagination and was widely published. Under the caption 'If you could see their national sport you might be less keen to see their cricket', it showed a policeman beating defence-less black citizens in Cato Manor township outside Durban.

The STST went ahead with plans to blockade the team at Heathrow Airport. Thousands of tickets were being bought up by local groups (the matches had been made all-ticket). Secret plans were being executed by the Special Action Group, which consulted me privately throughout. Ingeniously, the group had discovered an old underground train tunnel running right underneath Lord's Cricket Ground, with a disused but still functional air shaft that could facilitate a dramatic entry onto the pitch – potentially by hundreds of activists.

But, although much activity was nationally coordinated by the STST, local groups operated quite independently. Partly by design – to avoid acting like a conspiracy – this was mainly a product of the way the movement had evolved. There was also a considerable degree of individualistic autonomy in the campaign. I opened our front door one day to be faced by two young, bright-eyed if somewhat zany model-aeroplane buffs, with excitable plans to buzz the pitch during play from their aunt's flat, which overlooked Lord's. There were reports from all over the country of other novel protest methods. Some individuals were breeding armies of locusts, which they planned to let free on the turf. Others acquired small mirrors with which they intended to blind the bats-men. Newspapers had a field day reporting on such stories, and I was blamed for just about everything, regardless of whether or not I had any prior knowledge or involvement.

I was very much in the eye of a political hurricane, learning all the time while leading, and having to play daily media demands by instinct, and I was only too aware that saying the wrong thing could be calamitous. I was increasingly the target of hate mail and threats to my safety or life – something familiar to our family from our Pretoria days where the danger had been very real by comparison with what here seemed like the rantings of assorted nutters. But if the pressure on me individually was huge, at least I had the security of my close family and the rock-solid loyalty of the activists around me and the wider movement, for which I had become the figurehead.

The combination of sport, race and direct action had a toxic potency for many on the right in Middle England. For some, a cricket tour to England being stopped by 'radical agitators' seemed equivalent to the loss of empire, as revealed in letters sent by members to the MCC. One labelled me and the STST as a 'complete negation of all this country stands for'; another saw the MCC standing against us as 'the last bastion of what remains of the British way of life'. I was denounced as a 'dangerous anarchist and communist', the writer noting that if 'they' can 'smash this tour they will turn to other things'. Another described the STST campaign as 'persistent mob pressure and an attempt at neo-communist rule'. The anti-apartheid struggle was caricatured through a distorted Cold War prism, which the apartheid government deployed through its deliberate portrayal of all resistance as 'communist' – including my parents, both Liberal Party members.

But, despite the national and international furore, the cricket establishment held firm. In mid-May, with the first match just three weeks away, they were invited to meet the home secretary. James Callaghan was by now very concerned at the threat to public order, and the government was also deeply embarrassed by the impending collapse of the Commonwealth Games. After an unfruitful exchange in which he urged cancellation, Callaghan said he 'detected a lurking belief that they are a lonely band of heroes standing out against the darkening tide of lawlessness'. Certainly, the Cricket Council's members reflected old-world, right-wing political beliefs. And both they and our other opponents were no longer making their stand on their familiar territory of 'building bridges' and 'promoting sports relations', but instead on defending the rule of law against our alleged illegality.

But immediately after the Callaghan meeting came a decisive and unexpected boost to the anti-apartheid forces. As a result of SANROC's persistent work, South Africa was finally expelled from the Olympics. Events were scrambling to a climax. Harold Wilson was about to call a general election, and there was a notable shift in opinion. For the first time, EW Swanton, cricket correspondent for the conservative *Daily Telegraph*, and Ted Dexter, former England captain and one-time Conservative Party parliamentary candidate, both urged cancellation. The Cricket Council met in emergency session, with widespread media predictions that the tour would be called off.

Although I was hopeful, I was also sceptical that they would cave in, with something nagging away at me to this effect. And, indeed, the council meeting ended on a defiant note, though perversely conceding our case for the very first time by announcing a new policy that there would be no future tours until South African teams were selected on a multiracial basis. It was as if they hoped this switch would sugar the pill of their stubborn refusal to be 'bullied', as many of their diehards saw it.

But still the drama was not over. The home secretary asked to see the Cricket Council again and formally requested cancellation. Another hurried meeting was arranged at Lord's. This time the decision was indeed final. At long last, the tour was off, cricket's leaders bitterly complaining they had had no option but to accede to what they interpreted as a government instruction – in reality a face-saving excuse for their humiliation. From their sordid manoeuvrings over Basil D'Oliveira to their astonishing decision to proceed with the 1970 invitation to the South Africans, even after their own tour there had been stopped by the apartheid government, they seemed to me impervious to the modern world or to any appeals for human rights and equal cricketing opportunities.

I was both thrilled and intensely relieved. What would certainly have become a series of ugly confrontations had mercifully been avoided. I had become increasingly worried about the dangers of violence. For me, the direct-action strategy was designed to succeed because of the *threat* it posed. Although I would certainly have carried it through, I would have taken no pleasure in doing so. Others involved, however, saw things differently and some were even a little disappointed that the impending confrontation had been averted.

Some wanted the STST campaign to continue in an unspecified form with its own distinctive and now highly successful brand of direct action. But I was firm that it could not and should not. Of course, lessons must be learnt from its tactics and applied elsewhere. But the campaign had been set up for a very specific purpose and that purpose had been fully achieved. To continue would inevitably contaminate that achievement, and I believed that the same level of success was not sustainable.

In any case, there was an established organisation, the AAM, into which energy should be channelled. Its membership had more than doubled during the campaign (ironically, since, very early on, some of its leaders, who wanted to control the STST, had urged its incorporation into the AAM, which I politely but firmly rebuffed). Leadership, I had learnt, requires leading and taking decisions that might not be universally popular within the ranks, such as my announcement the very same evening that we stopped the tour that we would wind up the STST and encourage all our supporters to join the AAM.

'Hain stopped play' was the cricketing headline in a sympathetic feature in *The Guardian*. But the right-wing press trumpeted darkly about 'anarchy', 'lawlessness' and the threat to England's civilisation. A campaign whose nine-month gestation was in the minds of a few people had now won with mass support, the STST being one of the very few British protest groups to have completely achieved its objectives.

For the first time in ten long, bitter years, since Sharpeville, black South Africans and whites involved in the resistance had something to cheer about. From the Cape Reserve suburb in Pretoria came a simple but moving telegram from our activist friends Poen Ah Dong, Alban Thumbran and Aubrey Apples, who had waved us goodbye in 1966: 'And so say all of us.' (To have said anything more explicit would have invited police attention.) Messages of congratulation poured in. There were ecstatic celebrations as disbelieving STST supporters absorbed the full extent of their momentous achievement. And the link to the wider anti-apartheid campaign could not have been made clearer than by Moses Garoeb, a leading freedom fighter in the South West Africa People's Organisation (Swapo), when he told me that the STST had been an 'inspiration' to Swapo cadres in the bush when they heard the news on their radios.

It had always been the specious contention of apologists for sports links that maintaining contact provided a channel for encouraging South African whites to see how the rest of the world lived and so breed more liberal attitudes. This was pure fantasy, for during all the decades of so-called bridge building, apartheid – and specifically apartheid in sport – had actually become more entrenched. I was always convinced that an effective sports boycott would deliver a decisive blow. And so this proved. Hardly had the tour been stopped than top South African cricketers tumbled out to condemn apartheid in sport. Never before had they spoken out like this. Peter Pollock, the fast bowler who had been due to tour, was forthright. A week after the cancellation he told the Johannesburg *Sunday Times*: 'Sports isolation stares South Africa in the face, and to creep back into the laager is no answer. Sportsmen who genuinely feel there should be multiracial sport should say so.'

Where nine months before, I had been virtually unknown, now I was a national public figure attracting both idolatry and infamy, widely recognised when out and about, my privacy a thing of the past. Aware of adulation from supporters, I came to appreciate that this could be accompanied (sometimes simultaneously) by jealousy. All this attention was somewhat bemusing but simply came with the territory, a consequence of the leadership role into which I had been propelled. But I thought myself in other respects as still the same person, quite conventional, solidly rooted in my family, hardworking and happy. Some considered me 'boring' because I was too busy to socialise much and shunned the media celebrity circuit. Fame was not something I had sought, although with it came both opportunities and obligations to pursue the politics to which I was fiercely committed, and to uphold the values instilled in me by my parents during our Pretoria life.

❖

IN Australia there was an uncanny repeat. The Campaign Against Racialism in Sport teamed up with its more militant sister organisation, the Stop the Tours campaign, to focus on the mid-1971 Springbok rugby tour to Australia, to be followed by a cricket tour due that October. One of the organisers, Meredith Burgmann, explained: 'We were very influenced by the Stop the Springbok Campaign in England led by the exiled South African activist Peter Hain. We used to rush home to watch the news on telly and see how the protesters climbed up the goalposts and stormed the rugby fields.'

I was invited to support the campaign, and left for Sydney on a 31-hour flight after successfully sitting my first-year university exams. Arriving in Sydney early on the morning of 24 June 1971, two days before the arrival of the Springboks, I was greeted by my new comrades, including my opposite number, Peter MacGregor. I went straight into a press conference – the start of two weeks of non-stop media appearances, speaking engagements and private tactical briefings. I flew immediately to Brisbane and then straight to the field where the match was due to be played. It was completely open, with no visible defences, and there, in a television interview that was repeated for days, I said that it 'would be a piece of cake' to stop the match. It was switched to a more secure venue – an immediate victory for the campaign.

The Springbok tour began in conservative Perth on the west coast, but the campaign was able to achieve something that had eluded us in Britain (though not in Ireland), when trade unions promised to boycott the servicing of planes, and both the major domestic airlines decided they would not carry the team. So the team had to fly 2 735 kilometres to Adelaide crammed into a series of chartered light aircraft, the tiring seven-hour flight taking three times longer than on a regular airline.

I flew in on a scheduled flight from Brisbane to speak at a huge meeting in Adelaide's Central Methodist Church, finding the excellent response I received reminiscent of the STST. My message was clear: just as in Britain, the cricket tour would be stopped and the rugby one so badly disrupted that it would be the last. Over 1 000 demonstrators besieged the Adelaide match. There were interruptions to play and I watched from outside as smoke flares were let off under the floodlights. Police and stewards lashed out indiscriminately, even arresting a mild-mannered English gent who turned out to be the Australia correspondent of *The Times*.[1]

The campaign gathered pace. At student-union meetings I described STST tactics, encouraging activists to follow suit and delighting them with amusing tales of our ingenuity and the incongruity of apartheid sport. The spirit was very similar to that in Britain 18 months earlier, except that the distances between venues were so great that it was not feasible to bus in large numbers of demonstrators, as we had done. Seven current and former Wallabies (Australian rugby internationals) bravely and publicly opposed the tour, way beyond what was seen in Britain, where only John Taylor had refused to play.

Another difference, readily apparent, was the lower threshold for violence to be triggered, invariably by the police. In Melbourne armed guards with dogs patrolled the venue. At a rally attended by 5000 people, I was greeted enthusiastically, and said that the campaign was well on the way to emulating the success that we achieved in Britain. I went on: 'We are seeing a concentration camp-type atmosphere building up and I welcome that. It strips this tour of all its pretensions.' The demonstrators then set off to the ground, where 650 policemen with truncheons and horses started to wade into us. The *Sydney Morning Herald* reported the next day: 'Many Victorian policemen took the law into their own hands.' Sickening scenes of violence ensued. Even after the match, as we peacefully walked away, police on horseback charged us and we fled terrified – my most frightening experience in decades of demonstrating.

It was a tense day in another respect. That morning, calls were made to the media, purportedly from a right-wing assassin threatening to shoot me, so I was constantly peering around, knowing there would be no way of preventing such an attempt – if indeed it was for real, rather than the hoax I suspected but could not ignore.

By the time I left Australia two weeks later, after visits to Canberra and Sydney, the campaign was in full swing. I again enjoyed the company of so many committed people and enthusiastic young activists. One evening in Sydney, while briefing a private gathering on some of the STST's more covert methods, an attractive blonde student, Verity Burgmann, caught my eye. Her charismatic sister Meredith, a veteran anti-Vietnam War demonstrator, was a key figure in the campaign. In a few snatched minutes as we drove between destinations, Verity and I were drawn to each other. We promised to keep in touch, and when she later moved to London to take her university degree, we became closer.

On 8 September 1971, one month after the battered Spring-boks had departed, the chairman of the Australian Cricket Board of Control, the legendary Sir Donald Bradman, announced 'with great regret' that the cricket tour had been cancelled. The Australian campaigners were jubilant – job done, like the STST.[2]

It was another decisive blow against apartheid sport. Within months I was invited to give evidence before the United Nations Special Committee Against Apartheid. It was my first visit to New York, and I had little chance to see the sights, apart from a tour of the UN building, including the Security Council chamber, which meant such a lot to me. Not for the first (or last) time, I failed to take the opportunity to spend some leisure time in New York: politics came first, and there was more work to do back home.

❖

RUGBY remained a more difficult nut to crack than cricket: we had been able to stop tours coming from abroad, but it was very difficult to prevent teams visiting South Africa.

Despite opposition, England went ahead with their tour in 1972. By this time we had formed the Stop All Racist Tours, or SART, campaign, of which I was chair. A group of demonstrators disrupted the England training session at Twickenham. We also arranged for the team coach to be hemmed in at their hotel in Richmond prior to their departure for Heathrow Airport. Just before the coach was due to leave, we called the fire brigade, which descended on the hotel in force. Additionally, we requested several skips to be brought to the hotel, ostensibly to take away rubbish but in fact to block the team's departure.

The British Lions toured South Africa in 1974. Prior to their departure, I was one of a dozen people who broke through security and staged a rooftop occupation of the Rugby Football Union's headquarters at Twickenham. The Labour foreign minister Joan

Lestor, an AAM stalwart, instructed the British Embassy in Pretoria to withdraw the usual courtesy facilities for a visiting national side. We also demonstrated at the Lions' London hotel and occupied its reception area, forcing the hotel management to persuade the captain, Willie John McBride, to meet me. McBride was a giant of a man from Northern Ireland, and it quickly became clear there was no earthly chance of persuading him. Our exchange was polite enough, but we just talked past each other: the Lions were going to South Africa, regardless, imperiously indifferent to their collusion with sports apartheid. They played whites-only teams and returned in triumph, unbeaten, their dazzling play and legendary Welsh backs, such as Gareth Edwards, sweeping all opposition aside. (Over two decades later, as MP for Neath, I became friendly with Gareth, whose mother was a constituent still living in his home village of Gwau-cae-Gurwen. He interviewed me in the course of a BBC Wales programme in 2019, and I couldn't help but wonder how deeply he had confronted the anti-apartheid argument before.)

Afterwards, much was made of the support they had from black and coloured fans, but the latter always backed anybody against the hated white Springboks; more significant was the realisation among South Africa's white rugby fraternity that denial of international competition was damaging their own previous omnipotence.

The Lions returned to face a demonstration at a Heathrow Airport hotel reception. My sister Sally managed to throw a flour bomb that burst on the shoulder of Edward Heath, the former Conservative prime minister, who was there to greet the team. The Labour sports minister, Denis Howell, who had opposed the tour, also attended – hypocritically, I felt – ostensibly to welcome their sporting success.

By now barred from Britain and Australia, the Springboks were harried wherever they managed to go abroad. In 1973 we occupied the forecourt of another London hotel in which the visiting New Zealand rugby team were staying, in a protest against the Springbok tour scheduled for New Zealand later in the year. That tour saw a series of epic battles spearheaded by my New Zealand opposite number, Trevor Richards, and the Halt All Racist Tours campaign, which inspired mass opposition. The protests bitterly divided New Zealand society, including within families, until in the 1980s rugby tours involving the All Blacks were finally also stopped.[3]

In 1974 I was asked to visit France for several days to join the campaign there against a visiting white South African rugby side. I spoke no French and translators helped me at meetings and with the media. The protests were relatively muted, with the otherwise strong French left seemingly bemused by the mixture of politics and rugby. But it was an important first to take the battle into France, where the campaign against apartheid was much weaker than in Britain, and the organisers felt that my presence had raised their profile.

❖

THE *Financial Times* reported in 1970, shortly after the stopping of the cricket tour: 'Is it purely coincidental that the stepping up of the anti-apartheid campaign in Britain and America during the past year or so has been accompanied by a sharp falling off in the inflow of capital into the country? Those who follow these matters are convinced it is not.'

After the STST's victory, those centrally involved launched the Action Committee Against Racialism in July 1970, specifically to apply direct-action tactics elsewhere. Our small activist group – its core from the STST Special Action Group – discovered that a South African trade centre, financed by the South African government, was scheduled to open in St Martin's Lane, in central London. I wrote to the estate agents warning that the premises would become the target 'for an intensive campaign of demonstrations'.

The threat received extensive publicity and we sent copies of the letter to surrounding shops and offices, provoking paranoia in the complex in which the trade centre was to be located. We followed this up with a noisy picket. Shortly afterwards, the front doors of the complex were gummed up with solidifying agent. Then, a few days later, smoke flares were let off in the lifts during the lunch hour, and the fire brigade was called in. On each occasion the press were alerted and the estate agents informed. A week later, the firm acting for the organisers of the trade centre announced that they had shelved plans to take a showroom in London.

I also joined AAM protests against the British-based Barclays Bank, which had an important South African subsidiary and maintained the discriminatory staff wages and customer arrangements characteristic of apartheid; it bankrolled the South African economy, so underpinning apartheid. A 'Boycott Barclays' campaign spread across Britain, with direct-action protests on university campuses making it impossible for the bank to recruit new student accounts. Eventually, it took the extraordinary step of pulling entirely out of South Africa, signifying another major success for the British AAM.

In parallel with the AAM's consumer-boycott campaign, I helped orchestrate militant tactics in high-street supermarkets. Protesters plastered black-and-white stickers on South African goods with a skull and crossbones marked 'DANGER – PRODUCT OF APARTHEID'. We also filled carriers and trolleys with all the South African produce we could find, had the bill rung up at the till and then suddenly 'discovered' that the contents were all South African and refused to pay, leaving cashiers and managers with angry customers queuing up in frustration as the resulting chaos was sorted out. The boycott movement was by now spreading internationally, and in 1974 I spoke at a major international conference in the Netherlands focused on South African produce. It was organised by the Dutch anti-apartheid movement, which had been running a successful boycott of South Africa's Outspan oranges.

By now Verity and I had gone our separate ways, and I had begun going out with Pat Western, a friend of Jo-anne's. In early February 1975, while washing my old VW Beetle, I pondered our future. Probably time to get married, I thought. I looked at my diary, as usual full up with political commitments stretching way ahead, and discovered that the only Saturday free was the very next one. Pat was taken aback when I phoned her at work, but was fortunately free and agreeable too. Surprising relatives who wrongly suspected she was pregnant, we were married at a hastily arranged ceremony at Wandsworth Register Office on 8 February. A pack of jostling press photographers were determined to snap us – I was tieless and wearing my leather jacket – bang in front of the register office door, which was labelled number 10.

❖

THE annual Miss World pageant had only vaguely registered with me, but it offered another opportunity to highlight apartheid, because (like sport) only white participants had ever represented South Africa, and the event attracted enormous media attention.

The contest was the brainchild of Eric Morley, director of the leisure and entertainment conglomerate Mecca, and his formidable wife, Julia. They formed a powerful duo. I urged them to exclude the white South African candidate, Jillian Jessup, which they pompously refused to do, echoing the same incomprehension as British sports chiefs. The pageant, featuring 58 contestants, was to be staged in the Royal Albert Hall in November 1970.

I had been elected national publicity vice-chairman of the YLs six months earlier, and we publicly threatened to disrupt the event.

Just weeks before, with media interest around our initiative building, the Morleys, obviously on the back foot, contrived what they thought was a solution to the problem by hastily arranging for a black woman from South Africa to be invited as well. Pearl Jansen was plucked from her home in Bonteheuwel, outside Cape Town, and labelled 'Miss Africa South'. She joined the blonde Jillian Jessup, who had reached the position through a series of contests held across the country for the traditional title of 'Miss South Africa'. I suggested, ironically, that they be called 'Miss White South Africa' and 'Miss Black South Africa', which Eric Morley predictably opposed. He was seemingly unaware that his 'solution' played right into the hands of anti-apartheid activists by revealing, within his competition, that apartheid precluded a candidate's representing the whole country, unlike those from every other participating nation: it was merely 'whitewashing apartheid', I publicly insisted.

My intervention provoked the by now familiar outrage about 'interference' and 'bringing politics into entertainment', this time in a beauty competition, of all things. Meanwhile, however, a national Women's Liberation Movement had been launched in February 1970 at a conference held at Ruskin College, Oxford University. The feminist movement was gaining momentum, and our anti-apartheid initiative was understandably overtaken by opposition to the exploitative portrayal of women that the Miss World contest epitomised. In a media interview I described it as 'just a cattle market, debasing and degrading women'. Eric Morley retorted: 'Since when have the Young Liberals been a judge of the dignity of women?' The American comedian Bob Hope, who was to host the event and crown the winner, was gratuitously vitriolic about me when he arrived in London.

In parallel with anti-apartheid protests planned outside the hall, women's-liberation activists had decided to buy tickets and protest inside, insisting that the pageant 'reduces women to the condition of simple sexual symbols' and 'their dignity to that of a cattle market'. Their cause took precedence over our anti-apartheid protest and, thinking my attendance might prove a distraction, I decided not to attend. Helen Tovey, who was active in the Putney YLs (and who had also participated in the Davis Cup disruption in July 1969), assumed the leading role and did numerous interviews. She and other YLs took a pantomime cow to the event, demanding entry to the 'Miss World cattle market'.[4] Then, the night before, a clandestine anarchist group, The Angry Brigade, placed a home-made bomb under a BBC outside-broadcast truck, causing minor damage and raising the temperature even more.

Bob Hope came onstage for a few minutes of cheap misogy-nistic gags: 'I am very happy to be in this cattle market tonight,' was his opening quip. Outraged women's-rights protesters across the hall jumped up, blowing whistles and waving rattles, rushing towards the stage throwing leaflets, eggs and vegetables. A flour bag hit Hope, who was rushed off the stage, and the event was temporarily suspended amid the stench of smoke and stink bombs.

After security guards had cleared the protestors, Hope pro-duced some even poorer jokes: 'This is a good conditioning course for Vietnam' and 'Anyone who would try to break up an affair as wonderful as this has got to be on some kind of dope.' After com-plaints of 'rigging', with Julia Morley temporarily resigning, the declared winner was Miss Grenada, Jennifer Hosten – the first time a black woman had emerged victorious. The runner-up was Miss Africa South Pearl Jansen, who beat her white rival, Miss South Africa, into fifth place, to incredulity back home.

When she returned to South Africa, Pearl had a miserable time. She was totally ignored by whites, who had used her, and ostracised by some in her local community, who said she was a sell-out. Her father even lost his job. Many years later, in early

March 2020, she asked particularly to meet me when I was invited to the London premiere of *Misbehaviour* – a superb film about the whole episode, focusing rightly on the women's activists – and we had a good chat. The producers had kindly shown me the draft script for a scene of the actor playing my role, which I amended to reflect exactly the language I had used at the time.

Revenge

IT was an ordinary Saturday morning in June 1972 and we were all having a family breakfast at home in Putney, with 15-year-old Sally having fun opening my usual pile of campaign mail, watched by John Harris's eight-year-old son, David.

'What's this?' Sally asked. I looked up to see her pull something out of a large envelope. Recessed into a thick sheet of balsa wood were hideous metal cylinders and terminals with wires protruding. It was a letter bomb.

Mom and Dad were transfixed. We were all expecting it to explode. Seconds ticked by. Yet nothing happened. Horrified, and with hardly time to evaluate but anxious to get it clear of the house, I warily picked up the device and carried it gingerly outside, placing it alongside the garden path, while Mom called the police.

The Metropolitan Police's anti-terrorist squad – on red alert over IRA bombings in London – arrived with lights flashing and sirens blaring, and swarmed all over our house. They were friendly but formal, and I couldn't help noting that, for the very first time, I was apparently being protected by the police and security services, not targeted by them. They made the device safe and took it away for investigation, explaining later that it was powerful enough to have blown us and the house to smithereens. Curiously, they urged a news blackout: we were advised not to alert the media. In retrospect, it was a mistake to comply; everyone should have known about the package. And I heard nothing further from them.

Everything had happened so quickly that the deadly implications only settled in later. Just a small fault – caused by the gap between the spring-loaded contacts having been wrongly adjusted – had stood between us and oblivion. I had always accepted I was a target and had received many threats over the years – by letter, telephone or in person, and once from a fascist with a knife. But in practice there was very little that I could do to protect myself or my family, so we continued as if nothing had happened, albeit fully aware that South Africa had one of the world's most ruthless secret services, with a grim record of eliminating both internal and external opponents.

A number of anti-apartheid activists had been killed by similar letter bombs sent by BOSS, established in 1969. Its 'Z-squad', set up explicitly to mount such terrorist attacks, took the final letter in the alphabet because it specialised in final solutions: assassination of apartheid's enemies. The same year as the attempt on my life, a letter bomb blew up the Black Consciousness leader Abram Tiro after he had escaped to Botswana. Eduardo Mondlane, the president of Frelimo, the Mozambique liberation movement, whom I had met in London in 1968, had been similarly assassinated, as in 1982 was ANC activist Ruth First.

Why did the British police and intelligence services show no interest whatsoever in discovering who in BOSS was responsible for sending me this letter bomb? They never followed up. There was a great deal of cooperation and outright collusion between South African security services and those of Western governments such as Britain's. This was evident during the STST campaign, in which there were several instances of agents provocateurs deliberately inciting violence, one of whom was followed back to the South African Embassy.

Just before the start of the 1969–1970 rugby tour, BOSS printed a leaflet signed 'The Vigilantes', which appeared to come from loyalist rugby supporters. It stated that 'counter protest cells' had been established all over the country, and warned that any left-wing protesters who interrupted play would be 'carried off and walloped'. *The Times*, among other newspapers, reported on the leaflet. During the Springbok tour, BOSS distributed a press release from a hoax group, the 'Democratic Anti-Demo Organisation', which threatened to spray demonstrators with red paint and cover them with feathers.

At the time I was very suspicious of the provenance of these initiatives, and BOSS's responsibility only emerged in 1981, in a book titled *Inside BOSS*, by Gordon Winter. For instance, a Mr Peter Toombs had launched an 'Anti-Demonstration Association' from his house in Oxfordshire in 1969. According to Winter, Toombs had previously completed paid assignments for the South Africans. His 'organisation' had no members on the ground, but he seemed well connected and was put up to oppose me in TV interviews.

And, within hours of the 1970 cricket tour being cancelled, Gordon Winter's BOSS handler in London asked him to prepare a detailed report on me and the STST campaign. Winter wrote that it was to be used to 'pin him to the wall'.

❖

NO sooner had the STST been wound up than an eccentric English barrister and parliamentary draughtsman, Francis Bennion, announced he would be prosecuting me privately for criminal conspiracy.

Although virtually unknown, private criminal prosecutions had played a role over the centuries, and Bennion's initiative was soon backed by the right-wing Society for Individual Freedom (then with close links to British Intelligence), and Gordon Winter was instructed by BOSS to give material on me to them.

A 'Hain Prosecution Fund' was launched to raise £20000 for Bennion's venture, with links to the right wing, MI5 and BOSS. Bennion then flew to South Africa to raise money, and BOSS circulated subscription lists through the South African civil service, in what was described in the South African media as the 'Pain for Hain' campaign. There were also collection boxes in local bars, cafés and rugby and cricket clubs.

At Heathrow Airport in June 1971, just as I was about to depart for the campaign against the Springbok rugby tour in Australia, two Metropolitan Police officers served me with a summons relating to Bennion's criminal conspiracy charges. They were affable, even smirking. They obviously had me under surveillance because the timing was transparent: to try to dissuade me from departing, reminding me of how anti-apartheid friends in South Africa had often been stopped by the Special Branch prior to boarding.

But on returning from Australia I was relieved to be phoned by Larry Grant, legal officer of the National Council for Civil Liberties. Concerned about the way conspiracy charges were being deployed to suppress radical dissent, he offered to represent me. I was also relieved when volunteers organised a 'Peter Hain Defence Fund', which attracted a range of prominent people, including Lord Avebury, Labour MP Neil Kinnock and David Sheppard.

The case absorbed a great deal of time and energy, diverting me from anti-apartheid and wider political activism – a straightforward political trial. At our first 'conference' in their legal chambers, my lawyers, Michael Sherrard QC (Queen's Counsel) and Brian Capstick, stressed that the way the conspiracy law was then framed left me extremely vulnerable. Sherrard, leafing through my recently published book on the STST campaign, *Don't Play with Apartheid*, quietly explained that it could be construed as an admission of guilt, and that they had a hell of a battle on their hands to prevent my going to prison.

Four counts of conspiracy were levelled against me, covering the sit-down at the Bristol tennis court; the interruption of the Wilf Isaacs cricket tour; the disruption of the Springbok tour; and the stopping of the cricket tour. I was charged with conspiring with 'others unknown' – even though many were well known, or could at least have been easily identified. Laid at my door were literally hundreds of individual actions (one tally revealed over 900) across the entire United Kingdom (which for these purposes strangely included the Republic of Ireland because of a match played in Dublin). These included trespass, breaches of the peace, intimidation and violence against people and property. Also deployed was the antique offence of 'watching and besetting', which had formerly been directed at highway robbers and vagrants. Nobody could explain to me how or why it was being applied to stopping sports matches in the late 20th century.

Although some of these individual 'particulars' were not criminal offences, when prefixed with 'conspiracy' they were transformed into crimes. I found myself in an Alice in Wonderland world where words were simply reinterpreted to suit the purposes of the prosecutors. The law on conspiracy is ancient in origin, dating from 1304, and over the years judges had enthusiastically used their discretion to enlarge its scope.[1] For example, when I had been running onto sports pitches or helping organise others to do so, 'an agreement to commit a civil trespass' was then 'not indictable', as a leading legal textbook put it; that is to say, I could have been sued in a civil action by the owners of the sports grounds, though not criminally prosecuted.

But in 1972, in a case involving student protesters who had occupied the Sierra Leone Embassy, a judge declared that because the matter was of 'substantial public interest', conspiracy to trespass was, after all, a criminal offence. Despite the fact that this declaration came some *two years after* our protests (though conveniently *just before* my full trial), it was still applied to me retrospectively, defying one of the cardinal rules of British law. When my lawyers later disputed this on appeal, Lord Justice Roskill cheerily responded: 'Hain would not have done it had it not been

130

a matter of public interest.' The judges might well have said in my case: 'We don't like what he was up to, interfering with our enjoyment of cricket, tennis and rugby, and we shall find a way of reinterpreting the law to stop him doing it.' It was a reminder of Pretoria – shades of 'Go and find out what Ad Hain is doing and tell her to stop it.'

❖

THE trial in August 1972 became something of a *cause célèbre*, and lasted four weeks (fortunately, during my university vacation).

The courtroom was like a theatre, with everyone playing to the audience: barristers in long black robes and yellowing white wigs, sometimes studiously courteous, sometimes cuttingly sarcastic; the judge sitting on high, remote and dominating; the defendant in the dock, sticking out like a sore thumb.

However, there was one concession from the judge, Bernard Gillis, who was otherwise transparently hostile: I was allowed, as a 'person of good character', to sit in the well of the court alongside my lawyers, not in the dock. I was also allowed out on bail to be with family and friends during the lunch break, and to go home rather than be detained overnight.

It took fully seven minutes for the clerk of the court to read out the lengthy list of charges against me. Then the jury was sworn in: nine white men, one white woman, a black British Guyanese man and an Asian man. Very aware my fate was in their hands, I stared intently as each one took the oath and sat down: would they be fair, even sympathetic, or hostile?

As expected, the trial involved lengthy textual analysis and argument about my book, *Don't Play with Apartheid*. The prosecution was opened by Owen Stable QC, a large, portentous figure whose father, the retired judge Sir Wintringham Stable had, two years earlier, had a letter published in the *Daily Telegraph* calling for me to be prosecuted for conspiracy. This family 'heirloom' was now carried forward by his son, who asserted: 'Hain and his friends tried to set themselves above the law.' He then embarked upon a day-and-a-half-long opening speech, referring to my 'fertile, trouble-making propensities' and insisting that the 'very future of English civilisation' was at stake.

Although in English law one is supposed to be innocent until proved guilty, the reverse applied in my case. A judge in an earlier conspiracy trial had ruled that 'conspiracy can be effected by a wink or a nod without a word being spoken'. Basically, if it could be shown that I had advocated direct action and played a leading role, then I was guilty of conspiracy – even if I had had nothing to do with the individual acts carried out by those 'others unknown'. The only way I could prove I was *not* responsible was by calling some of those who *were*. For example, Peter Jordan was a school-teacher who on 31 December 1969 ran onto the pitch in Bristol and sprinkled drawing pins. Although I had had nothing to do with it – and strongly disapproved because of the injury risk to players – I was charged with conspiracy for his solitary action too. Calling Jordan as a witness was the only way I could prove that we had never met or communicated, and that, in his own words, 'it was a spontaneous act'.

The 1969–1970 Springbok captain, Dawie de Villiers, a member of the Broederbond (a powerful secret society devoted to Afrikaner advancement) and later an apartheid government minister, flew in to give evidence, as did Wilf Isaacs, who had sponsored the private cricket tour in 1969 and was an honorary colonel in the South African military. But they were only able to describe the events and could not directly implicate me. The prosecution's star witness was to be Gordon Winter, who later confessed he had all along been working for BOSS while London correspondent for the South African *Sunday Express*. (Other jour-nalists refused to cooperate.) He had been ubiquitous during the

STST, appearing at all the demonstrations, always popping up with notebook and camera to hand. Many anti-apartheid leaders suspected he might have BOSS links.

But, when called by the prosecution, Winter, to our utter astonishment, switched under questioning into becoming a virtual defence witness, alleging that Francis Bennion's team had asked him only for selective photographs showing the demonstrators in a bad light. Giving me a large wink from the witness box – disconcerting and embarrassing – he ostentatiously pulled out a wad of photos showing police attacking demonstrators. (One officer was actually convicted in 1974 for planting a knife on a black STST demonstrator.) Winter also corroborated our defence's reliance upon my role as a spokesperson for the campaign, rather than as head conspirator and organiser of all the demonstrations everywhere and anywhere. The prosecution were equally nonplussed. (Nearly ten years later, Winter revealed he had been instructed by BOSS to maintain his cover for a more important task – smearing the then Liberal Party leader, Jeremy Thorpe, of which more below.)

The court proceedings dragged on and on as Owen Stable tried – mostly unsuccessfully – to squeeze out any direct link to my involvement. His cast of witnesses were only able to describe what had happened at the various sports events, with little direct evidence relating to me. Even the Metropolitan Police's Commander John Gerrard was fairly neutral about my participation, appearing as a witness almost reluctantly.

Two weeks into the trial, it was crystal clear that the prosecution were relying almost exclusively on my book as a self-confession of guilt. Their last witness was Wilf Wooller, the former Welsh cricketer turned sports broadcaster and journalist. The right-wing Wooller was a colourful character, bombastic in the media, always denouncing me in the most personal and extravagant terms. His greeting when we met face to face for the first time at an Oxford Union debate was: 'I hope to see you behind bars before the tour is out. And I really mean that.' But he also was unable to implicate me directly.

❖

BECAUSE the oppressive, catch-all nature of the law on conspiracy meant it was almost impossible to prove my innocence, my lawyers recommended that I not go into the witness box, to avoid the probability of implicating myself.

Although certainly not guilty of over 90 per cent of the 900-odd particulars with which I was charged, I was nevertheless guilty of advocating and coordinating action to disrupt and stop the various sports events and tours. Michael Sherrard, my experienced QC, considered that Judge Bernard Gillis was after an exemplary prison sentence, and was especially concerned that he would be unable to answer a likely question from the judge as to what 'exactly was my defence in law'. It appeared there was no answer to this, in which case my defence would instantly collapse. However, the judge could not ask me that question because I was not a lawyer.

So, at a conference in chambers, and with my worried parents specifically invited, it was finally decided that I should effectively 'sack' my barristers and defend myself. By conducting my own case I could appeal directly to the jury on a basis of justice not to convict me. By making opening and closing speeches for the defence and by examining witnesses, I would be talking to the jury without having to be cross-examined in the witness box.

So when the prosecution case concluded, Michael Sherrard announced to the court that 'on my client's instructions' he and Capstick were withdrawing from the case. He cheerily added – expressly as a warning to the judge – 'We will be watching from the pavilion.' It was a dramatic moment.

As the experienced London *Sunday Times* journalist Derek Humphry reported, the prosecution were 'flabbergasted, as their preparation for the case had been on the certainty that Hain would have to give sworn evidence'. Judge Gillis was livid and tried to persuade me to change my mind. Humphry added: 'Lawyers said later that Judge Gillis came close to using improper pressure on Hain by his constant attempts to persuade him not to defend himself and his attempts to alter Hain's decision not to go into the witness box.'

It was nevertheless a daunting task. I had no legal training. I was on my own, facing the bewigged might of the prosecuting team, with only my solicitor, Larry Grant, and his assistants, Yvette Gibson and young trainee barrister (and years later famous QC) Geoffrey Robertson, sitting just below me in the well of the court.

Geoffrey soon provided a very good draft for my opening statement on the defence case, though I had to curb his rolling prose and penchant for outrageous wit. Initially nervous when I rose to deliver it, I soon got into my stride. I was by now an experienced public speaker, though addressing the court was something else entirely. Soon, however, taking my own defence seemed the most natural and obvious thing to have done, because it made explicit what had previously only been implicit in the rarefied atmosphere of the court. Instead of the political issues at stake being submerged in legal niceties, they could now be teased out through my own advocacy. What's more, my destiny was in my own hands. I was fighting for my freedom. I also saw it as part of the anti-apartheid fight, as my conviction could open the way for other South African-inspired prosecutions.

I told the court that I 'stood broadly by' what I had written in *Don't Play with Apartheid*, but insisted that it had not been written 'as a confession'. There had been no lawyer vetting every sentence in anticipation that the book would be transformed from something written for readability into a legal document in which the interpretation of even the most casual sentence was liable to land me in prison. Although it clearly exasperated Judge Gillis, my mention of 'prison' was premeditated in order to alert the jury, whom we rather doubted would have wanted that outcome, however tempted they might have been to convict me.

I emphasised my total opposition to violent protest and insisted that I was honest and open about my role and objectives. I had never hidden my commitment to non-violent direct action – indeed, I had publicly proclaimed it. This was no sinister, covert conspiracy. The STST campaign was disarmingly open and candid. Furthermore, I pointed out: 'The campaign was a loose movement. It was not a rigid organisation. We had no generals. We had no apparatus through which to conspire.' It was quite ludicrous to charge me with nearly a thousand offences committed the length and breadth of the British Isles.

Moreover, it was oppressive to frame the conspiracy charge in such a way that if I was found guilty of one particular offence, I was guilty of the whole lot. The jury's verdict would be given only on each of the four conspiracy *counts* rather than the hundreds of *particulars* that each contained. The latter was iniquitous because even if the jury found I was not guilty of hundreds of offences in each of the four conspiracy counts, there was no way for the judge to know this when he passed sentence. The jury might decide I was guilty only of the trivial offences or those that were strictly non-violent. But the judge could not know this and might assume guilt for the most violent offences. However, the iniquities of the then law on conspiracy meant that it was the *conspiracy* that mattered, rather than the *particular* actions or alleged offences – which made my defence almost impossible.

We had lined up a series of activists from across Britain to testify that they had organised local protests. But as they confirmed that they had never met or talked to me, the prosecution objected and Judge Gillis became increasingly testy. Eventually, I was stopped from putting questions. We had an increasingly tense battle as Gillis repeatedly interrupted me, sometimes legitimately when my inexperience showed and I found myself putting a question to a witness incorrectly in such a way that it was 'leading' towards a particular answer. However, on other occasions Judge Gillis was simply aggressive, reflecting his deep unhappiness at the manner in which I was evidently – and, observers thought, persuasively – getting my case across to the jury.

Once I overstepped the mark and cheekily called Owen Stable 'my learned friend' (the cosy parlance used between barristers in court). Gillis gave me a severe ticking off: 'Mr Hain, you are *not* learned. You must not say that again.' I apologised profusely, maintaining my posture of polite innocence, which always seemed to irritate him even more.

Among our list of distinguished witnesses was Archbishop Trevor Huddleston, president of the AAM, who appeared in purple robes, dignified and with imposing authority, straight from an overnight sleeper train from Edinburgh. But Judge Gillis and Owen Stable were transparently determined to thwart his evidence and he was constantly interrupted by both, almost being unable to reply to my questions. Tellingly, however, I was able to get on the record as evidence one reply from Huddleston: 'I would not support anybody who was advocating violence against the person and I never got the impression at any time that you were advocating violence.' He also confirmed that he supported any clergy involved in non-violent pitch invasions.

❖

THE defence witness subjected to the most hostile cross-examination was Ethel de Keyser, the indomitable executive secretary of the AAM. She was asked 218 questions by the prosecution spread over two days and, despite being on the receiving end of a QC skilled at tying witnesses up in knots, she never flinched. With almost uncanny precision she skipped deftly between his barbs, her composure never ruffled. She looked carefully at several STST campaign bulletins giving details of upcoming demonstrations, but said she had never seen one before, which meant they could not be presented as evidence before the jury. So effective was her performance that Stable was unable to make any use at all of her evidence in his final address to the jury.

But her appearance was notable for another reason. When Stable began asking her about the AAM's annual general meeting in October 1969, it became apparent that he was working from a transcript of a tape recording made secretly at the meeting. The prosecution must have felt they had a trump card, because I had spoken of the STST's direct-action plans at that meeting. If Ethel de Keyser had been able to confirm Stable's account of the meeting, then the prosecution would have got admitted as evidence before the court whatever transcript Stable was reading from. This would have included my contribution and would have been their first direct evidence to support the conspiracy charges.

But the meeting had taken place three years before, and Ethel was frankly unable to recall points of detail about what had been said in over six hours of reports, discussion and debate, especially since she was not a stenographer but had been busily engaged behind the scenes, making sure the day went smoothly. Stable would not reveal in court the source of the tape recording, but it must have been either a UCO or the South African security services, who regularly infiltrated AAM meetings, also bugging and breaking into the organisation's headquarters.

After Ethel's appearance – intended to confirm that the AAM operated autonomously from the STST as a perfectly legal and open organisation – we took stock as a team and decided not to call a string of other witnesses, some of them waiting outside and disappointed to be told they were no longer needed. (However, Mom and Special Action Group coordinator Mike Craft deliberately remained seated, so that the prosecution thought they would be called, though we had no intention of doing so.) With a hostile judge and the possibility that defence witnesses might provide ammunition for the prosecution, the danger was of unintentionally serving up new evidence against me. Other than my book, the prosecution had virtually no evidence of my culpability – not, of course, that much was needed under the conspiracy laws.

So we proceeded to the final stages of the defence case, with a pre-planned conclusion. We had dispensed with the conventional etiquette between defence and prosecution lawyers, in which they typically inform each other of developments, such as forthcoming witnesses; for me this was 'war'. The Labour MP Peter Jackson was stopped by the judge while answering a question confirming his publicly stated intention to run onto cricket pitches – again, quite independently of me. Anticipating a similar reaction to the appearance of the imposing, berobed Colin Winter, Bishop-in-exile of Damaraland, South West Africa (today Namibia), I had prepared my response. His evidence was duly blocked by a battery of objections. I protested that legal procedures were being used to stop me from mounting my own defence properly, and abruptly announced that in these circumstances, although we had plenty of witnesses ready to be called, I had no alternative but to close my case.

Judge Gillis was manifestly upset and flustered; he could see perfectly well how the jury would view me as a victim. Likewise, Owen Stable was caught completely by surprise. It was a delicious moment as he stumbled immediately into his closing speech, with the prosecutor's nightmare – a weekend break – intervening. Eventually, after an over-long and thoroughly boring summary of the prosecution case, which sent everyone to sleep, Stable, eyeing up the jury, contrived a final flourish: if I were let off, it would be 'an incitement to politically inspired law breaking' on such a massive scale – by, for example, homeless families occupying empty properties, Jews protesting at the Russian ballet, Palestinians disrupting performances by Israeli artists – that England's green and pleasant civilisation would be under dark and dangerous threat. All that stood in the path of these terrible and alien forces was the jury.

❖

OVER the weekend, meanwhile, I drafted my own closing speech, using Geoffrey Robertson's construction of the argument to underpin my own instincts. I, too, relied upon my book and tried to establish that it was not the transparent confession the prosecution were claiming. Addressing the jury, I took two days, dissecting all the evidence to prove that the STST was an open, honest campaign in which I had never sought to hide my role or objectives. This was a 'scapegoat prosecution' in a 'politically motivated' trial. I also reminded jurors of the honourable tradition of non-violent direct action – from the Chartists and suffragettes demanding the vote in Britain, to Gandhi over independence for India and African Americans demanding civil rights in the USA. Every sentence, every word, had to be judged carefully, for I knew only too well how my freedom depended upon the jury.

Throughout my speech I was repeatedly interrupted by Judge Gillis – another departure from court convention, which determined that closing speeches should be delivered without challenge. It was not as if what I was saying was legally or procedurally wrong – my legal team ensured that. Judge Gillis simply seemed determined to derail me. His laborious, three-day summing-up was, legal observers believed, so biased as to constitute a basis for appeal should I be convicted.

After a weekend break, he sent the jury out at 10.35 am on Monday 22 August 1972. I watched each juror rise and be guided out by ushers, wondering who might support me and who might not. Conscious that I could be sent to prison, I had packed a few clothes and toiletries. Although I had been on bail during the proceedings, I was now taken down and confined to the cells below the court to await my fate.

A canteen meal intervened as the hours dragged by, and other inmates in for 'proper' crimes were curious about my presence. They seemed to think it was all rather a joke, which was hardly my attitude. I was locked back in my cell, and the tension grew. There was nothing to do but wait, my mind going around in circles. Larry Grant came in to pass the time and we discussed possible outcomes. What could be going on in the jury room? Then he left me on my own again. Time dragged even more.

Finally, there was a jangle of keys and a warder said the court was reconvening, I assumed for the verdict. This time I was shown ominously into the dock. It was 4.21 pm, nearly six long hours after the 12 jurors had first retired. They looked strained, with the foreman nervously announcing that they could not agree on any of the four conspiracy counts. A frisson swept through the packed courtroom, the press section bulging. My spirits rose at this unexpected development. But what would happen next?

Judge Gillis informed them solemnly that he would now accept a majority verdict 'if ten of you are in agreement'. I was taken back down and locked up. On my own again, the tension became unbearable as yet another hour went by. Conflicting thoughts swirled around in my head, one minute hopeful, the next worried that a majority verdict might make a conviction easier.

Then, at last, I was taken upstairs. At 5.57 pm the jury trooped back in, and in vain I studied each face intently, desperate for a clue. But they all looked glum. 'Have you now been able to reach a verdict?' Judge Gillis asked. The foreman rose. 'Yes,' he replied. I was guilty on the third count, relating to the peaceful Davis Cup sit-down in Bristol – by far the least serious of the counts and the one where I was most culpable as charged.

But then came a dramatic twist. Pressed hard by the judge, the foreman stated that the jury could not agree on any of the remaining three counts. There were gasps of relief from spectators and smiles all round. I was overcome with both elation and vindication. The judge and prosecutors looked absolutely thunderous. As the London *Sunday Times* reported: 'It was evident that Hain had succeeded in going over the heads of the prosecution and the judge and influencing the majority of the jury with his political philosophy.' I managed to confirm later that the two black jurors had held out even against my conviction over the Davis Cup disruption. They were joined by others in refusing to convict on the much more serious (and imprisonable) counts relating to the rugby and cricket tours.

In the absence of a retrial (which the prosecution hastily confirmed they would not request), the judge then directed that 'verdicts of not guilty be recorded in Counts 1, 2 and 4'. He ticked me off, fined me £200 and I was free to go. So there it was: all the panoply and expense of a month-long trial, with the implicit backing of the apartheid government, and I now had a criminal conviction for sitting on a tennis court peacefully for a couple of minutes. I was elated, hugging my parents and my legal team, and delivering a defiant series of interviews to the media pack, television cameras and photographers jostling outside.

By this time I was 22 and more drained than I had ever been. The 'Pain for Hain' prosecution had failed in its fundamental objective: to remove me from a leading role in the anti-apartheid struggle. And the verdict was greeted with widespread disappointment in the white South African media. But it took several months out of my active political life – a minor consolation, perhaps, for those who wanted revenge for the defeat inflicted on them in 1970. Notwithstanding the verdict, however, England's green and pleasant civilisation remained intact.[2]

The order of the Companions of
the OR Tambo

in Silver
Awarded to

PETER HAIN

For his excellent contribution to
the fight against the injustices of
apartheid and his unwavering
support for the South African
Liberation Movement.

CHANCELLOR OF ORDERS:
R. CASSIUS LUBISI PHD
DATE: 08 December 2015

PRESIDENT OF THE
REPUBLIC OF SOUTH AFRICA
JG ZUMA

In December 2015 I was honoured to be awarded the Grand
Companion of OR Tambo in silver at a ceremony in Pretoria.

A bike race at the Hain family home, Arcadia,
Pretoria, in 1961. That's me crouching front centre.

The Arcadia Shepherds
Under-14 cup-winning
team, 1964. I am in the
back row at far left.

My mother, Adelaine
Hain, holding newborn
me, Nairobi, 1950.

Police removing me (in dark glasses) from the court during the Davis Cup protest, Bristol, July 1969.

A protest outside the South African Embassy, London, 1977, following the death of Steve Biko. I am in the background holding a placard.

With my sons Sam
and Jake, aged 4
and 2, London, 1980.

With my mother
outside the South
African Embassy,
London, 1986.

With Danie Craven at Stellenbosch rugby stadium,
during my secret visit to South Africa in 1989.

Above is a photo of
me at Hatfield Primary
School, Pretoria, in
1958. I returned to the
school in 1989 (right),
to find my name still on
the honours board.

Cape Times

WEDNESDAY, JANUARY 3, 1990

PETER HAIN'S SECRET SA VISIT

© AP & P Co Ltd

My secret visit in 1989 led to much interest in the media. Here is a street poster from January 1990.

With Nelson Mandela, on the eve of South Africa's first democratic election, Johannesburg, 26 April 1994.

Nelson Mandela with me, my wife, Elizabeth, father Walter and mother Adelaine, London, 2003.

With Ahmed Kathrada on Robben Island, December 2012.

In 2012 I paid a visit to my alma mater,
Pretoria Boys High School.

REVENGE

❖

THE next visible attack on me came in the form of a glossy 3 000-word smear sheet titled 'The Hidden Face of the Liberal Party'. It used various reports of my anti-apartheid activities taken viciously out of context. There were lurid photographs of the 1964 station bomb in Johannesburg, for which John Harris had been hanged, implying that as a 14-year-old I had been somehow responsible. Hundreds of thousands of copies were distributed in key parliamentary seats (including my home constituency of Putney) where the Liberals might have been expected to do well in the October 1974 election.

The screed (one was also produced on the Labour Party, with a joint print run of about three million) recycled the by now familiar themes of the hard right: extremism in the Liberal Party and Labour Party and allegations of subservience to Moscow. It was published by the Foreign Affairs Publishing Company, which had close links with white South Africa, British Intelligence and the Central Intelligence Agency (CIA), and was financed by the South African intelligence services, then engaged in disinformation, destabilisation and disruption.

During the 1970s, South Africa's Department of Information moved well beyond the normal bounds of foreign information and propaganda, with the active blessing of Prime Minister John Vorster. Ten years before, as justice minister, Vorster had signed my parents' banning orders and deliberately ignored John Harris's telephoned warning to clear the station concourse. In close cooperation with the head of BOSS, Hendrik van den Bergh, the Department of Information mounted 138 secret projects, spending billions of rands. They sponsored front organisations, spread disinformation, and secretly financed newspapers at home and abroad. Hundreds of people were victims of their nefarious activities.

143

One of their projects was the Committee for Fairness in Sport (CFS), established in 1973. Funded by wealthy white South African businessmen, and also by money laundered through the Department of Information, it undertook a programme of expensive newspaper advertisements featuring photographs of black and white athletes competing together in specially staged, one-off events (the underlying structure of sports apartheid from school to national levels remaining strictly unchanged). There was also a well-oiled public-relations drive, part of which included flying to the UK a black South African journalist, Leslie Sehume, to confront anti-apartheid leaders and rally support for the British Lions and New Zealand rugby tours to South Africa.

Sehume had a much-publicised half-hour debate with me on BBC television in April 1974, and his role symbolised a fresh tactic. As the sports editor of the black Johannesburg newspaper *The World*, he was presented as the 'true' voice of the black majority. Previously, I had faced white opponents in media interviews; having a black South African was designed to put me on the spot. Who did we think we were, foreign whites trying to dictate to black South Africans? Sehume was plausible (even acknowledging that people like me had helped 'accelerate change'), received some favourable coverage in the right-wing press in Britain and was feted by British apologists for apartheid. For several weeks, he held forth from a luxurious apartment in London's Waldorf Hotel, which was about as far from his township readers as it was possible to get.

In a melodramatic and doubtless rehearsed line, he told me during our television debate: 'If you returned to South Africa now, you would be stoned out of the country – by blacks, not whites.' Powerful stuff, and widely reported – but, unfortunately for him, not true. It was immediately denounced by *The World*. Although careful not to endorse our boycott strategy (for it remained illegal in South Africa to advocate sanctions and boycotts), an editorial in the paper took 'the strongest exception to Mr Sehume's remarks', and an accompanying page-long article reported the views of a range of black sports and civic leaders. Norman Middleton, president of the South African Soccer Federation, spoke for most when he said that Sehume was being 'used to exploit his own people', and added: 'Peter Hain would be welcomed to South Africa as a hero because he is a fighter for the blacks.'

After a similarly controversial trip a year later to New Zealand, Sehume was sacked by *The World* and ended up officially on the payroll of the CFS and therefore indirectly an employee of the South African government.

❖

IN 1967 South Africa had introduced conscription to increase the numbers of soldiers available for military service along the country's borders, which were under threat from Mandela's ANC and other liberation forces. This led to growing alienation, and an increasing number of young whites, including young Afrikaners, began doubting whether apartheid was worth fighting, and maybe dying, for.

A white underground group was formed in 1972 called Okhela – the Zulu word means 'spark'. The brainchild of exiled writer and activist Breyten Breytenbach, Okhela aimed to mobilise dissident whites on an underground basis. In its commitment to raising 'white consciousness', Okhela later saw its role in parallel with the growing Black Consciousness Movement led by Steve Biko.

In 1977, I received, via the then executive secretary of the AAM, Basil Manning, a covert approach to meet two members of Okhela. At their insistence, we talked in my car in London, ostensibly to avoid any surveillance, the arrangements contrived to underline the meeting's serious clandestine character. Both were tall, muscled, clean-cut young Afrikaners. They squeezed

145

into my Beetle and described the group's aims, appealing to me to join them.

Although they seemed plausible, and I replied that I would be happy to offer support, I explained that my most effective contribution to the struggle was as an anti-apartheid activist in Britain. They persisted, however, and in what I felt was an attempt to make me feel guilty at not being willing to lay myself on the line in the guerrilla struggle, tried to press me to travel to one of the frontline states (the apartheid state's nearest neighbours) and be infiltrated into South Africa. I was instinctively unenthusiastic and unimpressed at what sounded like a particularly foolhardy escapade. I was also suspicious: there was something about their demeanour that did not ring true. So I said I would think about it, and that they should contact me in a few weeks' time.

I never heard from them again, and later there was a revealing sequel to this mysterious episode. In 1980 the 'master spy' Craig Williamson was outed as a captain in the South African security police. He had successfully operated in London in the 1970s, posing as an anti-apartheid exile, and the two men who had tried to recruit me were also revealed as double agents who had infiltrated Okhela.

But two years before that Okhela encounter, I had the most surreal, Kafkaesque experience of my life ...

Thief

FRIDAY 24 October 1975 began as an ordinary day. After popping out to buy a typewriter ribbon, I grabbed a sandwich lunch. I was busy typing up a chapter for my University of Sussex doctoral thesis in the small Putney flat that Pat and I had purchased after our marriage eight months earlier.

There was a ring at the door and Pat returned to announce that some policemen wished to see me.

One of the officers asked if it was my car outside, pointing to our blue Volkswagen Beetle. Yes, I told him. It immediately crossed my mind that he must be investigating non-payment of parking fines by the previous owner, about which we'd been getting correspondence.

Had I been out in it recently, he asked.

Yes, I explained, to buy typewriter ribbons.

Well, they would just like me to go with them down to the police station. It shouldn't take longer than twenty minutes, the officer said.

The parking tickets were uppermost in my mind and it was only when he refused to let me finish eating my sandwich, and followed close on my heels as I collected my jacket and glasses, that I began to feel there was something awry.

Exactly what is this all about, I asked. Can't it be discussed here? Definitely not – I would find out when I got to the station.

The atmosphere had grown confused. Other policemen crowded into our doorway.

Was I being arrested, I asked. If so, what was the charge?

I would only go if I was given a proper explanation.

He turned for a quick discussion, and another policeman called out: 'Snatch at Barclays.'

Snatch at Barclays? What on earth had this to do with me? Pat, at my side, giggled nervously. 'You must be joking,' she said. My mind had become jumbled: parking tickets, policemen, bank snatch – me?

There was obviously a mistake somewhere, and it surely wouldn't take long to sort out. So I followed them, startled to see several squad cars and a police van, together with a further dozen policemen and policewomen.

One of the officers insisted on driving my car down to nearby Wandsworth police station and I was hustled into the back seat of the nearest police vehicle. As we pulled away, the officer sitting beside me reached for a microphone: 'The suspect has been arrested. Everything's under control.'

In my growing confusion I turned to him. Me, a suspect? Had I been arrested without even knowing what it was about?

As we pulled up to the police station I had an uncomfortable feeling I'd become hostage to events that could lead anywhere.

❖

UNKNOWN to me, almost exactly as I was getting into my car to drive down to buy the typewriter ribbon, a man of my age and appearance had snatched a bundle of £5 notes, totalling £490, from a cashier in the Upper Richmond Road branch of Barclays Bank. Barclays had been a target for anti-apartheid protesters, and I had participated in pickets outside that very branch.

The thief ran down Putney High Street, pursued by several bank staff, who were joined by four boys from nearby Elliott School. He then ran up Werter Road. When he reached Oxford Road, he turned round obligingly and said, 'All right, here you are then.' He tossed the money back, and conveniently disappeared.

Minutes later, and oblivious to what had gone on, I drove from our flat in Fawe Park Road down Oxford Road into Werter Road, and pulled up outside the WH Smith on the corner of Putney High Street. As I got out of the car, some of the schoolboys noticed me and thought I was the thief they had just been chasing. They followed me into the shop, decided I was their man, took my car registration number and walked to the nearby Putney police station to report it. Shortly afterwards, the police turned up in force at our flat.

I was locked up in a cell for the rest of the day, my thoughts a confusing swirl. Nothing happening. No explanations. Nobody to speak to. What made it worse was that I had not the slightest idea about the theft. *How* had it happened? *How* on earth I had been picked up? *What* was all this really about?

Bouts of jitters and fright overcame me. My world had suddenly turned upside down. Maybe I *had* done it? Perhaps I *was* a bank robber? I paced up and down the small cell in the dim light, peering at graffiti on one wall that asked: 'Am I guilty or not guilty? – somebody please tell me.'

Eleven long hours later – and on the basis only of statements by two 12-year-old boys – I was charged in the early hours of Saturday morning.

I had vehemently protested my innocence when formally questioned by a detective chief inspector, who seemed to have made his mind up and was just going through the motions. I didn't even know which branch of Barclays had been the scene of the crime (there were then two in central Putney, several hundred metres apart). Fingerprints (including, significantly, a fresh one) on the banknotes did not match mine.

There was no other evidence upon which to charge me.

During my long detention, my mother contacted Larry Grant, who had been my solicitor during the conspiracy trial and had become a good friend. Larry recommended John Dundon for this case. John talked to me in my cell and tried to persuade the police to drop the case, but without success: they were determined to prosecute.

I arrived home at around three on Saturday morning, completely shell-shocked. Later that day the police leaked the news to the media and Sunday's papers carried the headline 'HAIN IN BANK THEFT'; I was being propelled toward another trial just three years after the one for conspiracy.

This surreal sequence took another twist on the Monday when I was summoned to an identification parade. Standing in a line-up with other men drafted in from a local factory very roughly my age and appearance, I was extremely uncomfortable. I had been advised to try and be relaxed, and to stare straight ahead rather than peer at the witnesses as they walked by. But I could not help being nervous, not knowing what to do with my hands, where to look, what expression to have.

The deliberate police leaks had ensured huge publicity, including a portrait photograph on the front page of the *Evening Standard* with the caption 'Peter Hain, due to appear on an identification parade today'. Perhaps this was why the bank cashier from whom the money had been snatched came down the line and then straight back to me, placing her hand on my shoulder. How *could* she, I thought, feeling helpless, the prey of forces beyond me. Bank staff later confirmed in court that copies of the *Evening Standard* had been in their office and that they had all read and discussed it before attending the parade.

The cashier, Lucy Haines (variations on my surname were another quirky feature of the case), was a slight, nervy, grey-haired woman, probably in her late fifties. I had never seen her before in my life. Although none of the other witnesses from the bank (including those who had chased the thief at close quarters) identified me, the police were evidently pleased with themselves. They now had a 'positive identification' to corroborate that of the two 12-year-olds who had reported my car registration.

Later that evening, however, came just about the only break I got in the six miserable months in which the case consumed my life, and which led to my abandoning my full-time university doctoral thesis. Terry MacLaren, the elder of the schoolboys, who, it turned out, had refused to go along with his chums to report my car registration, was watching the ten o'clock news that night on television and saw me pictured outside the police station after the identity parade. 'That's not the man. They've got the wrong one,' he told his dad. Many, if not most, fathers would have told their young son to shut up and mind their own business, and few boys would have been as strong-willed as 14-year-old Terry. But, fortunately for me, his father contacted my solicitor the next day.

❖

QUITE spontaneously, journalists, political acquaintances and others began discussing whether I had been set up by BOSS. But although a South African connection seemed all too plausible, direct evidence was absent. For all we knew, I was simply a victim of the vagaries of identification evidence (which at the time was being exposed almost monthly for its notorious unreliability), combined with police malice. During my detention, one of the investigating detectives belligerently told me: 'You have caused a lot of trouble with your protests and we are going to make this charge stick on you.'

Then, on 3 February 1976, out of the blue, two months before the trial was due to start, a man named Kenneth Wyatt rang my parents' listed home number saying he wanted to talk to me about my case. I rang him back and he said he had some information that he did not want to give over the phone. Wary that it might be a crank call, I pressed him. He appeared calm and offered to come and see me the following day, arriving punctually. He was a large, bespectacled, shambling figure. Quiet and almost diffident, he seemed concerned that his car might have been followed.

At the suggestion of my solicitor, I took notes, as Wyatt talked in a disjointed, rambling fashion. But his manner was open and reasonable and gave no grounds for supposing that he was either unbalanced or devious. He began by saying that he might not be believed because he had been in the pornography business and had been convicted and served two years for distributing pornographic material. He then said he had been approached by a group headed by a Mr Fred Kamil, formerly a security officer with the South African mining conglomerate Anglo American, and told to contact me. He was instructed to inform me that the bank theft had been carried out by a South African agent specially flown in for the job.

Wyatt delivered his account quite flatly, without emotion or hyperbole. When I pressed him, he was unable to offer any direct evidence, maintaining that he was simply a courier. However, he did explain that information about my case, together with evidence of a plot against the Liberal Party, had come into the hands of the Kamil group. Apparently, Anglo American's extensive security service worked closely with BOSS, and one of Kamil's own intelligence contacts in the company had accidentally come across a confidential dossier in BOSS headquarters containing a plan to discredit members of the Liberal Party, including me, MP Cyril Smith and the party leader, Jeremy Thorpe. A document in the dossier stated that the operation against me had gone successfully and that 'action against Thorpe is going according to plan'.

According to Wyatt, the rationale was that the South Africans wanted to see a permanent Tory government in Britain: they believed that damaging the Liberal Party by discrediting its leadership would ensure a Tory victory at the polls. Their theory was that the removal of a serious Liberal presence in marginal seats would ensure that these went Conservative (a prognosis accepted by most political commentators at the time).

Wyatt further maintained that one of Kamil's female intelligence contacts had come across a picture of an agent who was my 'double' at BOSS headquarters and noticed the similarity. Further inquiries established that the agent in question had left South Africa for Britain in August 1975 and returned at the end of October (the bank theft took place on 24 October). The agent had since gone to ground, but not before boasting to colleagues that he had been given a bonus of £50000 for a 'very successful project'.

I was both intrigued and disoriented. The facts of the case simply did not add up, and here, completely unsolicited, was an explanation from a total stranger. But I couldn't afford to be seen as desperate by resorting to public allegations about a South African plot for which there was no direct evidence. Although I later arranged for Wyatt to repeat his story to the BBC journalist Roger Courtiour, who was making a documentary about my case, I was otherwise forced to keep the story quiet, consumed with frustration while trying to remain calm.

However, a fortnight later, events took a new turn when it was reported that some people had been charged with conspiracy to extort £1 million from the directors of the Anglo American Corporation, and I was startled to see Wyatt named as one of them. As details of the plot emerged in court, it became clear that everything Wyatt had told me about Kamil and his group was true, adding credibility to his account of the plot to discredit the Liberal Party.

Fred Kamil had been born in the Lebanon and had formed a group of mercenaries to successfully apprehend diamond smugglers operating between Sierra Leone and Liberia. He had worked briefly for British Intelligence and then fruitfully for Anglo American. However, he had lost his job in 1970 after a dispute over £500 000 that he claimed was owed to him. In a desperate attempt to get this money, in May 1972 he tried to hijack a South African Airways (SAA) Boeing, which he believed was carrying a relative of Harry Oppenheimer, the chairman of Anglo American. When the plane landed in Malawi, Kamil was arrested and sentenced to 11 years in prison. He served less than a third of the sentence, however, and was released in unusual circumstances with the assistance of the South African authorities. Still maintaining that he was owed the full £500 000, he went to Spain and hired Wyatt and four others to try and extort the money from Anglo American officials in London.[1]

At this point, events took an even more extraordinary turn. Several weeks earlier, the male model Norman Scott had made allegations that Jeremy Thorpe had had an affair with him.[2] Shortly afterwards, I telephoned Thorpe to inform him that I had heard that the *Daily Mirror* was about to publish a story about South African attempts to discredit him. The *Mirror* had been investigating my case, and a reporter told me that Gordon Winter had been involved in promoting these same allegations about Thorpe two years earlier. I told Thorpe of the belief in anti-apartheid circles that Winter was a BOSS agent, and he gratefully asked to be kept informed of developments.

So I decided to write a confidential memorandum describing the Wyatt approach and handed it to the Liberal leader at his grand West London home on 24 February 1976. To my surprise, he said that the Labour prime minister, Harold Wilson, would be interested. He picked up the phone, rang 10 Downing Street and dispatched the memo right away. (Within ten days Winter, by now back in South Africa, was handed a copy in Johannesburg by the head of BOSS, presuming it had reached him via British Intelligence, since the memo was still strictly confidential.)

Meanwhile I had been contacted by another complete stranger, Dan Hughes, describing himself as a London-based American academic, who claimed that a young doctor, Diane Lefèvre, had important information for me. Although frantically nervous and sometimes vague about substantiating details of the Wyatt allegation, she was anxious to reinforce its general validity. In several separate instances she was remarkably well informed. For example, among my often bizarre mail I had received, anonymously in an envelope postmarked Johannesburg, a photograph dated 1964. It pictured Gordon Winter swimming with Mary Oppenheimer, the daughter of the Anglo American chairman, in the pool at the Oppenheimer home in Johannesburg. Apart from my legal team and parents, this mysterious photo had not been mentioned to anyone else, but Dr Lefèvre asked me whether I had received it. (According to Gordon Winter, the photo was sent by Hendrik van den Bergh, who was anxious to promote rumours that Anglo American, not BOSS, was behind the plot against the Liberal Party. Winter stated that Lefèvre infiltrated the Kamil group on behalf of a section of British Intelligence hostile to apartheid.)

When Wyatt and his co-conspirators were eventually tried and convicted at the Old Bailey in 1977, it was alleged in court that Dr Lefèvre was a British Intelligence agent; she denied this, but was never able to explain her role. (Wyatt was imprisoned, evidently much to his surprise: he had told journalists beforehand that he would be 'protected'.)

Then, on 9 March 1976, Harold Wilson astonished the House of Commons when he answered a 'planted' question from the Labour MP James Wellbeloved, who maintained close connections with British Intelligence. 'I have no doubt at all, there is strong South African participation in recent activities relating to the leader of the Liberal Party,' he said, adding that there had been 'very strong and heavily financed private masterminding of certain political operations'. This South African participation, he stated, was 'based on massive resources of business money and private agents of various kinds and various qualities'. Later he also referred specifically to 'the Hain case'. This set the media off in pursuit of more details. My memo to Thorpe became public knowledge, Wyatt was widely interviewed and new, even stranger, actors soon appeared on the stage.

Frustratingly, however, we still had no direct evidence. Moreover, individuals such as Wyatt and Lefèvre could be discredited if called as witnesses: was their sudden appearance designed to achieve precisely that, we wondered. So I had to remain content with fighting for my innocence within the rules of a conventional criminal trial, while strongly suspecting that I was really the victim of a much larger South African plot.

❖

THE *Queen v Peter Hain* played to a packed house in court number 8 at the Old Bailey for a fortnight at the end of March and into April 1976. Between 20 and 40 reporters attended: 'The largest number since Christine Keeler,' an usher remarked nostalgically. One eyewitness gave evidence that the thief was 'South African' in appearance. And the prosecution tried half-heartedly to suggest that, since I had been active in the campaign to get Barclays Bank to withdraw from South Africa, I might have staged the theft as a political protest. Otherwise South Africa hardly received a mention.

There were no surprises in the prosecution evidence, except that in court it seemed, if anything, even flimsier. The unreliability – at times incongruity – of identification evidence featured throughout. As the *Sunday Times* reported:

A confusing picture has emerged of the culprit as a sharp-featured, dark-eyed man, sometimes wearing spectacles, sometimes not, aged between 23 and 30 and anything from 5 feet 10 inches to 6 feet 2 inches in height, of medium build, very skinny, quite slim, with a long face, very drawn and white, of normal complexion but needing a shave, a very 'sallow' complexion with a darkish tinge, foreign looking, possibly Spanish, Egyptian or 'Afrikaans', not foreign, with black curly hair worn collar length, not very long fluffy hair reaching just below the ears, shortish wavy brown hair with ginger tints, wearing light-blue jeans and dark trousers as well as a white check shirt, a blue check shirt, a cream shirt with puffed sleeves, a light shirt with dark stripes, a cream waistcoat made of thick velvet wool, white tennis shoes and brown suede 'Hush Puppies'.

The prosecutor, Michael Corkery, opened on the basis that it had been a 'spur of the moment theft'. He called Lucy Haines, the cashier who had picked me out in the identification parade. But she was hesitant, saying she had seen the thief only for a 'split second', and at one point was seemingly unable to pick me out in court – even though I was standing in the dock. She also confirmed that she had seen me periodically on television well before the theft took place, and in the *Evening Standard* newspaper just before the identification parade.

Apart from her and the two schoolboys – whose evidence was embarrassingly inconsistent – no other witness was able to identify me. The bank accountant, Timothy Hayne, had led the chase of the thief and told the court he knew my face well from television and the newspapers: he said I was not the man. None of the police officers called could implicate me. The photofit picture was nothing like me. The fingerprint analyst confirmed that my prints had not been on any of the notes – though there was a fresh 'unknown' print on the top note.

Nevertheless, identification evidence was a compulsive curse: once the finger had been pointed at me, I faced a conviction and effectively had to prove my innocence. There were echoes of my conspiracy trial: maybe I was destined to be a fall guy for the legal establishment. Fortunately, however, Terry MacLaren's evidence proved decisive. My solicitor, John Dundon, described him as 'a witness in a million' – remarkably composed, fluent and convincing. Terry said the other boys had been behind him throughout the chase – sometimes up to 30 metres. He added that he had initially got a clear sight of the thief some ten metres away across Putney High Street, and again later during the chase when the man looked back several times to glance at his pursuers. The prosecutor tried to trip Terry up by asking him to judge distances across the large courtroom, but he came up trumps on that too. He also described with astonishing accuracy what had happened when I went into WH Smith, including my having greeted a friend there. And he described in detail the differences between me and the thief.

The bank trial and the build-up to it imposed a much greater strain on me and my family than the conspiracy trial, which had been a straightforward political case. This one challenged my honesty and presented me as some sort of clumsy criminal. So I felt emotion welling up when my highly skilled QC, Lewis Hawser, summed up for the defence. He pointed out the string of contradictions in the case against me and how the prosecution had been forced to change their opening allegation of a 'spur of the moment theft': because their own witnesses had given evidence that the thief had been spotted beforehand acting suspiciously. 'Members of the jury, the bare bones of the story just don't hang together. This is a classic case of mistaken identity,' he concluded.

But I again found myself facing a hostile judge. Alan King-Hamilton was a member of the MCC, and I had been its bête noire during the STST campaign. Senior members of the legal profession later informed me that King-Hamilton had been keen to try the case and that court administrators were equally keen to give it to him. In a quite extraordinary summing-up, he suggested – without any substantiation – that Pat, my mother and a friend staying with her, Vanessa Brown (daughter of former South African Liberal Party chairman Peter Brown), might have been untruthful alibi witnesses. Yet not even the prosecution had made that allegation. He also introduced a preposterous new hypothesis to try to reconcile my clothing with that of the thief. He suggested to the jury that the jersey I was wearing when I drove to buy the typewriter ribbon had only been put on when I got back into my car after shopping – since the thief wasn't wearing one. It was wholly improper and false speculation, which he then had to withdraw under joint challenge from both defence and prosecution, the latter worried that it compromised their case. His open hostility to the defence shocked even the most experienced lawyers and was the talk of the Bar for some time. At best he might have confused the jury and at worst he raised serious doubts in their minds as to my innocence.

Perhaps that helped explain what followed: not an instant verdict at all. Wondering about my fate, which lay in the hands of 'twelve men and women good and true', I was taken downstairs to the cells. After five long and tense hours, during which the jury were called back and advised to reach a majority verdict, they quickly returned. I was led back upstairs, my senses dulled.

'Not guilty,' the foreman stated emphatically. But the sheer relief his words engendered hardly registered with me because pandemonium broke out.

The public gallery erupted with cheers and clapping. There were calls of 'order, order' as bewildered ushers rushed about. The floor of the court was alive as the people seemed to take over. The judge, who had ruled his fiefdom for two weeks, had finally lost control. I couldn't hear what he was trying to say amid the smiling, hugging jumble of people, as I struggled to control my emotions. Then I was let out of the dock at last and into the warm comfort of my family gathered around me. Justice had been done – despite the police, despite the judge and despite the South African security services and their helpers behind this 'Putney plot'.[3]

❖

AS played out in court, it seemed a straightforward case of mistaken identity; even my vehement feelings about the transparent police prejudice displayed against me in detention did not surface, because my lawyers advised it would detract from what was a strong defence.

But the South African dimension continued bubbling away – albeit frustratingly, only in the background. I had not raised it; other mysterious figures had done so. Therefore I had no alternative except to keep it below the radar. Nor could I afford to become obsessed with it. The case had been traumatic enough. I had met other victims of mistaken identity who had been so consumed by the injustice of their plight that their lives were virtually destroyed; it became such a haunting fixation that they couldn't focus on anything else, and their mental health was damaged. I tried therefore to get on with my life, determined not to be beaten by anybody, a trait that has stayed with me throughout a political life that has seen at least as many knocks as triumphs.

Our first child was due around three months after the trial and, with my PhD derailed, I started looking for a job. Fortunately, I found one: the Union of Post Office Workers appointed me as a research officer, though not after considerable anguish on the part of its general secretary, Tom Jackson, who knew the appointment would be very controversial among his national executive and membership. As indeed it was. 'Do you really hate cricket?' was one of the questions thrown at me during my interview by a union national officer who was a member of the MCC.

Nevertheless, the South African connection would not go

away. Not until five years and more after my trial, and then only when new books and evidence appeared, was I able to piece together an analysis corroborating an apartheid connection, which kept resurfacing in a series of exotic new developments.

A month after my acquittal, on 17 May 1976, a certain Frederick Cheeseman rang the office of the Liberal chief whip, David Steel MP, claiming to be an ex-intelligence officer with some information about a smear campaign against the party. When interviewed by Steel's aides, he claimed to have visited BOSS headquarters in Pretoria in September 1974 and to have been shown a series of dossiers profiling leading Liberal and Labour figures that were to be used as the basis for a smear campaign. After extensive reading of the documentation he provided, and checks on his identity with security services across the world by the BBC television journalists Barrie Penrose and Roger Courtiour (who, as 'Pencourt', had been investigating the South African angle), the BBC evening news ran the story as a lead exclusive, and other media followed it.

However, a day later, Cheeseman did a complete volte-face. In an exclusive interview with the *Daily Express*, he claimed to be a hoaxer: a Walter Mitty character on the dole. This effectively killed investigations into the possible role of BOSS and other intelligence operatives in my case, and that of Jeremy Thorpe and possibly other Liberal and Labour politicians. A few years later it emerged that Cheeseman, far from being bogus, was an intelligence agent on active service – and remained so.[4]

The former British Intelligence officer Colin Wallace told me when I interviewed him in 1987: 'The Colonel Cheeseman saga is known in intelligence circles as the "double bubble" because it contains a second dimension in deception and not only deflects attention from the main target, but also "bursts", leaving the investigator doubting everything he has uncovered so far. I have no doubt that Pencourt did get quite close – possibly too close – to the truth and various deceptions were put into action to discredit their investigations.'

❖

ALTHOUGH the Putney bank theft may have appeared an isolated event, a bizarre one-off, it coincided with an extraordinary period in British politics, from 1974 to 1976.[5]

By the mid-1970s key sections of the British establishment had become increasingly alarmed at what they believed was a leftward political drift in Britain. The escalating crisis in Northern Ireland, the growth of the left in both the trade unions and the Labour Party, successful extra-parliamentary protest and direct action such as STST, worker and student militancy – all were seen to pose a major threat.

Many on the right believed they really were faced with 'the end of civilisation' in Britain as they had known and controlled it. In 1972 striking miners using flying-picket tactics had emerged victorious against the Conservative government of Edward Heath. After imposing a three-day working week to limit energy demand, Heath called an election in February 1974 on the theme of 'who governs the country'. But he lost. Harold Wilson's Labour formed a minority government and then won a small majority in an October general election. Amid considerable disquiet at these events, the Conservative Party right moved against Heath, who was felt to be too liberal. He was eventually replaced in 1975 by an avowed right-winger, Margaret Thatcher.

The Thatcherites then began strengthening their hold over the Conservative Party, relying upon various research organisations and pressure groups, many of which were found to have clear links with British Intelligence. Among these were the Institute for the Study of Conflict, the Society for Individual Freedom (which had helped sponsor my 1972 prosecution) and the

National Association for Freedom (which BOSS helped fund).

In parallel, with the crisis escalating in Northern Ireland, the British Army in 1971 established an Information Policy Unit whose existence was officially denied but which became an instrument of disinformation and 'black' propaganda. Its leading operative was Colin Wallace, who served as senior information officer at the army's Northern Ireland headquarters outside Belfast between May 1968 and February 1975. When he left the service in 1976 after a distinguished career, Wallace provided detailed evidence on 'psychological operations' – or 'psy-ops' as they were known in the trade – including establishing front organisations and organising paramilitary projects.

Wallace confirmed that the distinction between 'legitimate' targets, such as the IRA or the Protestant paramilitaries, and 'illegitimate' targets became increasingly blurred, and his psy-ops work was steadily widened to cover individuals and groups in British politics not identifiably on the hard right, including members of the Labour and Liberal parties, and even 'liberal' Tories such as Heath. By 1973 Wallace and his army colleagues were working closely with the British security services on 'British' rather than 'Irish' intelligence projects. The 'Irish crisis' had come to be merged with what they perceived to be a 'British crisis'.

Colin Wallace told me early in 1987: 'We saw you as an important target in the long term. You were clearly on your way up in politics. Through your anti-apartheid activities and your involvement in radical campaigns, you had offended many people on the right and it was important to neutralise you.'

A former MI5 officer, Cathy Massiter, confirmed in a TV documentary in March 1985 that a fundamental shift of emphasis occurred between 1970 and 1984 when she was in the service. From being a counter-espionage organisation aimed at hostile foreign powers, MI5 switched towards a domestic-surveillance organisation, monitoring left-wing activists and trade unionists, with the service's F Branch expanding enormously to cover these domestic targets. Apart from tapping phones and maintaining surveillance, MI5 infiltrated individuals into various groups and organised illegal burglaries of target houses and offices. (My own phone was tapped and there was evidence of infiltrators in the various anti-apartheid, anti-racist and political campaigns in which I had been active.)

Wallace testified that intelligence information fed from MI5 to his office in Northern Ireland was then 'recycled' with the assistance of the CIA to news agencies in America, including Transworld News, the North Atlantic News Agency and Forum World Features (for whom Gordon Winter had written an article in 1970 on leading anti-apartheid figures, including me). When this planted information appeared in US papers or in international dispatches from these agencies, Wallace and his colleagues would then pick it up in Belfast as 'hard' information and supply it to MI5 and government ministers.

Thus, MI5 could use its own recycled information, disinformation or 'black' propaganda – Wallace told me all three types were involved – contained in apparently independent sources to give credibility to its activities against its political opponents, or to provide corroboration for its suspicions. Among the people who were targets in this process were Edward Heath, Harold Wilson and Jeremy Thorpe, who between them headed all three major democratic parties in Britain at the time.

Wallace confirmed that Heath was a target because he was regarded as 'too weak', Wilson because he was seen as the main alternative to rule by the right, and Thorpe because the Liberals might become influential enough to block the return of a new, rightist Conservative government. (This was much the same prognosis, of course, with which Kenneth Wyatt – entirely independently – had first approached me in 1976; and indeed in 1977 the Liberals *did* conclude a formal pact to sustain in power a Labour government that had by then lost its slim majority in the House of Commons.) Evidence of a plot involving elements in the British and South African security services to disrupt the Liberal and Labour parties was confirmed in 1987 by the retired MI5 agent Peter Wright in his book *Spycatcher*.[6]

When Labour came back into power in 1974, the attention of Wallace and his colleagues became even more directed at domestic British politics. Wallace recorded that MI5 was concerned that Labour would take tougher action against South Africa and the illegal Smith regime in Rhodesia – thus 'encouraging Marxist influence in southern Africa'. He explained: 'Most of my work during this period was being used by others for totally unconstitutional ends.' He also described how that created an atmosphere in which he and his colleagues found it steadily more difficult to distinguish between, for example, a suspected IRA bomber and a British anti-apartheid activist. Information on both was being fed across his desk. Both appeared on target lists and in his security files. Both represented a common threat and both therefore were legitimate targets.

❖

WALLACE spoke quietly and authoritatively during our meeting in 1987, his wife having made us a cup of tea in their modest house in Arundel, West Sussex.

The way in which intelligence information could be abused was evident from his contemporaneous files, in which it was eerie to see my name appear. For example, they contained a cutting from the *Irish Press* dated 7 February 1972 that described Soviet reaction to the events of 'Bloody Sunday' the previous week, when British soldiers killed 14 unarmed civilians in the Northern Ireland town of Derry (Londonderry). Wallace noted alongside the cutting: 'KGB – link to Labour activists. See also Bloody

Sunday Commemorative vigil Peter Hain. Hain's family deported SA 1966 for Communist activity.' As a leaflet in Wallace's file confirmed, I was one of the sponsors of that 1973 vigil.

Another article, clipped from the *Irish News* of 16 November 1972, reported the meeting of an international tribunal in Belfast to investigate army harassment of civilians. The tribunal was chaired by leading anti-apartheid activist Kader Asmal, then a South African exile in Dublin (and later a Cabinet minister under Nelson Mandela and Thabo Mbeki). Wallace had recorded alongside the cutting in red pen: 'Asmal is a SA lawyer. Hain's family deported from SA for Communist activity.'

Fifteen years after the files had been prepared and 12 years after my arrest, Wallace described to me this technique as 'guilt by tenuous association'. A false entry in MI5 records about my parents' 'communist activity' provided a pretext for my name to be associated first with Soviet communism and then brought full circle back to Irish terrorism. As Wallace also confirmed, it is not hard to envisage how, on this basis, action to discredit me could be rationalised by members of the security services. Wallace stated that he worked closely with MI5 and the CIA, and confirmed (as Gordon Winter had done) that both agencies then worked with BOSS. What began as part of a legitimate counterterrorist project in Northern Ireland widened significantly to cover intelligence work on, and psy-ops against, all manner of activity that had nothing to do with Irish affairs, and certainly nothing to do with terrorism.

❖

AT the time, there was also talk in senior military circles about organising a coup, as Field Marshal Lord Carver, Chief of the Defence Staff in 1974, later acknowledged. There were reports in 1974–1975 of private 'citizens' armies' being prepared by retired military figures, including General Sir Walter Walker (until 1972 commander-in-chief of NATO's Northern Command in Europe) and Colonel David Stirling (known for his wartime exploits in the Special Air Service), both covertly assisted by British Intelligence officers. One of General Walker's Kent area coordinators was Lieutenant Colonel Frederick Cheeseman, the 'double bubble' source in May 1976 of an alleged South African plot. Prominent right-wing figures Ross McWhirter and George Young were also involved: both had close links with British Intelligence and both were connected to my 1972 conspiracy prosecution.

Harold Wilson told the BBC's Penrose and Courtiour: 'I am not certain that for the last eight months when I was prime minister I knew what was happening, fully, in security.' During this period – spanning summer 1975 to his resignation in spring 1976 – Wilson had become more convinced of an earlier suspicion that there was 'a very right-wing faction' in MI5, and to a lesser extent MI6, that sought to smear him and others in his administration. In 1978 the author Chapman Pincher, a right-winger with extremely good intelligence sources, wrote: 'The undermining activities which Wilson complained of were not only genuine but far more menacing than he revealed. Certain officers, inside MI5, assisted by others who had retired from the service, were actually trying to bring down the Labour Government.'[7]

Colin Wallace added that what Harold Wilson had called 'this mafia faction' numbered at least 40 agents, explaining: 'Information supplied by the CIA to MI5 was used to justify a number of in-depth investigations into Harold Wilson's activities and those of other Labour MPs/supporters to find out if sufficient "hard evidence" could be gathered to wreck the Labour Party's chances of gaining power.'

The interests of the British hard right and apartheid's rulers coincided over my bank-theft case. Peter Wright testified that his faction of MI5 was openly sympathetic to white South Africa at the height of the Cold War because it was seen as an ally against 'international communism'. Colin Wallace corroborated this, adding that information was regularly 'traded' between MI5 and BOSS. Even joint operations were carried out where the agencies shared common objectives, as Gordon Winter also confirmed.

Consequently, in framing me for the Putney bank theft, BOSS was likely to have had the active or tacit support of officers in the rightist MI5 group. This would have given BOSS both the 'cover' and the operational back-up required. Assistance from MI5 agents would also have opened up channels to ensure I was linked to the crime.

Quoting his former London handler – later to be BOSS's head in the Transkei region of South Africa – Winter reported that a BOSS agent with a walkie-talkie radio had been watching my home from a parked car. When I left to go shopping, the agent alerted the real thief to act. This man had a criminal record and immediately after committing the theft was flown to Paris and then to South Africa to start a new life. (This account is uncannily similar to that given quite independently back in 1976 by Kenneth Wyatt.) According to Winter, the only minor slip-up was that the individual's hair had been styled to resemble mine whereas I had by coincidence changed my hairstyle shortly before the event. Winter added that immediately after the theft, BOSS arranged for Scotland Yard to be called to link me to the crime. The caller told the Yard to check in Special Branch files, where they would find I had campaigned actively against Barclays' involvement in South Africa and had taken part in a picket outside the very same Putney branch of the bank.

How does this account square with the facts? First, the intervention of the schoolboys must have been unplanned: they were clearly not part of any BOSS plot. But then their role was confined purely to implicating me through reporting my car's registration number. Second, one interpretation of the thief's behaviour (as reported by nearly a dozen eyewitnesses) is fully compatible with the role of a BOSS operative. About 20 minutes before I left the house, one of the cashiers had spotted the thief behaving suspiciously; she later told the court that he must have been 'casing the joint'. He had peered through the window and come into the bank.

Other witnesses reported seeing what they assumed was the same man in the area even before this. Uncannily, nearly an hour before the theft, one witness, Elizabeth Forshaw, spotted a man while she was shopping in Putney High Street: 'I saw a familiar face, and immediately I thought it was Peter Hain … Suddenly, when he was within a few feet, I did not think it was Peter Hain. Before, I was absolutely convinced, but when he came within two or three feet I knew it wasn't him.' (She explained that she was particularly interested in people she had seen on television and knew what I looked like.) After the theft, the thief turned round while running from his pursuers and threw the money back – not the behaviour of someone desperate for the money but maybe that of someone keen to allow witnesses to see his face, since everybody accepted that he resembled me.

Third – and perhaps most significant – is the reported phone call to Scotland Yard implicating me. Gordon Winter stated that this originated from a BOSS tip-off. And he could not have been aware of one fact that was never made known outside the very few most intimately involved in my defence team. When my solicitor, John Dundon, was in Wandsworth police station waiting to see me, the officer in charge referred obliquely to telephone conversations with senior officers at Scotland Yard, and to 'important evidence' he had gained thereby. But he would not elaborate.

Neither Dundon nor I could make any sense of it at the time, but if BOSS (or perhaps a British Intelligence source) did phone the Yard, as Winter described, then this could be the elusive factor in those key hours when the decision was made to prosecute me.

It would make sense of Dundon's conversation, of the lengthy delay while consultations took place and of the relative importance that the senior Wandsworth detective attached to those consultations. 'Evidence' via Scotland Yard could be corroboration of the schoolboys' account.

Colin Wallace told me that he had established, through a then serving British Intelligence officer, the contents of a record held by the security services stating that the Metropolitan Police were tipped off by MI5 almost immediately after the bank theft that I was responsible. This tip-off occurred *before* the schoolboys implicated me by reporting my registration number. Wallace said the security service record confirmed BOSS's involvement. The record also showed that there had been an earlier, but failed, attempt to set me up some weeks before. (And indeed, just before my trial, John Dundon was shown statements from a witness who had seen me on TV and reported to police that I looked like the suspect in a bank robbery that had taken place in Fulham, across the river from my home, one month before the Putney theft.)

Once my arrest had been accomplished, however, it seems that a section of MI5 or, more likely, MI6, wanted the South African plot to be known through a source that could not be traced back. Colin Wallace recalled that by 1975 the battle for power in Northern Ireland between MI5 and MI6 meant that 'they were much more at war with each other than with the IRA', and the two intelligence services were also known to be at odds over South Africa. MI6, the foreign intelligence service, tended to be more anti-apartheid, reflecting Foreign Office policy. By contrast, MI5 – particularly Peter Wright's faction – were actively pro-South Africa, reflecting their Cold War, anti-communist priority, which virtually 'equated anybody not blue with being red', in Wallace's words.

According to the authors of *The Pencourt File*, Kenneth Wyatt himself may have had British Intelligence links. Wyatt said the plot was intended to discredit the Liberals and thereby prevent them forming a pact with Labour to block a Tory government, an analysis shared by the rightist MI5 faction, as confirmed later in Peter Wright's *Spycatcher*. If Wyatt's allegations were encouraged or even inspired by MI6 officers, this might also explain the appearance on the scene of the mysterious and extraordinarily well-informed Diane Lefêvre. Her approach to me could have been timed deliberately to corroborate the Wyatt account. She actively promoted the South African connection at the same time as the prime minister, Harold Wilson, was doing so as a result of briefing by MI6.

Finally, BOSS had a history of disrupting anti-apartheid activity in Britain, in which framing me for a bank theft does not look unusual. It would also have been what is known as a 'deniable operation', which is precisely why it remained so difficult to prove.

When Nelson Mandela established the Truth and Reconciliation Commission, chaired by Archbishop Desmond Tutu, it was suggested that my case might be one to look at. But there were so many heart-rending cases of people who had lost loved ones to torture or assassination, frankly mine was of a lower order entirely and I thought it would be self-indulgent to apply to the commission.

During the Mandela presidency, there was an opportunity for anti-apartheid activists to inspect old security-police files, and my parents and I applied to do so. But, as others found, ours had obviously been ruthlessly culled, and there was nothing of interest left: only old newspaper clippings and the like. In 1994, with the ANC about to assume office, the National Intelligence Agency alone destroyed 44 tonnes of incriminating documents, 'the written record of countless acts of culpability', wrote investigator Hennie van Vuuren.[8] The scale of the destruction of Military Intelligence files is not known, but doubtless was massive too.

As with many South African intelligence activities across the world at the height of apartheid, the real bank thief was never identified. There was, however, a sequel of sorts on 25 July 2000 when the director general of MI5, Stephen Lander, came to see me at the Foreign Office when I was a minister.

This was after MI5 had been forced the previous September to open many of its secret files for the first time after an independent tribunal accepted that a blanket ban on releasing information was unlawful under the Data Protection Act. There were media revelations about old MI5 files held on senior Labour ministers Jack Straw, Peter Mandelson, Harriet Harman and myself, going way back to our youthful activist days.

Sitting on the sofa in my office, Lander courteously explained that MI5 had indeed opened a file on me in 1970 and I had been under regular surveillance, but my file had been closed in 1988 when I had ceased to be of interest, and had since 'been destroyed'. However, quite separately, there were voluminous Metropolitan Police Special Branch files on me, which I was shown during the Undercover Policing Inquiry in 2019–2021 – and was also told that a copy of my MI5 file remained in a microfiche store where, however, it could not be routinely accessed.

Lander assured me that I 'was never an operational target', merely that in my anti-apartheid and anti-racist campaigning I had had 'contact with communists and Trotskyists'. I had, he said, 'never been regarded by the Service as a communist agent'. Back in 1998 the House of Commons Intelligence and Security Committee did confirm that MI5 had handed over files to Prime Minister Tony Blair on his intended ministerial appointees, presumably including Jack Straw, Harriet Harman and me.

I asked Lander about the bank theft, and his calibrated reply was striking: 'South Africa would know. They almost certainly did it.'[9]

Secret Missions

BY the mid-1970s the international sports boycott had spread to cover almost all sports, and in response the apartheid authorities launched 'multinational sport'. This allowed the four officially classified racial groups in South Africa – whites, blacks, coloureds and Asians – to compete against each other as four separate 'nations' within the country, but only in major international events with foreign participation.

Although this manoeuvre confirmed the essential case for the boycott – that change would only be forced under the pressure of isolation – it was a concession in name only, and merely expressed the logic of apartheid: that each racial group should develop separately in their own 'nations' and compete in sport accordingly – provided, of course, that whites-only teams continued to represent the country abroad.

Crucially, Prime Minister Vorster added: 'I want to make it very clear that in South Africa no mixed sport shall be practised at club, provincial or national levels.' The fundamental structure of sports apartheid – both legislatively and practically – remained intact from school to national level. Yet there were attempts, backed by financial largesse, to co-opt certain black sportspeople willing to go along with 'multinational' sport, and in parallel attempts to persuade anti-apartheid campaigners such as me that progress was real.

So I formulated a response, as chair of SART, that focused single-mindedly upon sport. We had won the original argument for a boycott because South African sport was organised on the basis of race, not merit. Apart from racists or right-wingers sympathetic to South Africa in Britain or Australia or New Zealand, even those antagonistic to interference in 'their sport' had to concede that the very essence of sports opportunity should be merit, not skin colour. The more open-minded could be won over by an *argument about sport*, which in turn legitimised political intervention in an area that would otherwise have been seen as taboo. Therefore, I did not want anti-apartheid activists to be forced back upon the argument that we would not budge until the whole structure of apartheid was abolished, because that could have placed us in the position of having to justify singling out South African sport as opposed to other countries with tyrannical regimes that did not poison their sport.

By early 1977 I had formulated an agenda of changes in laws to 'exempt' sport from apartheid. It was pretty fanciful to imagine this actually occurring: how, in practice, could a black citizen be treated equally while engaged in sport, but then leave the stadium and resume a life still rigidly regulated and oppressed by apartheid? But because this reform agenda focused on 'sport' rather than on 'politics', the argument placed white South Africans once more on the defensive in the court of international opinion – and was deliberately intended to do so. I had the full support of the SANROC leaders, Dennis Brutus and Chris de Broglio, who knew the sports world inside out. However, I was privately criticised in some anti-apartheid circles on the grounds that you could not have 'normal sport in an abnormal society', the slogan of the internal South African Council on Sport (SACOS).

Although agreeing entirely with this as a *principle*, I was convinced it was not a *political strategy* for international anti-apartheid forces to retain the near-universal sports boycott we had achieved through direct-action protests and successful international lobbying, and I managed to win a carefully negotiated policy position after a difficult debate at an annual meeting of the AAM. I also held discussions with the Labour minister of sport, Denis Howell, and on 8 February 1977 drafted some notes for his department.

❖

OUR home telephone number was unlisted, and the phone very rarely rang with an unfamiliar call. But one evening in March 1977, there was a curiosity.

'Craven, South Africa,' the guttural voice said resolutely. 'I would like to talk. Will you meet me?' He seemed almost to choke on the request, as if hating having to ask a favour of me.

South Africa's 'Mr Rugby', Danie Craven, had been a bitter opponent during the STST campaign. He had regularly denounced me, often in the most lurid terms. During the tour he famously declared: 'There will be a black Springbok over my dead body.'

So for him to call personally was astounding to say the least. Was this some kind of manipulative stunt, I immediately wondered. The South African propaganda machine had been busily courting world opinion with all manner of ruses. But in interviews with white South African journalists, I had deliberately indicated that if *sports apartheid* was abolished, there might be a basis for the country's *sports isolation* to end. Perhaps Craven was responding to these?

I was warily courteous. What was the purpose? Would a meeting be strictly private? Having partly satisfied myself on these points, I agreed. Others in my position might well not have done so – it was dealing with the enemy, after all – but I felt instinctively that it was the right thing to do. However, his suggestion of a venue near the South African Embassy was not acceptable; we could meet only if he came to our flat in Putney.

The following day, at the agreed time, after I had returned from work, he arrived in a taxi and apprehensively knocked at our front door. Watching through the front window, I spotted a companion of his anxiously peering out of the taxi as it sped off. I was uneasy too, satisfying myself that he was alone, with no heavies or media in tow, before opening the door.

He entered distrustfully, brusquely declining the offer of tea or coffee, seemingly unsure whether to be aggressive or to return my respectful politeness. Gradually he thawed, obviously taken with the appearance of our seven-month-old baby son, Sam, in the cramped living room/study.

Was it correct, as he had heard, that I wasn't really 'anti-rugby' or 'anti-sport'? Yes, I replied – indeed, I was a bit of a sports nut, had played lots of cricket, football and even some rugby in Pretoria as a schoolboy. I had never been 'anti-South African sport' but was 'anti-apartheid sport'. Why had I not been allowed by law to play with or against black boys in the school or club teams of my youth?

We circled around each other, Craven part bristling, part reasonable, appealing to me that the youngsters he was renowned for grooming into great players were being thwarted by the absence of international competition to benchmark themselves against, as Springboks had always done so successfully before the boycott. So I suggested that we left 'politics' to one side and talked about changes that would be required in the way sport was played and organised in South Africa to warrant lifting the boycott. He warmed to that.

Surely he would agree that the aim would be to make sport truly non-racial – that is, free of all apartheid restrictions – even if these remained in other spheres of life? It turned the tables on his still-simmering suspicion that I was 'anti-rugby'. He agreed, and said that he wanted to move faster, but the government was blocking the way.

I responded by producing my proposed list of reforms. These included fully integrated club and school sport and a multi-million-rand programme immediately to improve black sports facilities and opportunities. He did not demur. There also had to be changes in a variety of laws affecting sport. These included suspension of the old pass laws, which meant African sportsmen or -women had to have prior permission to play at 'away' venues outside the municipal areas to which their passes confined them. There were a dozen other such pieces of apartheid legislation directly affecting the conduct and organisation of sport, just as they determined every other aspect of society. However improbable it might be to conceive of sport as some kind of non-apartheid oasis within the country, I knew full well that for Craven it was highly significant: because I was not demanding the abolition of the entire apartheid edifice, merely that sport be exempt from it. In return, the boycotts could be lifted and Craven could get his beloved Springboks on the world stage again.

I also told him he should talk to the ANC and black sports groups, principally SACOS, inside the country, stressing that their consent and participation was crucial, not mine. If they still said no to lifting the boycott, then that was that. (My whole strategy was to force white sports leaders such as Craven to deal with the people they were oppressing or denying.)

Craven took my list of reforms away with him. We had got on increasingly well as our talk went on. Underneath his gruff Afrikaner assertiveness was a traditional, well-mannered gentleman. I rather liked him and sensed the feeling might be mutual. He even presented me with a Springbok team jersey and tie, which I placed surreptitiously at the bottom of a drawer: the gift remained a secret, as it could have been misinterpreted as a sign of betrayal, so deep were hostilities at the time.

We both respected the confidentiality of the meeting – old enemies, old ogres, finding some common cause, perhaps? Although I wasn't under any illusions, I was convinced that, at some point, politics would have to take over from protest, and the meeting was a highly significant signal: maybe white sports leaders were beginning to recognise that they had to change, and change fundamentally, or their desperate desire to return to world sport would never be fulfilled.

Then, on 9 August 1977, the former South African Test cricket captain Ali Bacher, who had been due to lead the cancelled 1970 tour to Britain, also beat a path to my door. Acting as an emissary for the white South African Cricket Association, he aggressively sought to persuade me that things were changing for the better and we should call off the boycott. I did not agree, and our exchanges were acrimonious compared with the down-to-earth conversation I'd had with Danie Craven. It confirmed what my father had always told me: Afrikaners rather than English-speaking whites would ultimately be the ones to be won over when a settlement with the black majority finally occurred. He believed that the English interest in South Africa was historically mercurial, initially economically exploitative, subsequently fellow-travelling with apartheid, whereas Afrikaner whites felt they had a much greater stake in what became their country, not as colonists like English whites who could always return 'home'.

A couple of months earlier, the editor of the liberal *Daily Dispatch*, Donald Woods, had arrived in London. He was acting as a go-between for further discussions and asked to meet me. Despite his anti-apartheid inclinations and his growing reputation as an opponent of the system, Donald had been extremely hostile to the STST campaign. He had been used in television interviews (as was another, even more prominent, liberal South African, Helen Suzman) to criticise our campaign and especially its direct-action strategy; like most white South Africans, he could not stomach attacks on their sport and accused us of 'law breaking'. However, he was becoming progressively radicalised, especially through his friendship with the Black Consciousness leader, Steve Biko.

As a newspaper editor, Donald Woods had extensive contacts with Cabinet ministers and explained that he had been asked by sports minister Piet Koornhof to find out, as discreetly as possible, whether I, together with Chris de Broglio and Dennis Brutus, might be prepared to negotiate an end to the sports boycott in return for the dismantling of apartheid in sport. Koornhof was taking a considerable risk: if news of the initiative leaked, it could be used against him by his more conservative rivals in the National Party, who would be horrified at the thought of talking to the likes of us.

We were initially suspicious. Why was Donald carrying messages from the government we were seeking to destroy? But, he assured us, there was nothing to lose by testing Koornhof's sincerity and his ability to deliver. In return, we insisted that while we might present a set of reform proposals, progress would depend upon Koornhof's negotiating internally with SACOS leaders. An agreement could not be made unilaterally by international anti-apartheid leaders. Indeed, we had no authority from our movements to do so. At the same time, I was clear that we had to keep up the momentum – to push out a boat of reforms and see where it sailed.

So on 22 June 1977 I drew up a confidential memorandum, agreed with Chris and Dennis, for a 'Proposed South African Sports Summit'. We insisted on certain conditions for our attendance at such a summit: passport restrictions, bannings and harassment of non-racial sports officials must end; the government should declare an official moratorium on all sports tours for two years while the sports system was reorganised; a non-racial sports policy must be implemented, including the full integration of club and school sport, repeal of all racist legislation in so far as it affected sport, merging of separate sports groups into single democratic organisations and having non-racial overseas touring sides.

If these conditions were agreed in advance and in full, our statement concluded, 'we would be prepared to accept an invitation from SACOS to attend a formal meeting. If implemented, we would be prepared publicly to recommend dropping the boycotts and demonstrations, to take effect at the end of the moratorium period, subject to satisfactory progress having been made in establishing a non-racial sports structure.'

Donald Woods later wrote: 'When I handed Dr Koornhof the letter from Hain and the others he pondered it at length before looking up to say: "We can meet these conditions. We can do a deal. There are certain aspects of it that will be very difficult, but I am sure we can do it."'

Arrangements were discussed for me to meet Koornhof for secret negotiations in Switzerland in August 1977. But, before flying back from South Africa to discuss this with me, Woods was phoned by Koornhof and asked to meet Hendrik van den Bergh, the head of BOSS. Van den Bergh warned that Koornhof was going too far, too fast, and that *he* would like to meet me in Paris instead.

But Woods was by now becoming a target for the government that had asked him to act as an interlocutor. He was subsequently banned and had to flee the country following the murder in police custody of his friend Steve Biko. He decided against putting this proposition to me and I only learnt about it from him some years later.[1]

However, I was quite content with the outcome. Though intrigued by Koornhof's overtures, I hadn't expected anything to come of them. On the one hand, I was determined to formulate a reasoned response that could be publicly defended and put whites, desperate to regain world participation, on the spot. On the other hand, I was equally determined not to compromise our position, especially since a major advance had only just been secured at the Commonwealth summit meeting in Scotland: on 15 June 1977 the heads of government unanimously adopted the Gleneagles Agreement, under which each government pledged for the first time to take every practical step to discourage sports links with South Africa.

In the years that followed, as part of the lobbying operation then being undertaken by white sports leaders and officials, various South African newspapers invited me to visit the country 'and to see for myself'. Although I knew perfectly well what was going on inside the country, I did not want to be seen to be unreasonable. Despite criticism from others in the AAM, and to the horror of my parents, who were fearful for my safety, I said I would be happy to visit, to see and to talk – but on condition that a government minister write to me in advance to withdraw the ban on my entry first imposed in October 1969 and to guarantee my safety. As I expected, the letter never came – to my immense relief.

❖

BUT seeds had been sown. As internal resistance rose up again after the Soweto uprising in 1976, and South Africa moved inexorably towards ungovernability, the ANC, under the leadership of Oliver Tambo internationally and Nelson Mandela in prison, began reaching out to its oppressors.

There was an extraordinary, but again secret, meeting set up in October 1988. In Harare, Zimbabwe, Danie Craven and his close colleagues met a top ANC delegation led by Thabo Mbeki. After two days of talks, they reached agreement that the ANC would press for the ban on the Springboks to be lifted if rugby was reorganised on a fully non-racial basis. Thabo Mbeki indicated a softening in the ANC's position, stating that while the boycott should be maintained against racist institutions in South Africa, non-racial organisations had to be treated differently – a concession on the old position that apartheid in its entirety had to be abolished before sports links could be resumed. With the ANC still banned, the meeting was highly controversial. Within 18 years of stating that he would never have a black in his side, Craven, as the leading sports figure in South Africa, had finally done the previously unthinkable and met with the ANC – still regarded by most whites (and Britain's prime minister Margaret Thatcher) as the 'terrorist' archenemy.

But Craven was blocked, both within his own rugby board and by the government, which condemned him for 'plunging politics knee-deep into rugby' and spelt out 'the negative consequences of this kind of action for South Africa in its fight against terrorism'. President PW Botha publicly condemned Craven, insisting that the ANC was wrapping itself in a cloak of piety 'in order to stab you in the back with a dagger'. Sport, Botha added, was part of the ANC's terrain of 'subtle subversion' and 'there are still politically blind moles in this country who fail to see this'.

Although many anti-apartheid activists were privately equally unhappy with the ANC's initiative, I was always supportive. As Nelson Mandela was to show in political negotiations leading to the overthrow of apartheid, the ANC was extremely sophisticated – sometimes too much so for activists schooled in the harsh and necessary arts of 'no compromise'. In reality, our position had actually been strengthened by the ANC's demonstration of flexibility at Harare, for it revealed that all the blockages were from apartheid South Africa. But, from then on, sport – instead of being an important means of confronting whites with the realisation that they had no alternative but to change – became a means of offering them a glimpse of a new post-apartheid South Africa in which their beloved sports tours could resume.[2]

❖

IN December 1989 came a back-to-the-future moment – with a bump.

Turning around from the rear seat of the car I was in, I spotted a police van, driven by a white officer. The sight took me back to my Pretoria childhood a quarter of a century earlier. My companions were sceptical: nervy paranoia on my part, perhaps? But wherever we drove, the police van followed.

We were in the township of New Brighton, outside the southern seaside city of Port Elizabeth, and I was on a secret (and illegal) visit to make a film, *Return of the Rebel*, for Granada Television's renowned documentary programme, *World in Action*.

Our guide, Mkhuseli Jack – a prominent resistance leader in the eastern Cape – hastily redirected us to the local dry cleaners. The British camera crew hurriedly hid their equipment amid rows of clothing while the women running the place continued to serve their customers as if nothing untoward had happened.

I sat rigid, desperately hoping I would not be recognised as the police pulled up right alongside, the officers curtly engaging the charismatic Mkhuseli, a familiar figure to them who had recently been imprisoned. He was sitting in the front passenger seat and spun them a story that they clearly did not believe, making me even more tense.

Then *World in Action*'s formidable producer, Linda McDougall, stepped out in her full 'English lady' mode, asserting haughtily that this was her first time in a township. *Why* couldn't she travel about freely? *Why* was she being harassed? *Wasn't* this a country that welcomed tourists? *Where* was their superintendent?

The officers retreated in embarrassment, climbed back into the van and drove off. It was a narrow escape – and I insisted we abandon the Port Elizabeth leg of our visit. This disappointed Linda because she had planned to film me next in nearby Port Alfred, the seaside resort where I had spent happy holidays as a boy.

The whole idea for the venture had been Linda's. One of Britain's most original and incisive TV producers, she had first suggested a year before that I might return to make a film. I was incredulous: I was banned from returning; it would be very dangerous. Old scores could be settled. New evidence showed that officially sponsored death squads had been responsible for the assassination of over 50 anti-apartheid activists – some of them friends (such as Fabian and Florence Ribeiro, shot by gunmen outside their home on 1 December 1986). Linda explained that she had already secretly filmed township eruptions twice, surreptitiously entering the country by train from Zimbabwe or Botswana. But I was notorious and hated, I retorted.

Then two things changed. First, it was announced that the former England cricket captain Mike Gatting would lead a 'rebel' England XI cricket tour in early January 1990, organised by Ali Bacher – a serious breach of the sports boycott. Second, Linda came up with an ingenious solution. I was to change my name by deed poll and *World in Action* would negotiate a new passport with the authorities, as they had done for similar ventures behind the Iron Curtain.

I now had a family, a job as a trade-union officer and a mortgage, and Pat and my parents were implacably opposed to the plan. Nevertheless I decided to go ahead. Only Linda, the programme's senior editors and my immediate family were in the know. In case something happened to me, I also told our sons, Sam, aged 13, and Jake, aged 11. The night before I left I warned them that I might be captured if they breathed a word. (They did not.)

I organised a week's leave from work, assembled a new identity as a telecommunications businessman (an easy task as head of research for the by now renamed Communication Workers Union) and was booked on a British Airways flight from Heathrow to Cape Town. My new passport bore the name 'Peter Western-Hain'. Pat's maiden name being Western, this had provided a half-plausible reason for the Passport Office. Larry Grant, my solicitor friend, asked no questions. He accepted my explanation of a 'gesture to feminism' with obvious scepticism, confidentially making the deed-poll arrangements to change my name without being aware of the real purpose. We had calculated that the computer check on arrival would not spot the toxic but now hyphenated suffix 'Hain' in the new surname.

The overnight flight to Cape Town was edgy. I was booked in club class for the first time in my life. Seated among business travellers, wearing a dark suit and ostentatiously reading the *Financial Times* and various telecoms journals borrowed from my office, I hoped against hope there would be no chance encounter with someone who recognised me. We judged that the risk of recognition was slight because nobody would have imagined my going back to a country where I was such a bête noire. I also wore the glasses I normally used only for long distances and never in public.

Exchanging monosyllabic courtesies with the unsuspecting South African businessman in the seat next to me, I discouraged proper conversation, my mood both excited and worried. What would it feel like being back again? Would I get through passport control? If I was caught, what would happen to me and my hopes of being selected to stand for Parliament? (I had been invited to apply in South Wales.) Normally a good sleeper, I dozed fitfully as the jumbo jet whispered over the African continent of my birth.

The plane landed at Johannesburg before continuing on to Cape Town, and I decided to stay on board rather than risk brushes with officialdom by joining other passengers stretching their legs. Unexpectedly, there were familiar old sounds as black cleaners, whistling and chatting cheerily, appeared in the cabin to tidy up before we took off again.

Linda McDougall was waiting for me at airport arrivals in Cape Town. She had travelled out two weeks before, also under a pseudonym, to set up interviews and research locations; we had kept in touch clandestinely by phone as she furiously fed cash into public call boxes.

As the plane circled down, there was Table Mountain in all its glory, majestic in the morning summer sun, covered by a velvet white cloud. I emerged from the plane blinking at the brightness of the Cape sun. Feeling hot in my suit, I donned my prescription sunglasses and walked tensely across the tarmac, joining the queue of passengers at passport control, trying to appear relaxed. An official brusquely examined my passport, then looked up and stared. Was this the moment I would be exposed? Then he disinterestedly muttered 'purpose of visit?' I replied 'business' and he waved me through into the unknown.

Then all our careful preparation was suddenly threatened. My luggage wasn't on the carousel at baggage claim. I searched desperately, eventually going to inquiries. If I left it behind, a stray bag turning up might provoke unwelcome interest. On the other hand, I was attracting attention to myself as I started filling in a form, almost certain that the coloured clerk was looking quizzically at me with a half-smile.

Suddenly there was a shout. My case had appeared at the other end of the baggage area and I picked it up in relief, walking quickly through customs to find Linda, who was frantic with worry. Hardly speaking, we jumped into her hired BMW and started driving somewhere, anywhere, as I checked we weren't being followed. I remembered how Breyten Breytenbach had been allowed to enter in 1975 while the security police followed and picked up all his contacts before he was arrested and imprisoned.

❖

OVER the following nine days, travelling illicitly around the country felt like being on borrowed time – eerie, but exhilarating too.

I rarely display my emotions but they kept welling up, once severely embarrassing me when I burst out crying – something I had never publicly done as an adult before (only privately at the birth of our first son, Sam) – in front of Linda McDougall and the respected South African journalist Phillip van Niekerk (who had helped research the film and was accompanying us). We were flying from our close encounter outside Port Elizabeth and I was describing how moving it had been to meet vibrant leaders like Mkhuseli Jack and to witness the ANC's distinctive green, gold and black colours being worn so proudly and openly. ANC graffiti decorated townships to an extent unimaginable in my childhood.

In Oudtshoorn, while I was interviewing activists who produced a monthly newspaper, *Saamstaan* (Solidarity), security police were patrolling busily in cars outside. There was a phone call from one of their colleagues, who was bugging the office, and who issued threats over the 'shit' being told to 'these foreign journalists'. (Since my name was not mentioned, they were unaware of my presence.) Only four months previously, I was assured, the police would have burst in and rounded us up. Over the past two years they had harassed the paper's sellers, shot one of its journalists, burnt down its offices and restricted its editor, Reggie Oliphant. Yet here was Reggie telling me he had 'unrestricted himself' by talking to us and, though confined to his home between six at night and six in the morning, showing he would not be intimidated by threats, either to his family or his own life. The old certainties of the iron-fist regime were crumbling.

Reggie, who had lost his job as a teacher in 1981 because of his campaigns for non-racial sport, was a fierce opponent of the Gatting rebel tour. Whatever impression of reform was being projected abroad by white cricket officials, the very idea of mixed sport in a remote town such as Oudtshoorn was a notion he greeted with incredulity. Sports facilities for blacks and coloureds in the town were almost non-existent by comparison with the lavish provision for whites. Oudtshoorn's black pupils, deprived not just of sport but also of school places, were prevented by the government from filling an empty white high school, a training college and a technical college – all unused because of over-provision for whites. Together these could have offered nearly 1 000 places to desperate black children, along with ample sports facilities.

Carefully staged coaching sessions for blacks in a handful of well-known townships such as Soweto could not conceal the reality that sports apartheid was alive and well in Oudtshoorn, with its 80 000-strong population still rigidly segregated. Across the country, it was officially estimated at the time that well over 90 per cent of sport was still segregated.

Although some mixed sport existed in 1989–1990, it was overwhelmingly in the larger cities such as Johannesburg and Cape Town. In small towns in the middle of the country, such as Oudtshoorn, there was no mixed sport at all. A survey of sports facilities in the Natal town of Pietermaritzburg found that 11 567 white school pupils shared 32 cricket fields and 65 cricket nets; 13 608 coloured and Indian pupils shared just one field and five nets; and there were no sports facilities in black schools. In the black townships of Umlazi and Lamontville outside Durban, 330 000 Africans shared six football fields and two swimming pools. In Durban itself, 212 000 whites had 146 football fields and 15 public swimming pools. For the country as a whole, despite being under one-fifth of the total population, whites possessed 73 per cent of all athletic tracks, 93 per cent of all golf courses, 83 per cent of all hockey fields, 85 per cent of all cricket fields, 93 per cent of all squash courts, 80 per cent of all badminton courts, 98 per cent of all bowling greens, 84 per cent of all swimming pools and 83 per cent of rugby fields.

In Gugulethu township, outside Cape Town, several teachers spoke to me on the only football field, covered by an uneven stretch of fine grey gravel littered with glass; they could not give their names for fear of dismissal.

Outside Port Elizabeth, Ronnie Pillay and Khaya Majola, top black cricketers with the non-racial South African Cricket Board, told me despairingly how cricket was dying among their people because of abysmal facilities. Across the country, for every thousand rands the government spent on sport, just one rand went to blacks; of every 100 cricket fields, only 15 were available for blacks to play on – and most of these were of very poor quality.

The deliberate repression of non-racial sports bodies outside the white-dominated racial structures continued. When I interviewed him, the president of the Western Cape National Sports Congress (NSC), Ngconde Balfour, had only recently emerged from nine months in detention, mostly in solitary confinement. The NSC was then the leading non-racial sports group aligned to the ANC and the United Democratic Front, or UDF.[3]

Meanwhile, white companies refused to offer sponsorship except to government-approved bodies such as Ali Bacher's South African Cricket Union, which had invited the Gatting rebel tourists. The idea that cricket could be separated from politics remained incredible, especially since the government was bankrolling the rebel tour by granting 90 per cent tax rebates to companies providing sponsorship. Significantly, however, these sponsors, once keen to proclaim their support, were now keeping very quiet for fear of a black consumer boycott and trade-union reprisals – another indication of the changing balance of power.

❖

AFTER I arrived in Cape Town and was surreptitiously booked into a garden room at a hotel in leafy Constantia, we headed to an afternoon cricket match in Mitchells Plain, a coloured community on the Cape Flats.

First-class cricketer and anti-apartheid activist André Odendaal had been brought up in an apartheid-supporting Afrikaner household in the Queenstown area of the eastern Cape Province, where his father coached the local rugby club. As a rugby-mad boy himself, young André had kept a scrapbook of newspaper clippings on his beloved Springboks, which also contained reports of our 1969–1970 demonstrations, including hostile coverage of me, dubbed the 'Demo Mobster'.

But since his early youth, André had been on a life-changing journey, including courageously 'crossing the divide' by abandoning the whites-only cricket world (causing a rift with his family) and choosing to join the Mitchells Plain-based non-racial cricket team, United. He was getting ready to bat when we arrived to film the team at a Saturday-afternoon match at Rocklands ground, near the shore of False Bay. He was incredulous to find himself meeting and being interviewed by me. By then an increasingly prominent anti-apartheid activist, André had reluctantly switched from attending a crucial NSC conference in Johannesburg after a necessarily cagey call from London by Sam Ramsamy, head of SANROC, asking that he instead meet an 'important visitor'.

Afterwards, our crew of four – Linda, me, cameraman Lawrence Jones and sound recordist Phil Taylor – were invited to André's home in Woodstock under Table Mountain for a *braaivleis* (barbecue, often shortened to braai). It was a warm summer's evening and we chatted away until the early hours of the morning, helped by a couple of bottles of champagne supplied courtesy of Linda.

Apart from the episode with the police van, the rest of trip proved highly successful and we were not detected. None of the interviewees had known I was coming, only that a 'British TV team' wanted to talk to them. Nonetheless, Reggie Oliphant said he recognised me when I stepped off the plane in Oudtshoorn. (We had never met before.) Most people couldn't believe I was there. Some stared as if seeing a ghost, and the burly Khaya Majola had tears in his eyes.

I was even able to interview Danie Craven at his beautiful rugby headquarters in Stellenbosch. It was risky, but Linda was understandably concerned that there should be some balance in the programme. He reacted in amazement as I walked in on camera: 'Aren't you scared?' he asked (very appropriately). Linda had counted on his old-fashioned sense of honour in upholding a promise he had made to her beforehand not to mention the interview until we had returned safely to the UK. To his credit he stuck to this, and the meeting made a dramatic moment in the film.

The final hurdle was getting safely out through Johannesburg's Jan Smuts Airport (today OR Tambo International), which was notorious for its steely security. The tension obviously got to me because, despite a very smooth flight, I was sick on the plane. Although my tan attracted a few curious questions in the middle of a British winter, the venture remained secret until two weeks later when the film had been edited and was ready for transmission. The news was simultaneously broken in *The Guardian* and the South African morning papers. Val Rose-Christie, the civil rights worker who had shown us round the Cape Flats, was startled to see roadside newspaper posters proclaiming 'HAIN WAS HERE', as well as the headline in the *Cape Times*, 'PETER HAIN'S SECRET SA VISIT'. There were angry questions in the South African Parliament, and when they eventually discovered the 'Western-Hain' connection, the computer system at points of entry was expensively modified.

As an exercise in lifting the protest profile around the Gatting rebel tour, the venture was a triumph. After widespread media attention in Britain, the film got good ratings and video copies were smuggled into South Africa and distributed among ANC supporters. My predictions that the tour would be disrupted by angry demonstrators helped create a frenzy of interest within South Africa, with local media making the link between the STST protests and the opposition that the rebel cricketers were likely to face. (I had had private talks with some of the organisers about the tactical lessons that could be applied from the STST.)

The anti-apartheid sports campaign had come full circle. Where direct action had set the seal on tours abroad, now it was about to inflict fatal damage at home – a prospect inconceivable some 17 years earlier, during another rebel cricket tour, and when political conditions did not permit any protests.

At Heathrow the departure of the Gatting team was delayed for several hours after an anti-apartheid activist deliberately telephoned a hoax bomb warning. At Jan Smuts Airport, police used dogs, tear gas and batons to attack peaceful demonstrators, led by Winnie Mandela, awaiting their delayed arrival. This showed how worried the authorities were about the growing movement that threatened to disrupt and maybe even curtail the rebel tour.

Prominent in that movement was André Odendaal, and the bitterness the tour provoked had been seriously underestimated. The demonstrators – focused around the NSC, which was aligned to the Mass Democratic Movement inside the country and the ANC outside – mobilised across the country and the tour quickly degenerated amid demonstrations and police violence, compounding the grotesque miscalculation made in staging it in the first place.

This was a time of momentous political change. All of Nelson Mandela's closest comrades – including Walter Sisulu and Govan Mbeki – had just been released from prison. Negotiations with the government, secretly begun from prison by Mandela, were at last bearing fruit. Then suddenly the rebel tour threatened to undo a lot of the goodwill that had been carefully built up. Such was the pressure that, after one of the clandestine negotiating meetings in London then taking place between the ANC and individuals close to the South African government,[4] an agreement was initiated to stop the demonstrations in exchange for abandoning the second stage of the Gatting tour. Even tour organiser Ali Bacher conceded that it had been a mistake, and the humiliated cricket rebels came home prematurely, albeit amply comforted by payoffs averaging more than £100 000.

Following the deal to cut short the tour, Bacher began to negotiate with the NSC to agree upon a democratic, non-racial structure for cricket from school and club level up to national sides. From this followed the establishment, in 1991, of the United Cricket Board of South Africa – the first unified sports group in the country's history – led by Bacher. His deputy was Khaya Majola, a first-class cricketer who for years had spurned inducements to be co-opted into the white sports system. Change at long last.[5]

❖

MY secret visit had also provided a unique opportunity to make sense of the tumultuous changes about to be unleashed in the country.

Among ANC leaders such as Govan Mbeki (whom I interviewed on camera) downward to activists operating through the UDF and the Mass Democratic Movement, there was a mood of confidence I had not expected. People who had just emerged from long years of detention spoke with determined optimism about the inevitability of white rule ending in a negotiated solution.

For its part, white authority seemed rather punch-drunk, unsure about the new ground rules. Thus, while the press were still banned from publishing Nelson Mandela's picture, the ANC's colours were worn or displayed openly. Some protests were permitted, provided they received prior police permission and conformed to tight restrictions. Others were still repressed – as when the Gatting rebel cricketers arrived in Johannesburg. Despite having been agreed in advance, protests around the rebel tour quickly deteriorated into violent clashes with police. At the same time, morale among the previously omnipotent white police was collapsing.

Strikingly, the government was being forced to change, not out of desire but out of necessity. The pressure from an increasingly defiant black majority was growing; their trade unions were powerful and their consumer power threatened white business. Even the very limited foreign sanctions over loans and investment had

had an impact: the economy was in bad shape and whites complained constantly about depressed living standards and economic expectations. During the visit I was shown a confidential report
by a top consortium of white businesses arguing that an emerging
urban crisis threatened the development of a modern economy. It
called for the rapid eradication of all apartheid legislation.

Time did appear to be up for whites-only rule. There seemed
a realisation that they no longer had sufficient bullets. But I also
sensed that whites were losing their political will to govern in the
old way of ruthless force and sometimes outright terror. There
were parallels with the still fresh tumult in Eastern Europe following the reforms introduced by Soviet president Mikhail
Gorbachev and the collapse of the Soviet bloc: in East Berlin, the
demise of the old order saw people pour buoyantly into security-
police headquarters, which they had passed by in terror only days
before. The armed might of South Africa's police state was still
intact and the white political power still immense. But there comes
a psychological moment when that doesn't count any more, as
occurred in Romania with the startling ejection and execution of
Nicolae Ceausescu.

Nelson Mandela was gradually being transformed among
white commentators from feared ogre to national saviour. Back in
London on 2 February 1990, I gripped the chair in wonderment,
the hairs standing up on my neck, as I watched the live television
broadcast of President FW de Klerk opening the first session of
the new Parliament in Cape Town, the building I had been covertly filmed walking past six weeks before. De Klerk made good
on his promise of a 'new South Africa' and surprised everyone
by boldly announcing the unbanning of the ANC and other outlawed organisations. He also gave notice of the impending release
of Mandela and hundreds of other political prisoners. And he
declared his readiness to negotiate a new constitution in which
everyone would enjoy equal rights.

It was breathtaking, almost unreal. I suppressed a surge of tears, phoning my parents, my mother openly sobbing with joy. Relatives, friends and colleagues phoned each other or chatted excitedly as they gathered in front of televisions or radios. We could hardly believe it. But there was no going back. The new South Africa now beckoned at last.

❖

ON the eve of Nelson Mandela's release, I was in the South Wales Valleys, on what became the first step in my subsequent selection as the MP for Neath. Having slept the night at the home of Howard and Elaine Davies in the former coal-mining village of Seven Sisters, I was picked up at dawn by another local miner, Lyn Harper, and driven to catch a train back to London for media interviews.

When the world's most famous political prisoner, kept out of sight for over a quarter of a century, stepped to freedom through the gates of Victor Verster prison on 11 February 1990, it was one of those defining moments in history. Many would remember forever exactly where they were and what they were doing. I was back in Putney with my family. We hugged each other, tears in our eyes, and, like people around the world, wept openly.

Except for his obvious humility and humanity, Mandela looked almost regal: a slim, dignified old African statesman with a smile of destiny that hovered somewhere between the benign and the all-knowing.[6]

Self-evidently, his release was momentous, part of a transformation for which anti-apartheid activists had campaigned for decades. Unexpectedly, however, and almost subliminally, I started to be perceived rather differently: instead of being 'Public Enemy Number One', I became more accepted by mainstream opinion.

Over the following years, I found myself courteously stopped by total strangers – on several occasions people actually crossed the street: 'Mr Hain, I just wanted to apologise. I now understand why you did all those protests. I used to think you were just a troublemaker. I was mistaken. Good luck to you.'

Returnings

AS fate would have it, I returned openly for the first time to South Africa as an International Parliamentary Observer for the country's first democratic election in April 1994.

Excited and hopeful, the early morning bright and clear, I was collected from Jan Smuts Airport by the Welsh political journalist Max Perkins and his HTV (now ITV Wales) television crew, who were covering my homecoming. And it was to be an emotional one.

The last time I had seen Poen Ah Dong and Aubrey Apples was 28 years before, when I was 16 and they had waved us a tearful goodbye into exile at Pretoria railway station. Now I was 44, and tears were shed again, at Poen's house in Eersterust outside Pretoria. The TV crew had already been on reconnaissance for a few days and went ahead to knock on Poen's door as I waited until beckoned to walk in and be filmed. Climbing out of the car, I was suddenly overcome with surging emotion and had to check myself.

'Welcome home to the new South Africa,' Poen greeted me warmly with a big hug. With him was Aubrey, now blind, as well as scores of relatives, young and old, children and grandchildren lined up, some proudly bearing the names of my mother and father. Poen said that if he hadn't been asked to keep the meeting low key due to concern for my safety, the whole township would have turned out in a welcome.

With only a few hours to spare before my official duties, we tried to find our old house at The Willows. However, the surrounding area to the front and side had been completely altered by three decades of suburban property development. Eventually, there it was: the distinctive pair of linked rondavels seemed to have been preserved in time, although the grounds were markedly different and the swimming pool a great deal smarter than our scruffy, leaky old one.

There was the front door that I had opened to a security-police officer bearing Mom's banning order. The familiar *kopje* behind the house had been declared a protected area. I looked up, searching for the tree struck by the stone thrown by the security policeman 30 years earlier. Now the bush and scrub looked innocent and fresh.

We began filming a television interview outside the front door, having got permission from the person who answered it, without disclosing my identity. As the camera rolled, a car pulled up and a woman got out and walked up the terrace steps. Concerned that there might be a confrontation, I nevertheless continued answering questions. Then I caught her looking hard at me. It was Margaret Beerstecher, who had previously lived in the house next door, but had since moved into our old home. She called out excitedly and we talked of old times.

Pretoria was full of memories. Driving back, it was absolutely extraordinary seeing posters of Nelson Mandela smiling from the lamp posts – in Pretoria of all places! Not for the last time I wondered: was this really happening?

After a briefing on our duties as observers, the HTV crew drove me to see Hugh Lewin, who was back at home after many years in prison and exile. He was heading up the Institute for the Advancement of Journalism, which specialised in training black journalists. Hugh spoke of his time in jail when he had heard excitedly of the rugby-tour demonstrations, of the hated 'young traitor Hain' who was leading them, and of the boost to the political prisoners the news had been.

I was beginning to feel at ease, going that evening on an impromptu visit to a cabaret bar in Johannesburg's Market Square. The audience, mixed race and young, laughed together at the white comedian, a sharp observer of the absurdities of the old South Africa, who asked to meet me afterwards. But if the Market Square bar could have been in any modern metropolitan city, Alexandra township the next morning was an antidote to all illusions. Still an appalling slum covered in rotting rubbish, with dusty tracks, shanty dwellings, rudimentary sewerage and little running water, it was right next door to Sandton, one of the plushest suburbs in the world. Yet, despite Alexandra's squalor, the election atmosphere there was still infectiously buoyant.

Then it was off to the Wanderers cricket stadium, headquarters of the United Cricket Board of South Africa, to meet Ali Bacher. 'You were right, Peter, I was wrong,' he said generously as the cameras rolled, confirming how the 1970 tour cancellation had been a watershed. At the stadium there was a sign saying spectators who ran onto the pitch would be prosecuted – poignant for me to be filmed alongside.

Next to Bacher's office was that of Khaya Majola, now director of cricket development in the townships. Assisting Khaya was Conrad Hunte, the great West Indian opening batsman of the 1960s, out on an English-sponsored coaching programme for young players in the townships. I told Conrad I'd seen him at Trent Bridge during the 1966 Test match, and reminded him that at the height of the STST campaign, as a member of Moral Re-Armament, he had complained that I was too 'militant'; he laughed in embarrassment.

Back in Pretoria that evening, there was a reception at the British Embassy. The ambassador, Anthony Reeve, was modern, informal and astute – a contrast to the useless ex-colonial gents we knew in the early 1960s and who were obstacles to change rather than facilitators. An Afrikaner woman introduced herself from 'foreign affairs'. 'It's a real privilege meeting you,' she said. 'You have done so much for us.' Apparently I was no longer quite the 'Public Enemy Number One' of old.

The next day I went to Johannesburg's Carlton Centre for Nelson Mandela's packed eve-of-poll press conference. Although the lax security worried me, all went well and Mandela presided with his usual saintly, benevolent authority, patient but clear, grave though occasionally mischievously witty.

Unexpectedly, I was beckoned up at the end and ushered into an anteroom where I found myself alone with Mandela as he rested. We chatted amiably for ten minutes. He was tranquillity personified, even oddly downbeat: 'Peter, I suppose I should be jumping for joy. But I just feel stillness. There is so much responsibility, so much to do.'

Such a privilege for me; everybody treating him as extremely precious; the special 76-year-old president in waiting, who held the whole country's future in his hands.

❖

THE driver allocated to me was Desmond Khoza, a professional bookkeeper who had lost his job, and a well-informed ANC supporter. At the introductions, he turned round and gave me a hard look in amazement, his face breaking into a big smile. 'I can't believe it's you. After all these years, how wonderful to be driving you,' he exclaimed, inquiring after my parents, whose activities he had followed in the 1960s.

They, unknown to me, were also voting – for the ANC – having discovered that their old South African identity cards were acceptable, and queuing up joyfully with hundreds of others outside the Methodist Central Hall in Westminster, one of three polling stations in London.

On that historic Wednesday morning, 27 April 1994, we

left the hotel promptly at 6 am for Orlando West and East, the homes of Sisulu and Mandela, in Soweto. From the car we could see mine dumps looming in the early mist. Desmond came from Orlando, so we had no difficulty finding the polling stations despite being given lists of rather inadequate addresses – worryingly typical of the ramshackle organisation around the election.

Arriving at our first polling station at about 6.30 am, half an hour before it was due to open, there were hundreds, maybe thousands, already queuing up, their mood calm and expectant. More were streaming in out of the morning haze as the sun rose. It was soon evident that the democratic niceties were being painfully respected, and the calm seriousness with which the polling officials handled their first-ever democratic election was moving.

Because Desmond was an official driver for international observers he was able to jump the queues and vote first, waiting anxiously to have his hand sprayed. As he put his ballot form in the box, he caught my eye, smiling, part triumphant, part astonished – before leaving the polling station with a broad grin, punching the air in excitement. Hardly able to accept that, in middle age, he had actually voted for the first time in his life, he told me he had been worried in case his ballot paper might be snatched away at the last minute.

An old woman – perhaps in her nineties – was led shuffling away after voting, with a smile of eternity gracing her weathered face, as young men bounced confidently out in their trainers, giving high fives to friends. After all those years, all the bitterness, the killings, the violence, the lives wasted away in prison, here it was happening, amazingly, right in front of us: constitutional apartheid being exorcised.

However, the logistical problems were immense. Some polling stations did not open until midday because they didn't have elementary equipment such as stamps, the hand spray for identifying those who had voted, ballot papers, and so on. I bumped into the

Progressive Party champion Helen Suzman, clutching makeshift voting equipment and stationery she had purchased herself: 'This process must not be allowed to fail, Peter,' she said determinedly as she bustled away.

In Soweto, where murder and mayhem was a daily occurrence, crime and violence simply disappeared for those few days. Even the police were friendly. White policemen, carrying machine guns, welcomed me as an election observer and even allowed me a memento photo among them. Happy and relaxed in the sunshine, they expressed relief that it was going peacefully as they guarded the very democratic process that was ending their brutal history of repression.

The next day we went to Alexandra township and to the white suburbs of Edenvale, Lombardy East and Rembrandt Park. It was as interesting and moving an experience in another way, as blacks and whites queued together for hours, chatting for the first time as equals. The ANC polling agent Shantie Naidoo couldn't believe her eyes. Nor could a grey-haired white National Party city councillor, schooled in years of apartheid rule. 'Are you *the* Peter Hain?' he asked in amazement. He stuck out his hand, gave me a warm handshake and asked for my autograph. Not so many years before, he'd cheerfully have had me kneecapped. I ended up signing autographs for other whites. The new South Africa was stepping forward with a verve and excitement that was hard to believe but wondrous to behold.

Finally, on the Saturday morning I travelled to observe the counting with fellow Labour MPs Bob Hughes and Paul Boateng. We went to Benoni where Bob, chairman of the AAM, had been at school. We were able to see the ballot papers being unfolded for reconciliation purposes and turned upside down, the vote seemingly over 90 per cent for the ANC. By now my initial anxiety had evaporated in the euphoria and I was relaxed when people recognised me and came up to chat. One ANC agent, a coloured woman in her sixties, who had been with Trevor Huddleston when Sophiatown had been cleared in the late 1950s, suddenly threw her arms round me and kept saying, 'Thank you.' Yet people like her had suffered all those years, and whatever contribution we'd made from safety abroad didn't really seem to compare with theirs.

How did the white presiding officer think it would go? 'An ANC landslide.' What did he feel about that? 'No problem – actually it's a relief, having apartheid lifted off our backs.' Such equanimity from a former military policeman who had seen action in Namibia's Caprivi Strip, a notorious flashpoint where white soldiers had committed atrocities against infiltrating Swapo guerrillas. This boded well.

His courtesy and helpfulness notwithstanding, we could hardly observe any serious counting because of procedural delays and mix-ups. So we returned to the hotel and then went down to the ANC headquarters nearby, picking our way through the glass and rubble from an eve-of-poll bombing by right-wing white extremists. By pure chance we bumped into Walter Sisulu, standing around in the foyer like anybody else; the vice-president of the ANC, vital mentor to Mandela, had lost none of his earthy humility. He graciously handed me fresh 'Mandela for President' posters, which ended up framed in our home and my constituency office, and later followed me around to sit above my ministerial desks during the 12 years in government when I held eight different posts, and then in my Lords office.

Before flying out, I glimpsed the election results on television: the ANC was standing at 54 per cent and rising. It was an incredible lump-in-the-throat feeling to watch the citadels of white power falling as the votes piled up. Although I had no illusions that an election observer could really know what was going on, our presence was an important deterrent to any potential wrongdoing. But it was an honour to have observed spellbound as all the long bitter years of struggle finally bore fruit.

I watched on TV in my House of Commons office as Nelson Mandela was solemnly sworn in as president on 10 May 1994 at the Union Buildings, the grand neoclassical government offices that lord it over Pretoria. On the broad lawns below, where I had played as a boy, a multiracial crowd of over 50 000 heard their new president declare: 'Never, never and never again shall it be that this beautiful land will again experience the oppression of one by another and suffer the indignity of being the skunk of the world.' As the cheering died away, from a ridge across the city came the roar of helicopter gunships trailing the new South African flag and jet fighters in acrobatic flights swooping in to salute their first ever black commander-in-chief.

❖

'MANDELA'S BOKS': the banner brandished six months later in the crowd for the South Africa-Wales rugby international at Cardiff Arms Park said it all.

For my parents and me, invited guests at an arena once fiercely supportive of the apartheid Springboks, it was a thrill to see black winger Chester Williams scoring tries for his reborn country. However, the official programme brochure for the match never mentioned the reason for the Springboks' two-decade absence, remarking only that Danie Craven had been 'deeply saddened by South Africa's exile from the company of the rest of us'. Rugby resumed, the 'absence' never explained.

A week before, on the eve of the tourists' match against Swansea, I had joined the new sports minister, Steve Tshwete, at the top table. In 1969, when I had been organising to disrupt the Springbok tour, he had been organising rugby matches as a political prisoner with Nelson Mandela on Robben Island. I also found myself a guest of honour at dinners welcoming the South Africans at my home ground in Neath, The Gnoll, savouring the moment with Arthob Petersen, coloured executive committee member of the new, united South African Rugby Football Union. (A year later, on 15 November 1995, the Springbok captain Francois Pienaar shook my hand enthusiastically at an official reception for his World Cup-winning team in South Africa House, the Trafalgar Square building outside which we had held so many protests and vigils.)

Yet, while many South Africans embraced the new, non-racial rugby era, for a good few of their Welsh, Scottish and English hosts the Springboks' return was – after an inconveniently indecent interlude – 'business as usual'. They had been just as happy to welcome the old racist South Africa, and seemed not to have absorbed the lesson of history: that apartheid would not have been defeated without uncompromising opposition, including rugby isolation.

My old Welsh opponent Wilf Wooller was unrepentant at a pre-match reception in Cardiff: 'That bastard Peter Hain – thank God he's a socialist,' he fulminated. (This was some progress since the STST days, when he used to denounce me as a 'communist'.) Amid the celebrations, I took the opportunity to remind British rugby that, by failing to take a stand early enough, it helped to ensure that generations of young black rugby players never had the chance to play for their country. There was a debt to redeem: to ensure that young blacks in the poverty-stricken townships got the facilities and the opportunities to play and to tour – unlike their fathers, grandfathers and great-grandfathers.

On such occasions, the moments to savour continued to pile up for all anti-apartheid activists as we greeted each other in amazement. In July 1994, I was invited to Lord's by Ali Bacher as a guest of the visiting South African team for the first Test since 1965; I couldn't help celebrating South Africa's win. However, when I climbed up high in the stand to the BBC commentary box to do a long lunch-time interview on the history of apartheid in cricket, a number of old gents eating and drinking from their hampers made clear their displeasure at my presence. Following me up, my teenage cricketer son Jake observed: 'They still really hate you, Dad.' One of the 1970 would-be South African tourists, Barry Richards, now commentating for the BBC, shunned me, as did famed English cricketer turned commentator Trevor Bailey.

That day I met Basil D'Oliveira for the first time, when he was also a VIP guest at Lord's. By then D'Oliveira was long retired, and I could sense both a pride in his achievements for what had become his team, England, but also a wistful sadness at what might have been his team, South Africa.

A few weeks before, I had volunteered to welcome the South African cricketers at Heathrow. While some in the English cricket establishment were unhappy, the South Africans were delighted to see me, including their coach Mike Procter, a world-class fast bowler whose international career had been terminated by the stopping of the 1970 tour.

The following year, in July 1995, the first-ever tour by the Soweto cricket club took place, the team of youngsters appropriately captained by Khaya Majola. I escorted them on a tour of Parliament's inner sanctums and helped organise one of their matches in South Wales, near my home in the Neath Valley, against the leading village club Ynysygerwn of which I was patron. It was an unusually sunny day for Neath and the tourists said afterwards that it was the highlight of a most successful tour. Ali Bacher travelled from London to join us, and I also invited Tom Cartwright, by now one of my constituents, who had been replaced by Basil D'Oliveira in 1968, adding to the sense of history coming full circle.

After a press conference packed with TV, radio and newspaper journalists, the mayor of Neath put on a pre-match lunch and civic reception, declaring, 'The name Soweto rings throughout the world wherever men want to be free.' In his report on the tour, Soweto chair Edward Cebekulu wrote that 'they treated us like veritable VIPs'. The day ended very late with celebrations, presentations and Khaya Majola, a big man in every sense, crying on my shoulder. Welsh songs from the Onllwyn Male Voice Choir competed with the singing from the Soweto players, who had earlier performed an ANC toyi-toyi and chant as they left the field.

The afternoon match was drawn on the last ball, the teams sharing 444 hard-fought runs. 'There I was wondering who I wanted to win, when Nelson Mandela swooped in and made it a draw,' I quipped at the post-match presentations. It had indeed seemed like divine intervention. Edward Cebekulu described it as 'a truly democratic result'. Top scorers for Soweto were Harmony Ntshinga with 72 and Solomon Ndima (nickname 'Duiker') with 28.

However, the Soweto boys were visibly apprehensive when a police car roared up to the clubhouse, siren on and lights flashing in the dark – until they realised it was a prank. The smiling police officer was the batsman who had plundered runs off them before going on duty. A white police officer, yes, but nothing like the ferocious ones they had normally encountered.

❖

ANOTHER moving occasion to witness was in London on 29 October 1994 when the AAM, for nearly 40 years the leading such group in the world, wound itself up.

The ANC deputy secretary-general, Cheryl Carolus, who had flown in overnight from Johannesburg, paid ringing testimony to the AAM's work. There were tributes from the veteran Labour MP Joan Lestor and from AAM stalwarts, including Ethel de Keyser and Abdul Minty. Bob Hughes, Labour MP for Aberdeen North, had carried the movement's banner as its chair for many crucial years. Dick Caborn, Labour MP for Sheffield Central, had been its treasurer, at one point helping rescue the organisation from near bankruptcy. Mike Terry, executive secretary, had worked tirelessly and selflessly during the critical period since the late 1970s: he was a towering figure in the British campaign, both dedicated and strategic in his direction of the AAM.[1] In a simple ceremony, and to a standing ovation, the three of them lifted the AAM's banner and folded it up: job done in supporting the struggle inside and maintaining the pressure for sanctions and boycotts outside. As Abdul Minty poignantly remarked: 'The AAM was a movement committed like few others to bringing about its own early end.'

We had steadfastly maintained our strategy against an onslaught from apartheid apologists. The hypocrisy of Conservative MPs still rankled with me, such as John Carlisle – nicknamed the 'Member for Pretoria Central' – who had shamelessly backed the Nationalist government, and accepted generous freebie trips from its front organisations. It rather stuck in the craw to be present as many of these Conservative MPs queued up to be seen with President Nelson Mandela when he spoke to both Houses of Parliament in Westminster Hall on 11 July 1996; Margaret Thatcher scuttled down to the front, having notoriously denounced him as a 'terrorist' only a few years previously. But history had vindicated the AAM and all who had supported it.

❖

BY now I was an established British MP, my two boys were British and my parents had British grandchildren and active roots in their southwest London community. We had never expected to return to South Africa, and Mom and Dad still had a residual apprehension about going back.

Partly, this was out of fear of what they had fled from. Partly, it was that they had buried so much psychologically in leaving South Africa, what effect would going back have on them? But the sheer exhilaration of the country I had discovered on my election-observer visit convinced me that a holiday for the whole family was a must, and I persuaded them to return over Christmas.

Mom and Dad – now excited though also still nervous – Pat, sons Sam and Jake, sister Sally, her partner Arthur and baby daughter Connie flew out from London's cold winter to sunny Cape Town. My cousin Liz had arranged to greet us at the airport, but, totally unexpectedly, limos were waiting, indicators blinking on the tarmac in the fresh early-morning sun to whisk us off to the VIP lounge for a surprise welcome.

Later, visiting the city's V&A Waterfront marina, we could see the old railway tracks on the dockside where, three decades earlier, we had boarded a ship for Britain under security-police surveillance. It was hard to imagine those dark days as we lunched, seals lazily bobbing at the quayside. After ascending the majestic Table Mountain by cable car, we looked out over the beauty of the Cape Peninsula, surely one of the sights of the world. And, yes, there beyond the Atlantic breakers, shimmering in the haze, was Robben Island, where Nelson Mandela and so many others had spent the prime of their lives.

'Isn't our president simply wonderful,' whites said to us. *Our* president? We encountered a touching tribute to Mandela's extraordinary influence at a braai at the home of André Odendaal, who wanted to meet and welcome my parents. André explained how his Afrikaner mother had for several years refused to recognise his marriage to his Muslim wife, Zohra Ebrahim, a fellow activist, or to meet her and their mixed-race children. Then came the months after the election. Slowly, the fear ebbed as Mandela mutated from Satan to saviour. Blacks weren't going to burn her out of her farmstead after all.

She invited his family to visit, though not yet to her home (a mixed marriage would still shame her in the eyes of her white neighbours). They booked into a nearby hotel and met in the car park. He stood there with her grandson in his arms. She paused, then reached for the baby, cradling him gently as her own.

Suddenly, she seemed to emerge from a trance, asking to meet Zohra, who had remained discreetly in their car.

As we enjoyed the braai, Grandma was upstairs babysitting – André's first Christmas with his mother since the marriage. Although his mother was still fearful of meeting me, André insisted on introducing us as she rocked the baby to sleep. (Over the years she would warmly greet me whenever I visited.)

It was as if a great millstone had been lifted. The old South Africa we had left had been descending relentlessly into a pit of human depravity. The new one was buoyed by an infectious optimism from whites and blacks alike – though in those early times they too were caught by the same sense of wondering whether it was actually true.

It was difficult to find anybody who admitted to ever having supported apartheid. And of course most whites had just gone along with it, turning a blind eye to the misery and the oppression while enjoying the immense privileges: over 90 per cent had never visited a black township, choosing not to know.

But there seemed to be a desire to exorcise guilt. Some of our relatives had kept a studious distance when my parents most needed support in the dark early 1960s. Now they gave us generous hospitality, a small example of the healing process that was such a moving feature of the new country.

We drove east to Port Alfred, nearly 970 kilometres along the coast from Cape Town, past long sandy beaches and turquoise sea, in a hired Volkswagen minibus, recalling idyllic summer holidays spent swimming, boating and fishing. Port Alfred, like the country, had changed a lot in 30 years. The yuppie marina seemed out of place, but the Kowie River was as we remembered it, especially upstream where it was protected by a nature reserve. The wide, expansive beaches remained a delight. 'It's not right. We should never have been forced to leave all this,' said Mom, tears streaming at the emotion of her return to Mentone, her childhood home on the banks of the river. Her parents had died there during our absence and she had not been allowed to attend their funerals.

In nearby Grahamstown (now Makhanda) is Victoria Girls' High School, much as Mom remembered, and where she won a 'deportment girdle' for 'good behaviour and standing up straight'. The English colonial feel of the town had been engagingly preserved. But it was startling seeing blacks and whites in the same queues in shops and banks, and the odd black family in restaurants and pubs. Later on our travels it was also pleasantly strange to enjoy mixed-race swimming on previously segregated beaches (on one occasion amid a school of dolphins surfing in the waves).

❖

CHRISTMAS Day 1994 was like an action replay of my childhood: sunburn weather by 7.30 in the morning, pre-lunch drinks on the lawn and roast turkey on the verandah.

We spent Christmas with Peter Brown and his family at their farm, Lion's Bush, in the KwaZulu-Natal midlands, north of Pietermaritzburg. A long-standing friend and Liberal Party chairman, who had recruited my parents, Peter was celebrating his 70th birthday as we arrived – a reminder of another talent wasted. He should have been in government, but he too was imprisoned, then successively banned from the 1960s onward. The peaceful atmosphere was striking. Political violence appeared to have vanished just eight months after the election, yet barely 16 kilometres away, at Mooi River, there had for years been scenes of awful carnage between rival Zulu supporters of Inkatha and the ANC.

After our reunion with the Browns, we hit the road for Johannesburg and by late afternoon, the city was in sight, the yellow glint of its mine dumps visible through the baking heat haze. Another group of old friends embraced us in a welcome-back party hosted by Jill Wentzel, Ernie's wife. She said that the sports protests of 1969–1970 had been 'decisive' in pushing whites into accepting change. 'The government must have bitterly regretted kicking out the Hains,' Jill chuckled.

The goodwill among blacks was remarkable. But a disturbing cloud was the ubiquitous wave of crime and muggings. However, another old white friend brushed this aside: 'It's just redistribution of wealth. What else do you expect with 60 per cent plus black male unemployment?' But in the plush Joburg suburb where we lodged with friends, every home was guarded by security gates and burglar alarms. Whites travelled only by car – and even then felt themselves vulnerable to hijacking at gunpoint.

Although South Africa had been liberated from constitutional apartheid, the poverty and destitution was much, much worse than when we had lived there. Over seven million blacks – a quarter of the total black population – subsisted in squatter settlements ringing the cities. On the Cape Flats, we were shown the latest grim squatting areas, not by accident named 'Beirut' and 'Vietnam' by their inhabitants.

South Africa is certainly a rollercoaster land. After witnessing some of its grim downsides, we travelled to the renowned Kruger National Park for a delightful few days with Jill Wentzel. Nwanetsi camp, isolated on the Mozambique border, gave a real feel of the African bushveld: hyena and baboons patrolling the perimeter to a cacophony of birds and cicadas. Mom and Dad stood emotionally holding hands outside at dawn, soaking up once more the smells and sounds they loved, recalling what they had given up. The experience made them admit something that, in order to avoid the limbo life of an exile, they had repressed for a quarter of a century: how sorely they missed their old homeland.

And then came the *pièce de résistance*. Some of the black activists who had struggled alongside my parents in Pretoria, suffering much worse harassment than we did, celebrated our return after 30 years. Poen Ah Dong and Aubrey Apples turned out with dozens of their relatives and gave my parents a special rendition of the national anthem, 'Nkosi Sikelel' iAfrika'. When we knew them, they had lived in shacks. Now we partied at the sumptuous family homehad of Poen's daughter, Mee Ling, in Pretoria's exclusive Waterkloof Glen. She would never have been allowed to live here in the old days, and it would have been illegal to hold such a multiracial party, where liquor was served – and certainly unthinkable that two white Afrikaners happily barbecued a lamb for the predominantly black guests.

At Pretoria Boys High my father pointed out the spot where, as a banned person, he had had to watch me play cricket from outside the school fence. Hatfield Primary School's honours board still bore the name 'P Hain' as head prefect in 1962: the gold lettering had survived even my denunciation by the media and government ministers in the early 1970s. At the Union Buildings Mom pointed out where she'd been spat upon by civil servants during a picket. Now all was at peace in the morning sunshine, the country's new flag fluttering proudly overhead. Once the seat of white oppression, it now housed Mandela's office.

The Old Synagogue, which had acted as a court when Mom had attended Mandela's trial in 1962, and where she and my sisters had met Winnie, was now boarded up. But she couldn't help breaking down outside the Supreme Court, where John Harris had been sentenced to death and Hugh Lewin jailed for seven years.

The prison where my parents had been detained, and where in the old days blacks were hanged at the rate of over a hundred each year, was hidden behind a new, less threatening façade. It made me wonder what all those agents of the police state who had intimidated, tortured and killed in the name of apartheid were doing with themselves these days. Were we passing them by as we walked in the city centre?

Although that holiday, following the secret visit and then the election, meant I had returned to South Africa three times, my emotions still churned. And I had only spent my childhood there. Mom and Dad had lived there for about 40 years, and they had to adjust to returning home all in one breathtaking go, experiencing both the delight and the turmoil of old friends and old places that carried such deep meaning, such emotional highs and lows. Although thrilled at the visit, they were for several months not quite themselves, and were extremely unsettled on their return to Britain.

Having fought to defeat the old South Africa, we found ourselves unapologetic evangelists for the new one. The country, for so long a pariah, seemed at last able to reveal itself, in Alan Paton's immortal words, as 'lovely beyond any singing of it'.

Mandela

IN June 1998 Nelson Mandela visited Cardiff to address a European Council summit hosted by Prime Minister Tony Blair. He was
granted the Freedom of the City and I, a minister for Wales in my
first government job, was deputed to escort him from his hotel.

The ceremony in Cardiff Castle was majestic in the sunshine,
the packed crowd expectant, and a queue of VIPs were swelter-
ing in the unusually hot weather for South Wales. But Mandela
ignored my guiding arm to introduce them all, and stopped
when a group of primary-school children caught his attention.
The VIPs sweltered on while he began conducting them to sing
'Twinkle, Twinkle, Little Star'. (He once told me that the Robben
Islanders had missed the bubbling sound and sight of children –
including their own – more than almost anything.)

Cardiff that day experienced a vintage Mandela performance –
singing and dancing with the children, and electrifying his ador-
ing audience. Seeing my dad for the first time since they had
been together in South Africa in the anti-apartheid struggle 40
years before, Mandela quipped: 'Are you still causing trouble?'
And spotting the former Labour leader and Welsh anti-apartheid
stalwart, Neil Kinnock, he boomed: 'Hullo, Neil. Why are you
hiding from me there at the back?'

The following year I was promoted to minister of state in the
Foreign and Commonwealth Office, under the foreign secretary
and good friend Robin Cook. He sat me down in his grand office
overlooking 10 Downing Street and Horse Guards Parade with a
map of the world to discuss my new responsibilities. 'It must have

been like this dividing up the world in the days of Empire,' he said mischievously.

He appointed me minister for the Commonwealth, on top of the Middle East and South Asia, the environment, human rights and the United Nations. Against the advice of officials, he also allocated nuclear non-proliferation: 'We share the same stance on nuclear disarmament and I know you will do what I agree with,' he told me. But my real delight was being made Africa minister too – the only ever African-born holder of that office. Cheryl Carolus, who was by now South African high commissioner in the UK, was thrilled, and there was a lump in my throat when I called by to see her at South Africa House.

Partly because of the stress of being a foreign minister (I flew more than 400 000 kilometres around the world in my first year), Pat and I separated after nearly quarter of a century together. Fortunately, however, both she and I were to happily remarry and we remain good friends. I married Elizabeth Haywood in June 2003, and the tables at our joyous, bubbling wedding reception in Neath were labelled with the names of freedom struggle heroes, including Nelson Mandela, Oliver Tambo, Ahmed Kathrada, Chris Hani, Steve Biko, Joe Slovo, Ruth First, Helen Joseph and Albertina and Walter Sisulu.

❖

'AH, Peter, return of the prodigal son!' Mandela beamed, welcoming me to his Johannesburg home in February 2000.

Ten years earlier, when he was in prison, I was still banned from entering South Africa and I wasn't an MP, still less a government minister. And ten years before *that*, I had never even considered being an MP: I was more steeped in extra-parliamentary protest and activism, the roots of which lay in my parents' brave anti-apartheid work.

It was always special to be in his presence. A humble icon without an ounce of self-importance or arrogance, he had a unique aura: a sense of deep tranquillity and gentleness with everyone, yet also a worldly shrewdness that made you feel simultaneously at ease and in awe.

With a twinkle in his eye, Mandela – or Madiba, his clan name, used affectionately – courteously poked fun at the elegant British high commissioner, Dame Maeve Fort, who had arranged the meeting with him; he was especially taken with English ladies – the Queen included. But soon we moved on to talk about African policies, including his efforts as a mediator in the civil conflict in Burundi. Then, the meeting over, we walked out together in the bright summer's day to a battery of television cameras, photographers and journalists gathered under the trees in his front garden, his hand resting across my shoulders, part affectionately, part because (now aged 81) he found walking increasingly difficult.

'I wanted to welcome my friend Peter Hain,' he said, generous to a fault. 'He was a noted supporter of our freedom struggle and we thank him for that. Except for people like Peter, who was a leader of the anti-apartheid movement, I might not be standing here, a free man today, and our people would not be free.'

It was a proud and almost magical moment for me, standing alongside both my hero and my interlocutor, the global giant who inspired such universal affection and admiration.

Now aged 50, I was feted as a returning VIP, not just from the days of the freedom struggle but also as the representative of the government of the former colonial power, the United Kingdom – which in past decades I had vigorously attacked for its responsibility in sustaining apartheid.

The British High Commission threw an official reception in Pretoria to mark my visit, with Mom and Dad (who had flown out on their own) also honoured guests. We wryly observed how my Aunt Marie – who had publicly disavowed Mom in 1962 – now basked in the admiration of guests for being connected to us.

I was welcomed to speak at a Pretoria Boys High School assembly by head teacher Bill Schroder, and was moved to see that a third of the boys were black: in my day that would have been unthinkable. However, there was a throwback on the tarmac as we drove through the school gates: 'Go Home Peter Hain' had been freshly painted in white. Funnily enough, this was similar to what British rugby and cricket fans had trumpeted at me 30 years earlier during the anti-Springbok campaigns, 'Go Home Hain the Pain'.

A few days later Mom and Dad joined me overnight as guests of André Odendaal, who had become the founding director of the Robben Island Museum. The island was both eerie and thrilling, a place once synonymous with horror and oppression but now a gentle environmental sanctuary and a memorial to hope and the triumph of the human spirit. As I stared back at Cape Town from the island, I reflected on how time can change places and buildings from places of horror to places of healing. The following year, Elizabeth and I stayed overnight on Robben Island in the former prison governor's colonial-style home, complete with four-poster bed, to see in the new millennium.

Over the next few years Mom and Dad visited their homeland periodically, experiencing a mixture of joy, jarring nostalgia and jangling emotion. In December 2004 Sally organised a surprise 80th birthday party for Dad at the home of our cousin Liz and her husband, Kent, in Noordhoek on the beautiful Cape Peninsula. Present were friends and activists from the past, including Eddie Daniels and Randolph Vigne, both Liberals and former ARM cadres, and George Johannes, once of the ANC's London office and latterly a diplomat. And of course André Odendaal and Zohra Ebrahim. There were reminiscences of past struggles and campaigns, bannings and detentions, breathing the air of democracy and freedom on a warm, sunny Cape day.

But, although invigorating, these return visits were still

psychologically charged. 'I like visiting but I don't like leaving,' Mom explained.

❖

MEANWHILE, reunions and intertwinings with my personal history kept occurring as those who had fought against me extended invitations, if not always fully to reconcile, then at least to recognise.

Ali Bacher invited me as a guest to the launch in July 2004 of his biography, *Ali: The Life of Ali Bacher* by Rodney Hartman. The event was held at Lord's Cricket Ground, where 34 years earlier barbed wire had ringed the pitch to deter us from wrecking the tour he was due to captain. Ali asked for a photo of the two of us with the hallowed pitch behind, and kindly sent it to me with a note thanking me for attending.

Lord's was an example of places that had shunned me but now welcomed me, albeit with some mutterings in the undergrowth. The same was true for Twickenham, for the Welsh Rugby Union, for Newlands Cricket Ground and for white South Africans generally. President FW de Klerk's key negotiator during the transition to democracy, Roelf Meyer, invited me to lunch when we met for the first time in February 2020, when he was an adviser to President Cyril Ramaphosa. 'I used to hate you with a venom,' he said with a smile – he really meant it, and I quite understood as we then proceeded to enjoy each other's company.

❖

IN September 2000 I escorted Nelson Mandela down in the lift from his hotel room for a meeting with Prime Minister Tony Blair, before Mandela's address to the annual conference of the Labour Party, in Brighton.

As we entered the lift, he asked me his usual question: 'How's the family?' On hearing Mom was in hospital with a fractured femur, he stopped immediately. 'I must speak to her.'

Out came my mobile, and the minutes ticked by as I tried to track her down. Meanwhile, the prime minister was kept waiting as Mandela chatted happily to a line of hotel cleaners, porters, bar and catering staff waiting for him outside the lift.

Eventually, Mom answered from her hospital bed in Swansea.

'A special person to speak to you,' I told her and passed the phone over.

'Hullo. Nelson Mandela here, do you remember me?'

Of all the public figures, kings and queens, international politicians, sporting and entertainment celebrities I have met – and there have been many – none had Mandela's capacity for engaging self-deprecation, wit and the common touch. In retirement, while on a visit to London, we talked in his hotel and he said that his wife, Graça Machel, would be along later: 'She is much more important than me.'

When Mandela announced in August 1997 that he would not serve a second term as president, he downplayed his role: 'Many of my colleagues are head and shoulders above me in almost every respect. Rather than being an asset, I'm more of a decoration.' Another saying of his was to claim that 'I am just a country boy.' After he stepped down as president in 1999, there followed busy years of retirement supporting various causes around the world, and in 2003 he announced that he was 'retiring from retirement'.

Mandela's capacity for mischief was also very evident when, a few weeks after my marriage in 2003, I introduced Elizabeth.

'Is this your girlfriend?' he asked.

'No, she's my wife,' I replied.

'So she caught you then?' he chuckled.

And when Elizabeth exclaimed indignantly that she'd taken a lot of persuading, he laughed: 'That's what they all say, Peter, but they trap you in the end!'

By then she realised he was teasing her, and we all ended up laughing. He apologised for not coming to our wedding, having instead sent a message: 'But perhaps I will be able to come the next time!'

On his 90th birthday, in 2008, Mandela took a phone call from Buckingham Palace to speak to the Queen. 'Hullo Elizabeth, how's the Duke?' he said. Perhaps only he could have got away with such disregard for royal protocol. When Graça reprimanded him, he retorted: 'Well, she calls me Nelson!'

❖

INHERITING an apartheid society in 1994, where 80 per cent of people lived in endemic poverty, the challenge for Mandela's new democracy was how to create a prosperous, united, rights-based society with routes to decent living standards for all.

He faced immediate hurdles from a fast-growing African population with high expectations, complicated by continuous migration from impoverished rural subsistence economies to harsh urban squatter destitution, and an influx of several million African immigrants from countries as diverse and distant as Somalia and Zimbabwe. Demands on government for basic services seemed insatiable: as fast as new houses were built, new shacks appeared beside them.

On the credit side, in the first 20 years of democratic government, the ANC built millions of new homes and created four million jobs. Millions more South Africans secured access to running water and electricity. Some economists say that income per capita, in real terms, rose by almost a third, assisted by a new ANC welfare state. This provided a vital safety net of social-security payments: a lifeline for up to 17 million people, from the elderly to the unemployed, constituting a third of the population. Substantial state bursaries opened up the country's universities to over 400 000 new mostly black students. Life expectancy improved, with child mortality dramatically reduced.

Basic infrastructure remained by far the best in Africa. The country's economy accounted for fully a fifth of Africa's total GDP, with just a twentieth of the continent's population.

Nevertheless, violent crime and gender-based violence, including rape, soared to grotesque levels. The legacy of Bantu education, the apartheid policy of preventing black South Africans from acquiring the necessary education to work in a modern industrialised society, adversely affected three-quarters of the population, and black unemployment hovered around 40 per cent, unlikely to be much reduced until at least a younger generation obtained skills.

❖

INDEPENDENCE of mind was a characteristic that Mom and Dad encouraged in me, and it was sometimes troublesome for the party leaders to whom I paid allegiance – especially Tony Blair and Gordon Brown.

This also proved the case with the ANC after Mandela stepped down as president in 1999, notably over Zimbabwe's President Robert Mugabe. I had enthusiastically saluted Mugabe's landslide win in 1980 over the London/Washington-backed favourite, Bishop Abel Muzorewa. But when I became Africa minister, I was particularly angered by the brazen way Mugabe prostituted the ideals of the freedom struggle, which he had once led with distinction. They were the same ideals of democracy and human rights I had fought for in the anti-apartheid movement, and that Nelson Mandela and his comrades had sacrificed so much for. I also felt strongly that where I had once condemned white tyranny, consistency demanded the same stance over black tyranny.

Black victims of Mugabe's rule sent me messages applauding

my outspoken stance, saying that their morale was boosted by knowing they had support not from right-wingers delighted to side against a black dictator but from the left and from someone with a credible record of support for liberation struggles. One, Sekai Holland, was international officer for the Zimbabwean opposition movement, the Movement for Democratic Change. I had first met her during the 1971 Springbok tour campaign in Australia, where she was living in exile from Ian Smith's racist regime. Now she urged me to maintain my stance, despite being savagely beaten, her life constantly endangered.

I was also fortified in the knowledge that Nelson Mandela was equally contemptuous of Mugabe. Speaking at a UN event in Johannesburg in May 2000, Mandela gave vent to his anger when he referred to those African leaders who 'once commanded liberation armies and despise the very people who put them in power and think it's a privilege to be there for eternity. Everyone knows well who I am talking about.' He never once disagreed with my position when we discussed Zimbabwe; on the contrary, he gave me every encouragement. He was, however, circumspect over his own government's sadly pusillanimous role. At a private meeting in his London hotel in 2002, his frustration was all too evident. He started to spell it out, then abruptly dismissed the subject, waving his hand: 'Peter, you must speak to my president,' he said, evidently concerned that he was tempted to breach his self-imposed protocol of loyalty to his successor, Thabo Mbeki.

Mandela remained tormented by the havoc and terror unleashed by ZANU-PF, Zimbabwe's ruling party. In July 2008, with Zimbabwe almost destroyed and Mugabe clinging to office despite having lost the presidential election, Mandela denounced 'the tragic failure of leadership in our neighbouring Zimbabwe' at a fundraising dinner in London. During his own presidency, Mandela's relations with Mugabe had been poor, the prickly Mugabe openly resenting a much bigger liberation hero than himself, and Mandela abhorring Mugabe's rising despotism and self-serving corruption.

My old comrade and then president of South Africa, Thabo Mbeki, was especially culpable. His government toadied embarrassingly to Mugabe when they could have pulled the plug on the tyranny – as, ironically, had happened to Ian Smith under apartheid's rulers. Pretoria supplied electricity and other vital strategic necessities to Zimbabwe, yet it chose not to exert serious pressure. Some of the arguments deployed were embarrassing, echoing the specious propaganda of apartheid apologists. 'Outside interference' was condemned, sanctions against Mugabe and his henchmen 'would hurt the masses'. Other arguments were insulting: we had no right to criticise a former liberation leader, even one now a tyrant; as a minister now representing the former colonial power, I was out of order. There was speculation that as an old liberationist, Mugabe was regarded by his peers in the traditional 'African chief' sense as the most senior, and they deferred to him.

On an official visit to South Africa in early January 2001, I questioned the strategy adopted toward Mugabe by the other southern African leaders: 'Constructive engagement seems to have failed.' The *Sunday Independent* put a front-page spin on the story, written by the highly respected journalist John Battersby. South Africa's foreign minister, Nkosazana Dlamini-Zuma, wrote a furious letter of protest to Robin Cook, which she then leaked. Although I couldn't but feel she had a bit of a chip on her shoulder, we had got along fine until this attack, and she deserved credit for being the country's first female foreign minister.

I also warned in the interview that failure to deal firmly with Mugabe would rebound upon neighbouring states, as indeed later occurred. Foreign investment slowed, and refugees flooded across the border, millions into South Africa, triggering ugly attacks from indigenous residents, which tarnished the rainbow nation's reputation. Zimbabwe blighted Thabo Mbeki's noble vision of an 'African Renaissance' based upon democracy and good governance. And I met potential foreign investors who were even put off from doing business in South Africa, fearing contagion because of the failure to bring Mugabe to heel. Although I remained on good terms with the South African government, Mbeki included, it remained a big disappointment that they failed to live up to Nelson Mandela's – admittedly exacting – standards.

❖

MY arguments with Thabo Mbeki extended to Angola. Under apartheid, South Africa, together with the CIA, had sponsored a brutal civil war there by arming and funding the rebel forces of Jonas Savimbi's Unita against the MPLA government, a liberationist ally of the ANC. In 1995, I went on a parliamentary visit to the country, witnessing how it had been all but destroyed, the aftermath of the still-simmering civil war starkly evident in towns, with buildings blown apart and burnt-out tank wrecks everywhere.

Once a thriving country, with enormous mineral and oil resources, highly fertile, with an abundance of food for export to neighbours, Angola was now a basket case. Starvation and poverty were rampant. Limbless people begged in the streets and children stepped accidentally on landmines planted across once-lush fields by Savimbi's militia.

As Britain's Africa minister, I was able to change the policy of Her Majesty's Government towards Angola and visited the country again in 2000. Previously, Britain had sat on the fence between the notoriously corrupt MPLA government and Savimbi. But people power was unable to assert itself in the murderous civil war fomented by Savimbi's forces. We had to defeat Savimbi, I insisted. Soon afterwards I listened to a UK intelligence recording of his operatives discussing what to do about 'that man Hain', and complaining that I was 'causing big problems' by targeting Unita. I issued instructions for Britain to help identify Savimbi's whereabouts, and to pass this information on to the Angolan authorities. As a direct result, in February 2002 Savimbi was trapped and killed by Angolan forces in remote eastern Angola.

Before that, Thabo Mbeki had taken me aside at a summit meeting in 2000 in Cairo and sought to persuade me to back off. 'Whatever his activities, Savimbi is an African,' Thabo told me. 'The MPLA are *mestiços*' – meaning of mixed African and Portuguese blood.

'But Savimbi was sponsored by apartheid and he has been destroying Angola for years,' I retorted.

'Yes, of course. But you must understand, Savimbi represents an important African majority in Angola,' he said. I nodded politely, but resolved to take absolutely no notice and to push on regardless. Although I held no brief whatsoever for the corrupt MPLA governing elite, Savimbi needed to be destroyed to enable an alternative politics to assert itself. Thabo's spurious attempts at Africanism cut no ice against Savimbi's primitive fascism.

After Savimbi's death, Angola began to recover, restoring the shattered towns I had witnessed, and began booming.

❖

BUT early in 2003 I had a very different encounter with Nelson Mandela. My ministerial office excitedly informed me that he wanted to phone me, and a time was fixed.

This was shortly before Tony Blair backed President George W Bush in invading Iraq to topple its dictator, Saddam Hussein, an intervention Mandela had outspokenly condemned. He was more agitated than I had ever known him, almost breathing fire down the line, asking me to get a message to Tony, who, unusually, was not taking his call: 'A big mistake, Peter, a very big mistake. It is wrong. Why is Tony doing this, after all his support for Africa? This will cause huge damage internationally.' I had never heard him speak so angrily. But, as history showed, he was proved correct: the Iraq invasion and its aftermath were indeed a disaster.

After Iraq, all the foreign-policy achievements of the Labour government seemed to be forgotten – much as Nelson Mandela had foreseen in his call. Yet I was proud of our record. We had secured an international treaty to ban antipersonnel landmines and the Comprehensive Nuclear-Test-Ban Treaty, helped to set up the International Criminal Court, trebled Britain's overseas aid budget and led the world to try and make poverty history, cancelling debt that crippled poor nations, and tackled climate change. We reformed arms-export legislation to prevent the export of military equipment that might be used for either external aggression or internal repression; ministers like me had to scrutinise each application according to strict criteria. This was a world away from the Tories, who had scandalously sold British arms to almost anybody anywhere.

I was also proud of our achievement in negotiating the UN Nuclear Non-Proliferation Treaty in May 2000 in New York – another example of how ministerial initiative and political values could make all the difference. In the build-up to the UN conference, the usual stalemate seemed likely. Negotiations always polarised between the 'P5' nuclear-armed countries (the five permanent members of the Security Council) and the non-nuclear states. The New Agenda Coalition – formed two years earlier and composed of Brazil, Egypt, Ireland, Mexico, New Zealand, South Africa and Sweden – wanted full disarmament. I never liked going to events for no purpose and resolved in advance to try and make some progress if at all possible.

Once there, I got chatting to my old friend Abdul Minty, formerly secretary of the AAM, and now South Africa's chief negotiator – appointed by Mandela. I told him that if the New

Agenda Coalition had some flexibility, I was keen to get the P5 to do a deal. Abdul's role proved key when I repeated the same message to other countries in the non-nuclear coalition, who also seemed sceptical until they realised I was serious. My officials, used to stonewalling, were equally wary. But they quickly saw the opportunity once they also realised I was determined. Effectively, with Abdul's indirect assistance, I changed UK government policy in line with my own values and those of my boss, Robin Cook, who had specifically entrusted me with the remit.

The result – against all expectations – was a deal: the other P5 countries, including the US, swung behind Britain and it was unanimously agreed that, for the first time, all countries of the world would work towards the global elimination of nuclear weapons. The P5 had conceded that objective while retaining their capability, and as a result the New Agenda Coalition had been able to move the non-nuclear states away from their previous insistence on immediate disarmament. This achievement was ultimately down to two former London anti-apartheid comrades, one a Pretoria boy and the other a Hartebeesfontein boy.

❖

IN 2000 another phone call from Nelson Mandela was politically more convivial. I say 'politically' because he was always friendly to me, even when angry with Tony Blair over Iraq.

I had been deputed by Tony Blair to represent Britain in the negotiations to settle the civil war in Burundi, and Mandela wanted to be certain that I would be present in early August 2000 at a key summit in Arusha, northern Tanzania: 'Bill Clinton is coming, African presidents also. It's a real shame Tony cannot make it but it is important you come for Britain.' It was a request I couldn't have turned down, and my diary was accordingly abruptly changed.

But whereas foreign ministers in equivalent countries, France for instance, had their own government jets, I went on a scheduled flight to my birthplace, Nairobi, and then flew on a small twin-engine charter, landing at night at Arusha's little Kilimanjaro International Airport. I asked what the large contraption was by the main runway. 'President Clinton's portable landing gear for Air Force One,' came the laconic reply. When he landed, Clinton's security detail virtually took over the entire town with a whole cavalcade of armoured vehicles and Secret Service agents in dark glasses with crackling earpieces: US presidents don't just arrive, they occupy.

Mandela convened the gathering with a genial warmth, shrewdly appearing to defer to African presidents such as his successor, Thabo Mbeki, while cajoling everyone into making progress. Eventually, he did broker a Burundi peace deal, enabling Hutus and Tutsis to join a new power-sharing government in Burundi in November 2001 and end what was described as its 'slow genocide' – a civil war in which about 300 000 people had died. Mandela spent two years in what he called these 'alarmingly slow, painful and costly' talks, after replacing Tanzania's Julius Nyerere as mediator. But while Nyerere was seen as hostile to the Tutsis, Mandela's authority enabled him to bring the 19 parties into a productive though inevitably imperfect and still choppy outcome.

❖

IN my 2018 biography, *Mandela: His Essential Life*, I wrote: 'Perhaps long-standing ANC supporters like me expected too much of the "rainbow nation". Perhaps it was naive to think that Mandela's ANC – for all its noble history and tradition of moral integrity and constitutionalism – could be immune to human frailty, especially in the face of such immense social inequality and global power imbalances.'

But could any political party anywhere (including in rich, old democracies like Britain) have done any better? I served for 12 years in Labour's social-democratic British government, and we found it tough to advance social justice while delivering economic success in a world gripped by the inequality-increasing, growth-stifling economics of neoliberalism.

The problem also for the rainbow nation is that Mandela set such high standards after the depravity – including deep corruption – of the apartheid era, that the world expected better of it than from other countries. Speaking as president as early as August 1998 he warned: 'We have learnt now that even those people with whom we fought the struggle against apartheid's corruption can themselves become corrupted.'

The notion of the 'Mandela miracle' was grounded in reality, but it also engendered myth. The transition from brutal apartheid to rainbow democracy encouraged a tendency to frame the South African story too simplistically. Moreover, outside observers have never been able to view post-apartheid South Africa in a nuanced way: they either romanticise it or cynically dismiss it. But neither of these perceptions is accurate – and they never were. After the relatively painless transition from apartheid under Mandela, it was always going to be a bumpy road.

❖

IN December 2012 I travelled across South Africa to make a film for the BBC. *Marikana: The Massacre that Shocked a Nation* was broadcast in April 2013 and revealed not simply the grotesque details of the massacre but also the systemic sickness that allowed it to occur.

In scenes eerily reminiscent of apartheid, police opened fire on striking black mineworkers at Lonmin's Marikana platinum mine near Rustenburg, west of Johannesburg, on 16 August 2012.

However, unlike the 1960 Sharpeville massacre, in which white police attacked black citizens, this was black workers being killed by predominantly black police under a majority black government.

Thirty-four people died and 78 were injured. Even more shocking, at least 14 of the dead were hunted down and shot from behind, some distance from the main protest area. Lawyers representing families of the dead miners insisted that the massacre was pre-planned by senior figures in the police and the Zuma government, invoking chilling testimony that 'weapons of war' were used instead of proper riot-control procedures. Guns were planted on some of the corpses, and witnesses claimed to have been intimidated and tortured.

As I walked around the Marikana complex, talking to miners and managers present on the day, it seemed to me that the massacre symbolised the unresolved legacy of apartheid: a wealthy white-owned corporation pitted against its poor, black migrant workers. Most of them lived in the shadow of the mine at Wonderkop, a sprawling informal settlement of 40 000 people, with no running water, no proper electricity and no sewerage or sanitation.

Some 1 200 kilometres to the south, close to Mandela's birth-place in the rural Eastern Cape, we drove around five hours from East London to meet the widow of one of the murdered strikers. But our vehicles got stuck in deep mud and we had to get out and walk, carrying between us the camera equipment several kilometres in the rain to her bleak turquoise-green family rondavels. But, disappointingly, she wasn't there.

We were advised to trudge back, and fortunately came upon her walking out of the mist carrying a small baby on her back. Her situation was desperate, because the family's meagre income had suddenly been destroyed. Despite the government's system of social grants, like the one she had just walked 20 kilometres to claim, it was hard to see how two decades of democracy had made any improvement to the living standards of the rural poor like her.

Afterwards, President Zuma gave me an interview at his office in Pretoria's Bryntirion Estate. Much to the chagrin of the BBC's Johannesburg office, he had turned down repeated BBC requests before, but obviously felt I would be more sympathetic. However, his media and political advisers were politely tetchy, especially when we persuaded him that it would be better to set up outside in the sun overlooking the city rather than sitting hunched in the gloomy interior.

I began the interview by discussing the ANC government's many positive achievements. But when we turned to Marikana, Zuma became shifty, inexplicably blaming the shootings on the company and disclaiming any culpability for the police of which he was ultimately in charge.

The problem for Zuma and the whole of the ANC – including Cyril Ramaphosa, who was on Lonmin's board of directors at the time of the massacre – was that it symbolised the unresolved apartheid conundrum. Under apartheid, government and big business were run exclusively by the white minority for the exclusive benefit of that white minority. But when Mandela and his ANC leadership comrades began negotiating a transition from apartheid with the white ruling elite, the fear was that white businesses and investors would flee. And it was a fear grounded in grim reality: white capital and skills could well have flooded abroad.

Instead, under Mandela's guidance, a deal was struck, and compromises were made for the sake of a peaceful and economically stable transition. Thus, a black majority now ran the government but the white minority still ran the economy. Although it is fashionable among radical critics to accuse Mandela and the ANC leadership of 'selling out', that is an ahistorical and completely prejudicial stance, for it is hard to see how they could have adopted any other course. It was a perilous moment in South Africa's history. On the one hand, the country was becoming ungovernable and the economy was plunging over a cliff. On the other hand, more radical change at the time would undoubtedly have triggered a flight of wealth, resulting in financial calamity and political turmoil.

There would also have been a real risk of national rather than partial civil war. Mozambique and Angola – societies for decades torn apart and plagued by landmines, infrastructure destruction and economic chaos – are salutary examples of the consequences of non-negotiated transformations. But some, such as former ANC underground hero and intelligence minister Ronnie Kasrils, who played a part in the transition, subsequently saw this as 'the devil's pact': a terrible betrayal of the poorest of the poor.

The problem that radical critics haven't resolved is that the revolutionary change they appear with hindsight to advocate would have led to violence and mayhem. The ANC leaders with Mandela were only too aware that the white ruling elite had virtually all the firepower – the army, the police and the full resources of a brutal state. And the history of Leninist-type insurrection is not a happy one, whether in the Soviet Union, China or Latin America: dictatorship, economic failure and institutionalised corruption have always been the result.

No balanced assessment could reasonably accuse Mandela of being a sell-out. However, where radical critics are justified is in the ANC's failure to deliver 'radical economic transformation'. That very slogan was disingenuously appropriated by the Zuma faction to justify their looting and to empower their cronyism, and also opportunistically grabbed by Julius Malema's EFF.

Under ANC rule, companies such as Lonmin did bring black South Africans into their senior management. A new black business elite was empowered – even creating some billionaires – and South Africa gained a sizeable and growing new black middle class, including state bureaucrats, ANC politicians and ANC-linked trade-union leaders affiliated to the Confederation of South African Trade Unions (Cosatu). But the fundamental

233

divide bequeathed by apartheid remained, and the inequality gap grew, contradicting the agenda of the 1955 Freedom Charter and the ANC's original mission.

If that trend continues, there could well be a revolution of rising expectations and frustration, in which South Africa could once again become as ungovernable as it was during the darkest years of apartheid. By 2010, Zwelinzima Vavi, the former general secretary of Cosatu, and one-time ally turned critic of President Zuma, was already warning: 'We're headed for a predator state, where a powerful, corrupt and demagogic elite of political hyenas is increasingly using the state to get rich.'

Under the choking universal fog of global neoliberalism, implementing policies for greater equality and social justice is extremely difficult. But it is also extremely necessary, both to avoid destructive popular uprisings and to ensure opportunity and justice for all, and for the ANC to do much more than replace an old white elite with a new black one, and old white corruption with new black corruption. Mandela would never have settled for that.

Mandela's reputation continued to soar long after he had stepped down as president in 1999. He never claimed to be a saint and nor was he, any more than even the best of us could be: we all have our frailties. His greatness derived not just from his courage and leadership, but from the humanity that he radiated. He had a common touch, humility, self-deprecation, a sense of fun and dignity.

Prison could have embittered him, adulation could have gone to his head, and egotism could have triumphed. The clutching of the crowd and the intrusive pressures of the modern political age could have seen him retreat behind the barriers that most top figures today erect around themselves – partly to retain some individual space – but which all too often end up either in cold aloofness or in patent insincerity and its companion, cynicism. But none of this happened.

Throughout everything, Nelson Mandela remained his own man, not seduced by the trappings of office nor deluded by the adulation of admirers, always steadfastly principled, friendly and approachable until he faded forlornly away in his last year or so, dying in December 2013.

President Zuma reaped his just reward when he was booed at the FNB Stadium in Soweto as he spoke at Mandela's memorial service.

Betrayal

IT was quite sudden and proved a career-changing question: 'Would you go to the Lords?' the Labour Party leader Ed Miliband asked me in 2014 after I'd spent 23 fulfilling years as MP for Neath.

'But I don't agree with the place! It should be elected,' I replied, taken aback.

'That's why I want you there,' he said. 'When I'm prime minister I plan big reforms.'

Members of the House of Lords (also known as peers) are mostly appointed by party leaders roughly in proportion to their share of the vote at the previous election, and a small minority through an independent commission.

Having sought a categorical assurance from Ed that I would be nominated regardless of whether he became prime minister, I pondered long and hard, talking only to Elizabeth and my trusted former political agent, Howard Davies.

Eventually, I decided it was time for a change and I would stand down from my beloved Neath constituency (where the local Labour Party had unanimously selected me to re-stand) when the general election came. I had spent 12 rewarding but demanding years as a minister, working 80 to 100 hours a week, and wasn't enjoying being in opposition nearly as much as I had fighting to get into power in the 1990s. Also, my parents were getting frailer and needed care; Dad was 90, Mom was 88 and five years earlier they had moved from Putney to Neath to be near Sally and her daughter, Connie, as well as to Elizabeth and me.

So it was 18 months later, in September 2015, that I found my way to a Harry Potter-type building in central London to meet someone I'd never before heard of called the Garter King of Arms. His post, I discovered, was the most senior of 13 officers of arms who make up the College of Arms and are styled 'heralds in ordinary'. Thomas Woodcock, a courteous, middle-aged member of the Royal Household (who had held the position since 2010), led me up some winding stairs to his office, which looked rather like nothing much had changed since the 19th century.

We sat down at his desk: there were formalities to go through before I could take my seat in the Lords. First, my title. I'd toyed mischievously with 'Lord Hain of Pretoria'. But Neath was always my preference. So that was signed off. My full official title would be 'The Right Honourable The Lord Hain of Neath in the County of West Glamorgan'. ('The Right Honourable' is a prefix I'd first been given when sworn in by Her Majesty the Queen as a Member of her Privy Council in 2001.) So far, so good.

Then came the two more awkward bits. My ermine robe would be £9000. 'What?' I protested. It was a huge amount; no way was I buying it. I didn't want one anyway.

Garter added that the daily hire rate was £180. What? I again protested. And there was one day when 'there is no charge' and that was on introduction to the Lords, when the robe came free.

'I really don't want to wear it,' I replied, testing his polite patience now to the limit.

'That's quite impossible,' he said, not a little irritated: the long and the short of it was that I would be introduced wearing the red ermine robe or not at all.

Also, he explained, with a peerage came the entitlement to my very own heraldic shield. He had been thinking about its design, and a few springboks could be accommodated. He smiled, having kindly shown some consideration to this Pretoria boy – not the usual type he was used to putting through their introductory paces. By the way, my new heraldic shield would cost £8500.

'I'm very grateful, but I really don't want one, sorry,' I replied.

'But it will remain in your family for ever; your sons will inherit it,' he pleaded.

'Thank you again, I appreciate the trouble you have taken over me, but I don't want one, and my sons I'm sure wouldn't either.'

Garter, though meticulously courteous, looked disapprovingly disappointed.

The formalities over, we had a little chat, the afternoon darkening in his large, dimly lit room. He laughed at my story about the Queen being tickled pink after delivering the Queen's Speech in the 2005 Parliament when I was Leader of the Commons, and deputed to both welcome and bid her farewell. I'd asked her what she would have done if, when the kneeling Lord Chancellor had bent down to retrieve her speech from his pouch, it was empty. 'I'd have had a cunning plan,' she replied, laughing – mystifying the BBC commentator David Dimbleby who had covered the occasion for decades and remarked that he'd never seen the monarch so amused before. Garter and I agreed she had a good sense of humour that was only rarely displayed publicly.

'So is your salary as a member of the Royal Household paid by the Civil List?' I asked.

'No, our whole office is financed quite independently,' Garter replied proudly.

I was surprised: 'Where do you get your funds, then?'

'From the sale of heraldic shields,' he said wistfully.

❖

IN Britain, the doctrine of parliamentary privilege is a part of the rule of law itself, and dates back to arguably Parliament's finest historical moment, in 1642, when King Charles I and his soldiers invaded the House of Commons to arrest five MPs who had spoken there critically of his rule.

The Speaker courageously defied him while MPs chanted 'privilege, privilege' – a cry taken up in the streets by the people of London – and eventually in 1689 the right to free speech in Parliament was entrenched in the Bill of Rights. It means that when speaking in Parliament, MPs or peers cannot be sued and what they say can be reported in the media without the rich or powerful being able to suppress it with legal injunctions or asset seizures.

Despite outrage from the legal establishment, parliamentary privilege has been used to good effect, to name, for example, the notorious spy Kim Philby. That said, it is indeed a privilege not to be abused, and should be used with absolute integrity – responsibly, sparingly and only when necessary to name guilty individuals or to expose wrongdoing.

During my 30-year career as a parliamentarian I have used it just three times – first in 2000 when as minister for Africa I utilised information from UK intelligence agencies to name traffickers selling arms for 'blood diamonds' fuelling wars in Angola, Sierra Leone and the Democratic Republic of Congo, putting most of them out of business. One, the notorious ex-KGB agent Viktor Bout, whom I dubbed 'The Merchant of Death', ended up serving a prison sentence. Several (including white South Africans), unaware that parliamentary privilege protected me, angrily threatened to sue: they never got anywhere.

The third time was in October 2018 to name businessman Sir Philip Green, who had abused the system of non-disclosure agreements to suppress allegations by his employees of sexual and racial harassment. That provoked outrage from senior legal bods, the former Supreme Court Justice, Lord Brown of Eaton-under-Heywood, denouncing it in a special debate in the Lords on 24 May 2019 and effectively insisting I had overridden a court injunction keeping the alleged abuse secret and had therefore undermined the rule of law. My response was that, if true, the abuse was unlawful and that the courts should not be party to covering it up.

There were legitimate arguments on both sides, but the point is that those two occasions were examples of a responsible use of parliamentary privilege, namely, to expose evidence of injustice and elucidate a matter of public interest: the first to block arms fuelling bloody wars in Africa, the second to protect victims of apparent abuse.

Its contemporary justification therefore was living proof of the principle of parliamentary sovereignty – irrespective of the wishes of the executive, the powerful and the wealthy, and even rulings by the legal establishment when it covers up allegations of misconduct. I insisted that in such cases, a parliamentarian's right to exercise privilege, conscientiously, rarely and responsibly, is an important safeguard for the liberty of the subject. It should not be whittled away by making the sovereignty of judges override the sovereignty of Parliament.

❖

BUT a year before the Sir Philip Green controversy, and when Parliament reopened in September 2017 after the August holiday recess, I had been preparing to expose evidence of international connivance with state capture, looting and money laundering under President Zuma, as I had been asked to do in Johannesburg by Pravin Gordhan and his ANC colleagues. My primary source, Deep Throat, was ready and waiting to help. But I was still uncertain how my use of parliamentary privilege could do this.

Then a perfect vehicle presented itself: the Sanctions and Anti-Money Laundering Bill the government planned to take through the Lords, starting in November 2017. The advantage was that, rather than asking a necessarily brief question, I could make detailed speeches, both on second reading and on amendments during the committee and report stages of the Bill – all on the record and under privilege.

The key was to focus upon any involvement or collusion of British-based corporations, because the British government – through the Serious Fraud Office, the Financial Conduct Authority or the National Crime Agency – could be pressed to take enforcement action against them. Otherwise, complaints about what was going on in South Africa could be ruled out of order.

But first, an obvious target came up: the UK-based global public-relations company, Bell Pottinger, founded by Lord Tim Bell, Margaret Thatcher's favourite media guru. It had attracted some British media attention because of a dispute between Bell, its flamboyant chairman, and its chief executive, James Henderson, who was trying to force Bell out, arguing that he was not bringing in enough work to justify his £1-million annual salary. But the underlying issue was a lucrative £100 000-a-month contract signed in January 2016 with Oakbay, which Tim Bell had previously flown to South Africa to initiate. Oakbay was among many companies, some of them 'shell' or 'front' companies, established by President Zuma's cronies, the Gupta brothers, to facilitate their alleged looting.

South African investigative journalists and opposition politicians were up in arms over the lucrative Bell Pottinger contract, which had generated a campaign of racist 'fake news', social-media abuse, outright lies and prodigious use of so-called bots with bogus Twitter accounts. Bell Pottinger's campaign also smeared and targeted journalists who were exposing allegations of corruption by the Zuma/Gupta state criminal conspiracy.

But it was an astute operation, manipulating entirely legitimate popular resentment at the lack of economic transformation for the black majority since the demise of apartheid. It fiendishly presented the culprits as agents of 'white monopoly capital', neatly avoiding Zuma's role in South Africa's increasingly dysfunctional public administration, corrupt governance, economic decline and rising inequality. Bell Pottinger's seamy racial ferocity – designed

241

by its white South African team to exploit legitimate grievances – conveniently diverted attention both from the shameless looting going on and from the reality that it was actually the 'Zuptas' who constituted South Africa's primary 'monopoly capital' centre of power and elitism.

I applied for and was successful in a 'topical question' ballot in the Lords on 7 September 2017, the first time 'state capture' had been raised in the UK Parliament. I asked that all Bell Pottinger's widespread work for British public bodies be called in and reviewed after it had run 'a pernicious and poisonously racist smear campaign in South Africa for the wealthy Gupta brothers, whom President Zuma has enabled to capture the state and bankroll his family and friends through corruption and cronyism'. I added that 'since the respected former finance minister Pravin Gordhan has stated that the Guptas and Zumas have benefited from R6.8 billion of money laundering', the government must investigate whether any British banks were involved.

Within South Africa the heat had been rising around the 'Guptagate' scandal. A year before, in November 2016, a damning 355-page report by South Africa's indomitable Public Protector, Thuli Madonsela, had been released, despite attempts by President Zuma and his ministers to suppress it. The report, entitled 'State of Capture', stated that Bell Pottinger had attempted to stir up racial anger by mounting a 'hateful and divisive campaign to divide South Africa along the lines of race'.

But the outside world had not yet focused upon either Guptagate or its own responsibility. My task was to try to ensure that a global political fuss around the banks and other financial institutions would shine a global light on the problem, and thereby help confront and resolve it.

Just before I asked my question, British pressure had started to build on Bell Pottinger. It had been expelled from its trade body, the Public Relations and Communications Association.

The following week – whether or not triggered by my question and the wide political and media attention it generated in Britain and internationally – Bell Pottinger went bankrupt, the architect of its own demise. A company whose very mission was to protect the reputation of its clients had, through pure financial greed, neglected its *own* reputation to such a degree that it collapsed. It was a salutary lesson for all corporates and a case study for all business students.

❖

BUT there were bigger fish to try to fry.

My primary motivation was the anger and pain felt by many anti-apartheid stalwarts at the flagrant trashing of the values of the freedom struggle by Zuma and his coterie, and the way that the ANC had converted itself into a gravy train, an invitation for members to help themselves to the looting. The freedom struggle was supposed to secure human rights, equal opportunities, social justice and equality. Its leaders – Mandela, Tambo, Sisulu, Mbeki, Kathrada, Mlangeni – never pretended to be saints. But integrity, morality and the common good were in their very core. As Nelson Mandela eloquently stated in March 2001: 'Little did we suspect that our own people, when they got a chance, would be as corrupt as the apartheid regime. That is one of the things that has really hurt us.' 'We just assumed everyone was honest,' an obviously anguished Ahmed Kathrada said when he took me around Robben Island in December 2012.

Hundreds had died for those values in the struggle. Thousands had been beaten, tortured, imprisoned, banned or exiled. Mandela and his Rivonia Trial comrades had sacrificed the three prime decades of their lives in prison. My own activist parents had been forced to leave the country of their birth and I had been a target for the South African security forces.

What was happening to the new South Africa we had all fought for? Its democracy perverted by patronage. Its governance polluted by corruption. Its public administration – from electricity and water supply to municipal services – disintegrating under incompetent cronyism and looting.

❖

MEANWHILE, Deep Throat and I had established an encrypted channel of communication. The second reading of the Sanctions and Anti-Money Laundering Bill was on 1 November, and I decided to write to the Chancellor of the Exchequer (finance minister), Philip Hammond, in advance of the debate, naming members of the Zuma and Gupta families and their associates, and requesting that sanctions be applied to them, and that the banks they were utilising to allegedly launder billions of rands be prosecuted. Deep Throat supplied me with a first draft of the letter, including (I was astonished to find) the South African identity numbers of each of the 27 individuals concerned – the Zuma family, the Gupta family and their associates.

Also listed were 14 Gupta-linked entities apparently set up to transnationally launder their illicit proceeds, most (such as the business consultancy Trillian) well known to investigative journalists in South Africa but unfamiliar to the British authorities.

In order to make clear that the UK government had the ability to act, I deliberately headed the letter 'Financial crimes allegedly committed in South Africa, UAE and Hong Kong, through UK headquartered financial institutions'.

I then wrote: 'Having recently visited South Africa, it is clear the country is gripped by a political, economic and social crisis, precipitated by a vast criminal network facilitated by an Indian-South African family, the Guptas, and the Presidential family, the Zumas. Such is the extent of this criminal network that the South

244

African state is indisputably regarded as having been "captured", with corruption and cronyism plundering taxpayer resources on an industrial scale. In consequence, economic growth has plummeted, international investor confidence is rock bottom and state institutions have been hollowed out in this great country.

'However, this Gupta/Zuma criminal network is not localised to South Africa – indeed, it has been enabled by a transnational money-laundering network that these individuals have established, including bank accounts at global financial institutions.' I explained that several Standard Chartered US-dollar accounts in Dubai were suspected to have been used by the Gupta network to launder the proceeds of their illicit gains from the South African state. Multinational companies, including McKinsey, SAP, Bain & Co and KPMG, had been implicated in facilitating the Guptas' financial-crime activity.

Explaining that the majority of the illicit funds had seemingly flowed through the United Arab Emirates (UAE) and Hong Kong, where two of the UK's largest financial institutions – Standard Chartered and HSBC – had their biggest footprints, I asked for the UK law enforcement and regulatory authorities to investigate both this and the 27 people I had named.

I concluded: 'Could you please immediately refer this letter to the Serious Fraud Office for investigation and the Financial Conduct Authority too?'

Before sending the letter, I had phoned the Chancellor's political adviser to say that my letter was not an adversarial one from an opposition Labour politician but a genuine request for him to act immediately. He replied unusually speedily and positively: 'I have referred your letter to the Financial Conduct Authority and relevant UK law enforcement agencies, including the National Crime Agency and Serious Fraud Office. My officials have also been in touch with the British High Commission in South Africa. The government takes allegations of corruption and money laundering extremely seriously and is committed to preventing the proceeds of corruption from entering the UK financial system.'

I followed up with a question in the Lords on 19 October 2017, stating that India's Bank of Baroda should be added to the list for investigation because it had allegedly been a conduit for the corrupt proceeds of money stolen from their taxpayers and laundered through Dubai and Hong Kong.

Having alerted South Africa's media to these initiatives, and especially the feisty online news outlet *Daily Maverick*, supplying its indefatigable editor, Branko Brkic, in advance with speeches, there was an immediate news impact in South Africa. Coverage in Britain also started to grow.

❖

PREVIOUSLY, in early October, I had flown to speak at a business conference in Cape Town and travelled back via Johannesburg for some teaching sessions at Wits Business School. In my office there, I met Branko Brkic and showed him, on an embargoed basis, the text of the letter with all the ID details of the Zumas and Guptas.

By now I was anxious about security. I was travelling around on my own, albeit with pre-booked regular drivers whom I knew and trusted, but Zuma's grip on security was ubiquitous.

Soon, however, my intervention went global when I was able to supplement the excellent draft speech supplied by Deep Throat for the Bill's second reading on 1 November with information given to me by a whistle-blower within the South African wing of HSBC.

On 31 October 2017, hand-delivered to the Chancellor at the Treasury in Horse Guards Parade, Whitehall, I enclosed HSBC print-outs of transactions handed to me and asked that these be referred for investigation. This information detailed Gupta-linked money transfers over the last few years from their South African bank accounts held with HSBC to its accounts in Dubai and

Hong Kong. As HSBC did not have the relevant foreign-exchange licences, they used South African banks, specifically Nedbank and Standard Bank, as intermediate banks. The print-outs showed the relevant banks involved and account numbers used, some for legitimate transactions, many certainly not.

For example, there were records of minor debit-card payments by Gupta family members using motorway service-station cafeterias in England mixed in with much more serious transactions. I wrote in the letter to the Chancellor: 'The latter illicit transactions were flagged internally by the HSBC FIC department as suspicious. But I am informed that they were told by HSBC UK to ignore it. That is a major breach of FCA [Financial Conduct Authority] practice which I am sure you would never countenance and is an incitement to money laundering which has self-evidently occurred in this case, and also been sanctioned by HSBC, as part of the flagrant robbery of South African taxpayers of many millions. Each originating transaction would start with one bank account and then be split into a number of accounts a couple of times to disguise the origin. Can you please ensure that such evident money laundering and illegality is not tolerated and that HSBC is investigated for possible criminality?'

In my speech the next day, 1 November 2017, I explained the background for a UK and international audience. Corruption within, and money laundering from, a monopoly capital elite around the president's family in South Africa and their close associates the Gupta brothers had demonstrated, I argued, that winning the war against financial crime required coordination, influence, action and accountability between multi-jurisdictional law-enforcement agencies.

I explained that my regular visits to South Africa had left me stunned by what seemed like a systemic transnational financial-crime network facilitated by the Guptas and the Zuma family. I argued that if there had been more proactive and genuine cooperation between various law-enforcement agencies, and within and between the banks that had been moving money for the Gupta/Zuma laundering network, the devastation wrought on South Africa could have been significantly reduced.

'Urgent action is needed to close down this network of corruption,' I insisted.

I then gave a practical example of how a community in the Free State, one of the poorest provinces in South Africa, with nearly one in two people unemployed, had been devastated by what seemed like international money laundering.

In February 2013 the Free State government announced that it would spend R340 million (£18 million) to build, in a small town called Vrede, a dairy farm that would be part-owned by 80 impoverished locals. As I explained in my parliamentary speech, these aspiring farmers unknowingly became pawns in a swirl of international money laundering, which involved some British and other financial institutions.

In May 2013, three months after the Free State government announced the dairy-farm project, a company called Estina – ostensibly the vehicle for the 80 beneficiaries but which was actually linked to the Guptas – was handed a farm to begin building the dairy. Estina's sole director was an IT salesman with no farming experience. The project was not put out to public tender.

Next, the government almost immediately transferred about R180 million (£6 million) to Estina.

But instead of investing this in the farm, Estina transferred most of the money to a Gupta company in the UAE called Gateway Ltd, registered in Ras al-Khaimah, one of seven emirates making up the UAE and a highly secretive offshore company jurisdiction. At the time, Gateway held its account with Standard Chartered.

Based on information given to me by my source, I explained that once the funds were in Dubai, the Guptas engaged in what appeared to be a classic laundering cycle, transforming illicit money into ostensibly legitimate assets. In arguably the most eye-watering example, they transferred over £2 million of the Estina dairy money in two separate tranches through two shell companies, ultimately consolidating it in their Standard Chartered account for another of their UAE-based companies, called Accurate Investments.

They then transmitted this money into an entity called Linkway Trading, banked with the State Bank of India, back into South Africa.

Once in Linkway, the Guptas used these funds to pay for a lavish four-day family wedding at Sun City, where, among other extravagances, over £1 000 was spent on chocolate truffles, £120 000 on scarves for guests and £20 000 on fireworks. At about the same time that the Guptas were celebrating at the wedding, veterinarians in the town of Vrede were called to the dairy farm because of the reeking stench of dead animals. They found at least 30 cows that had been buried in a ditch, having died from, 'an unknown condition that could be caused by malnutrition'.

The Vrede dairy criminal catastrophe proved, I argued, that the laundering was effected through a transnational triangulation between South Africa, the UAE and British and other global banks such as Standard Chartered, HSBC and the Bank of Baroda.

What struck me time and again is why an internationally respected bank such as Standard Chartered would open accounts for shell entities registered in a free-trade zone such as Ras al-Khaimah, whose primary attraction is as a highly secretive offshore jurisdiction. What was it doing this for? Shell companies, by virtue of their ownership anonymity, and as used by the Guptas in the Vrede dairy tragedy, are generally classic vehicles for money laundering and other illicit financial activity, moving funds from one part of the world to another to facilitate mafia crime, terrorist activity and looting, as in the South African case.

I concluded my speech by insisting that global corporates,

whatever pressure they may come under from their clients, and whatever the cost to their commission or fees, must conduct themselves according to the highest professional standards. Surely the complicity of UK financial institutions should make UK government ministers and UK parliamentarians hang their heads in shame? Just as they were complicit in sustaining apartheid, so today they were complicit in sustaining the corrupt power elite in South Africa, betraying the legacy of Nelson Mandela and the anti-apartheid struggle.

In South Africa, the estimable *Daily Maverick*, which again had been given the text in advance, ran large chunks of it. The popular news outlet Radio 702 ran much of the speech live. The independent TV station eNCA gave it extensive coverage. Suddenly, my name was headlining in my old homeland, just as it had in STST days.

But something more important also happened. The speech led to a front-page report in the *Financial Times* linking my initiating the UK investigation into HSBC with a probe into the bank's US division for money laundering in Mexico. *The New York Times* and *The Wall Street Journal* followed up, and *The Economist* ran a major feature splashed over its front cover. Once confined to Johannesburg, the story went global and the corporates involved found themselves in an uncomfortable spotlight in New York and London. Their global bosses did not like that one little bit.

❖

STRAIGHT away I had the worried corporate-relations director of HSBC and former top UK diplomat, Sir Sherard Cowper-Coles, on the phone wanting to see me urgently. We had worked together when I was a minister of state in the Foreign Office some 17 years before. 'Your action could lead to HSBC being barred from the US,' he complained, agitated about the impact on the corporation's future and the risk to its employees' jobs.

I readily agreed to meet a top HSBC team in my Lords office, where they pressed me hard about the identity of my South African HSBC whistle-blower. It was the usual ruse of company bosses in these situations, and in this case my source feared for his/her life, let alone job, so I refused. But I did arrange for my source to meet with representatives from the Financial Conduct Authority.

After the HSBC visit to my Lords office came senior figures from Standard Chartered. The common refrain was that although both banks had indeed had Gupta accounts, these had been closed a while back, so why all the fuss?

What about tracking the laundered money through the digital footprints the laundered funds had left in their systems and handing this to the South African Treasury and the British enforcement authorities, I asked. Sorry they replied, that would breach 'client confidentiality'. This was the habitual excuse, I was to discover, of the global banks; having passed looted billions through their channels, they would shut their stable doors only after the criminal horses had bolted.

By now social media was flooded with Zupta attacks on me straight from the Bell Pottinger playbook; the company may have gone bankrupt but its fiendishly manipulative and cynically racist programme was still in full cry. I was presented variously as 'a white colonialist', an 'agent of white monopoly capital', a 'foreign imperialist', some almost reincarnations of my old 1970s apartheid label, 'Public Enemy Number One'. There were crude semi-pornographic faked montage images of my wife Elizabeth and me nude in bed covered with red pimply splodges. Others had me as a crude puppet dangled by caricature fat white capitalists, some transparently antisemitic. These attacks were almost universally presented as coming from various black South Africans on Twitter who did not exist but had been digitally invented.

My normal practice with outright abuse, racism or lies was to block those from tweeting my handle @peterhain. But every time I did this to the Zupta tweets, another 100 or more immediately flooded in. 'Don't bother, Grandad,' my IT-savvy 15-year-old grandson Harry told me. 'Just ignore them. They are all fake – they're spam posts being uploaded automatically and repeatedly by bots. They will be run by some form of algorithm.' That didn't mean a hell of a lot to me, so I asked Harry to clarify. 'It's similar to how you might receive spam advertising emails constantly sent to your inbox, except this is on social media so it is directly to you,' he patiently explained.

Some well-informed South Africans thought these bots were run from India or Dubai, where the Gupta brothers were also based, but Harry thought they could have come from anywhere across the world. Clearly, the monster created by Bell Pottinger remained alive and kicking.

But there was more promising news from within the ruling ANC, though some believed it irretrievably corrupted. Deputy President Cyril Ramaphosa's campaign for the party leadership might well win, according to a briefing given to me by two Cape Town friends, former ANC London organiser Lawson Naidoo and academic and constitutional-rights campaigner Richard Calland. They had a different model from other surveys for re-searching what was happening in local ANC party branches and had detected an underlying swing away from the Zuma machine: many delegates to the forthcoming ANC conference at Nasrec, Johannesburg, where Zuma's successor was to be elected, were not declaring their real intention to vote for Ramaphosa.

There were reports of local branch secretaries being offered R10 000 and ordinary delegates R3 000 to swell the Zuma camp's votes. The money was said to be from Vladimir Putin's Russia, which was determined to secure a deal for a massive proposed nuclear build programme, from which Zuma would get a big rake-off. 'Take the money and still vote for Cyril,' was the advice.

Key members of his campaign team seemed optimistic, whereas back in late July, when we had first met up, I had thought they were displaying the usual overenthusiasm of party campaigners.

❖

WHEN the Sanctions and Anti-Money Laundering Bill went into the committee stage on 6 December 2017 I again deployed a draft speech expertly supplied by Deep Throat, to describe how President Zuma and the Guptas allegedly used state-owned enterprises (SOEs) as vehicles for large-scale looting and money laundering, to benefit their families and friends.

Former primary-school teacher Dudu Myeni is a person near and dear to Zuma (he is rumoured to have fathered a child of hers, although he has publicly denied it). In 2012 Zuma ensured that Myeni was appointed chair of SAA, the national airline. In early December 2015, the then minister of finance, Nhlanhla Nene, rejected her request to renegotiate a fleet renewal deal for the airline because it was clearly not in SAA's best interest. Within days, the president sacked Nene.

I outlined how Myeni had not only facilitated alleged looting by the Zuma and Gupta families, but apparently also sought to control, instruct and manipulate the running of the state-owned power utility, Eskom, from which the Gupta family, through an intricate network of companies, reportedly siphoned off billions of rands, via various banks, including London-based banks. I again argued that this needed investigating.

I gave chapter and verse of information at my disposal showing how Tony Gupta had phoned a senior Eskom executive accusing him of not 'helping us with anything', adding, 'We are the ones that put you in the position you are in. We are the ones who can take you out!' A few days later, President Zuma himself allegedly called the executive with more instructions to act illegally.

That, I explained, resulted 'in one of the most notorious examples of looting in South Africa's recent history. This Zuma-Gupta conspiracy ... in less than 18 months had bled the power utility dry. It now faces bankruptcy and has been downgraded by international financial institutions due to governance failures.'

It was clear to me that each South African SOE was looted using the same modus operandi by the same elite individuals at the very top of the chain – President Zuma and his family, and the infamous Guptas. Hundreds of millions of rands were siphoned off these important public companies.

I asked for an immediate investigation by the City of London Police, the Metropolitan Police and the financial regulatory authorities into all bank accounts held in London by any South African state-owned company, beginning with SAA, to ensure that its UK accounts had not been used for the illegal laundering of funds from the proceeds of financial crime in South Africa.

Armed with Deep Throat's expertise, which went way beyond my own, I explained how, when dirty money from a global criminal network infected one financial institution, it sequentially infected a number of others. This is the result of what is known as 'correspondent banking' – a term that Deep Throat had taught me – which because of its complex nature is often misunderstood. Correspondent banks are international banks that clear smaller transactions, generally the foreign-currency transactions of domestic banks, through large financial centres. In practice, this means that one transaction can move through a chain of financial institutions from the point of payment before it reaches its intended beneficiary. This creates significant money-laundering and terrorist-financing risks, because each bank in the chain has to rely on the other to correctly identify the customer, determine the real owner and monitor the transaction. In essence, the correspondent bank is only as strong as the weakest link in the chain.

I warned that umpteen domestic and regional banks inevitably became caught up in the chain. These included, in South Africa, Nedbank and Standard Bank; in the UAE, Habib Bank; in China, Citibank China and Bank of China; and almost certainly every well-known bank in continental Europe. I insisted that in the UK, Barclays Bank, which has a significant presence in South Africa and Africa,[1] together with Santander, which also has a global footprint, should be given a red-flag warning to check their exposure to Gupta transactions – both direct and indirect. I also argued that it was essential that all UK banks refused to have anything to do with the Guptas or Zumas. I urged the UK government to act and to give the same warning to RBS, Lloyds and any other UK banks – indeed, any bank that had had any contact with the Guptas or Zumas, inadvertently or knowingly, because they were infecting the whole UK financial system.

For over ten years the Guptas had washed their money, I added, aided by a labyrinth of correspondent banks – names that we all bank with. Had these banks closed the Gupta accounts of their own volition even five years before, and not late in the day after political and investigatory journalist pressures, South Africa might not have been brought to its economic knees.

I urged my fellow British parliamentarians to give a loud and clear message that no UK commercial entity should have anything to do with the Guptas or Zumas, and that UK financial institutions should stop being used to pilfer public money from countries around the world and ensure that banks do not put profit before ethics when handling risky money.

By now the global chiefs of KPMG and McKinsey were flying into London to join their UK counterparts in coming to the Lords to meet me. They reported that they had sacked their top South African managers who had failed to act against corrupt public-sector contracts that had brazenly facilitated the Zupta looting. Embarrassed at finding themselves in the global media and political spotlight, they assured me they had cleaned up their acts, and that money obtained from these dodgy contracts would be repaid to South African taxpayers.

To reinforce this point, at the committee stage of the Bill on 12 December, I cautioned 'all our banks which face allegations of money laundering. Usually, their initial stance is to deny, then admit, and then apologise. I caution them that with this disease of money laundering it is better not to deny in the first instance.'

❖

AT another Lords session, on 15 January 2018, again speaking from a Deep Throat draft, I explained that I had referred the international law firm Hogan Lovells, headquartered in London, to the Solicitors Regulation Authority (SRA) for enabling a corrupt money launderer to be returned to his post as second-in-command of the critically important South African Revenue Service (SARS). I asked the SRA to withdraw Hogan Lovells' authorisation as a recognised body and to examine what other disciplinary action could be taken against its leading partners, including withdrawing their permission to practise as solicitors.

I argued that Hogan Lovells had shielded two of the most notorious perpetrators of state capture in South Africa, Tom Moyane, head of SARS, and his deputy, Jonas Makwakwa, from accountability for their complicity in and cover-up of serious financial crimes. In so doing, I said, Hogan Lovells were complicit in undermining South Africa's once revered tax-collection agency and thereby effectively underpinning former president Jacob Zuma and the Gupta brothers in perverting South Africa's democracy, damaging its economy and robbing its taxpayers. When Hogan Lovells was engaged by the corrupt Moyane in September 2016, I said, it was well known that he and Makwakwa were synonymous with then president Jacob Zuma's capture of the state. Hogan Lovells should therefore not have pleaded ignorance as they walked right into that web of corruption and cronyism for a fat fee.

I explained how, in order to help protect himself from 783 counts of corruption, fraud, racketeering and money laundering levelled against him when he came to power in 2009, President Zuma had systematically dismembered and manipulated the once highly functional SARS and the National Prosecuting Authority (NPA). Zuma's key man in this process was, I said, his long-time comrade Tom Moyane, whom he appointed as head of SARS in 2014 and who from day one loyally set about obliterating all of its investigative capacity, with the assistance of his deputy, Jonas Makwakwa. These two turned the institution, which under the leadership of Pravin Gordhan had consistently overdelivered on revenue collection, into one facing a R51-billion (£3 billion) revenue shortfall.

I described how Hogan Lovells had been brought in to investigate Makwakwa's unethical behaviour and became either a willingly gullible or malevolent accomplice, explaining that the firm issued what was regarded as an incomplete, fatally flawed whitewash of a report, which ultimately cleared Makwakwa, despite reams of evidence to the contrary. Makwakwa had answered to only a fraction of the allegations levelled against him, with explanations described by legal experts as 'utter nonsense'. Hogan Lovells' cover-up, I argued, led directly to Moyane's exonerating his deputy and welcoming him back on 30 October 2017 – 'to continue their looting and the dirty work of robbing South African taxpayers'.

But to my mind Hogan Lovells ducked and dived over what I believed to be its complicity in propping up corruption and money laundering in South Africa.[2] I therefore asked the British government to issue an edict that no British-based firms should do any business whatever with any member of Zuma's family, or with any member of the Gupta family, and that any work for any state agency or SOE in South Africa must be undertaken only with total integrity.

Hogan Lovells repeatedly and aggressively denied being party to any collusion, publicly denouncing me for 'misrepresentation'. Their South African chair, Lavery Modise, emailed me with a request to meet in London, which I refused to do until, like the other corporates, he had publicly apologised. He wouldn't and so we never met. Hogan Lovells, in my view, seemed to be taking a lawyers' stance of regurgitating a dodgy client's brief regardless of its validity, especially as in this case they were their very own client. The firm issued comments saying I had failed to understand the work it did for SARS.

The SRA did mount what I was assured was a 'thorough investigation', but then accepted what in my view amounts to Hogan Lovells' specious and transparently expedient defence that it was an international firm for 'branding purposes only'. The UK entity therefore had no direct connection with, let alone responsibility for, the South African one. In other words, if there were any questions to answer, they were local, not global. Looking at its global publicity, you could have fooled me, for the firm had long explicitly projected itself as an international corporate. Clearly, however, the publicity had an impact, for Lavery Modise and his team left the firm in 2019.

❖

BY the time I was able to publicly raise these issues for a global audience, in early January 2018, the tectonic plates of ANC politics had shifted.

Having narrowly won the election to succeed Jacob Zuma as ANC president, Cyril Ramaphosa began moving to establish his authority over a party split right down the middle between his supporters and the devotees of Zuma. He was therefore hemmed in, something people naturally impatient for rapid change seemed not to appreciate. Half of the party's 'top six' leadership were Zuma-ites, including the secretary-general, Ace Magashule, the former premier of the Free State and the subject of a coruscating book by renowned investigative journalist Pieter-Louis Myburgh.[3]

Almost straight after Ramaphosa's victory, the Zupta social-media attacks on me seemed to expire, as if they were exhausted – or maybe now irrelevant. I felt a little safer, though had no illusions that, just as during the apartheid era, any professional wishing to attack or even kill me would in practice be able to do so whatever precautions I took.

The Guptas themselves fled the country, abandoning their plush gated family compound in Johannesburg's exclusive Saxonwold suburb.

A new chapter was to open for a very troubled country, which had gone from hero under Mandela to zero under Zuma.

Corruption

WHEN I was asked to give evidence before the Commission of Inquiry into State Capture, headed by Deputy Chief Justice Raymond Zondo, I submitted a detailed paper, with considerable help from supportive experts (both British and South African).

A few weeks before I appeared on 18 November 2019, Jacob Zuma had brazenly and defiantly denied before Zondo that he'd done anything wrong – his chutzpah was limitless. My focus on his alleged looting was the massive collaboration of international financial institutions, global corporates and foreign governments (notably in India, Dubai and Hong Kong).

Advocate Paul Pretorius – a former banned anti-apartheid activist and student leader – led me through my written evidence, with Judge Zondo occasionally asking questions or seeking clarification. I had prepared carefully, and had been rehearsed by the experts who'd helped draft my statement, because I was concerned I might be out of my depth on the intricacies of financial crime. Fortunately, it went off without a hitch.

I explained how instead of working in partnership with the National Treasury to recover the billions of rands looted from South African taxpayers, much seemingly laundered abroad, international players had turned a blind eye to it. Without that global dimension, I said, state capture could not have been as monumentally lucrative to its perpetrators, the direct and indirect costs of state capture having been estimated at around R1.5 trillion.

According to the United Nations Office on Drugs and Crime, around five per cent of global GDP, or $2 trillion, is laundered each and every year. Developing countries are particularly vulnerable, and it leaves their citizens in perpetual and abject poverty. Unless there is global action and global coordination by governments, businesses, banks and non-governmental organisations, the state capture of South Africa or another country will happen repeatedly.

It was international actors, I argued, who helped corrupt individuals to enjoy their spoils by offering them the means to move their ill-gotten gains out of South Africa, and then sometimes back in, undetected. It was international actors who helped corrupt individuals create complex corporate structures disguising the true ownership of funds and complicating the tracing and repatriation of stolen funds while earning huge fees out of the looting. It was international actors who provided refuge to corrupt individuals and the means to continue their activities through less regulated 'open' economies, such as that of Dubai.

Therefore, international actors across the public and private sectors surely have a duty to strengthen regulations, improve corporate governance, increase transparency and coordinate globally to reduce financial crime, including the recovery and return of stolen funds to South Africa. Without cross-border cooperation and engagement of the public and private sectors, no country will be emancipated from financial crime.

❖

ELECTRONIC banking remains the simplest and fastest means of transferring funds between people and across borders. It allows criminals to move their money to more convenient (often also less regulated) jurisdictions and it 'cleans' the money by mingling it with other funds and disguising its source so that it is easier to spend.

The Guptas, I explained, used a number of international

banks – many of them household names such as HSBC, Standard Chartered and Bank of Baroda – to transfer money, disguise payments and hide the source of their funds. The banks assisted the Guptas by allowing bank accounts to be opened and, in so doing, granting access to the global banking network to transfer illicit funds out of the country and then back in.

Suspicious activities by the Guptas should have been spotted much sooner, or immediately, I argued. These included: secretive transactions to obscure the ownership of the accounts; unexplained payments to and from third parties with little or no apparent connection to the underlying transaction; and the transfer of funds around shell companies, which do not conduct trading and obscure the persons who control them; and unexplained connections with and movement of monies between jurisdictions. All of this, I said, occurred when South African media outlets were exposing corruption under then President Zuma and identifying the Gupta brothers' key role, and when legitimate funds created by the Gupta enterprises were dwarfed by the funds they amassed through illegal activity.

A specific example I cited of a transaction that should have been stopped, or at least investigated by Bank of Baroda South Africa (part of India's state-owned, global Bank of Baroda), was a loan on 18 January 2017 by Trillian Management Consulting (then majority-owned by a Gupta associate, Salim Essa) of R160 million to Centaur Mining (a Gupta-owned company) via Trillian Financial Advisory (a Gupta-owned company). Bank of Baroda simply waved this through.

Similarly, South African government funding for the state-financed Estina dairy project was transferred via the Gupta-controlled Estina (Pty) Ltd to a Standard Chartered account held by Gateway Limited (a Gupta-owned company registered in the UAE) in May, August and September 2013. Standard Chartered did not stop these transactions, despite the fact that government funds were leaving the jurisdiction to a company beneficially owned by the Guptas with no material explanation provided for the suspicious payment structure. Standard Chartered simply waved this through.

Given that banks ought to have access to customer data and transaction data for all accounts they open and transfers they facilitate, they are well placed to monitor the legitimacy of any and all transactions, in addition to having regulatory and moral responsibilities to recognise and stop illegal money flows. But I found a great reluctance from HSBC and Standard Chartered – who cited 'client confidentiality' – to cooperate fully when I specifically asked them to trace and track the money laundered by the Guptas under the Zuma administration.

That is simply unacceptable, in my view, and it is important that banks take full responsibility for monitoring transactions and ensuring that adequate compliance policies and procedures are properly implemented to prevent money launderers from disguising and disseminating their illegal profits and exploiting weaknesses within the banks' infrastructure.

❖

THEN there are the 'professional enablers' – lawyers, consultants, auditors/accountants and estate agents – who 'clean' the money for a fee. Their role is to disguise the source, location and ownership of funds. Lawyers typically assist by setting up complex shell companies enabling money to be moved from one country to another country where there is low transparency. Accountants typically audit incorrectly, leaving suspicious transactions hidden in the accounts. Estate agents typically receive laundered money into their client accounts during property purchases.

Global brand names such as KPMG, Bain & Co and Hogan Lovells in effect assisted the Guptas in their looting from the South

African people. They profited while the Guptas hid stolen funds that could otherwise have been spent on essential public services and on helping to repair the colossal damage caused by apartheid, still a huge deadweight on the country.

KPMG South Africa was responsible for auditing various Gupta companies in South Africa for around 15 years up until March 2016. During that period, it seemingly ignored warnings about the integrity and ethics of the Guptas and accepted the categorisation of certain spending (such as the Sun City wedding in 2013) as 'business expenses' while earning significant fees for performing auditing services (such fees ultimately being paid in looted or laundered funds). Eventually, the firm conducted an internal investigation that led to eight senior South African executives being fired and a promise to donate the R40 million it had earned from auditing Gupta-related companies to anticorruption charities.

Another example is that of Bain, the Boston-based consultancy firm, which was named in the Commission of Inquiry into Tax Administration and Governance (the Nugent Commission) as having 'coached' Tom Moyane on how to capture and manipulate SARS a full year before he was appointed commissioner by then President Zuma. Several of these meetings took pace at Nkandla, Zuma's private 'palace' in KwaZulu-Natal. The Nugent Commission recommended criminal prosecutions against Bain & Co because it found that the firm had engaged in a 'premeditated offensive against SARS': Moyane's interest was to take control of SARS, Bain's simply to make money.

Global firms such as Bain and KPMG have access to client data, and it is high time they established robust compliance policies and procedures to recognise and prevent money laundering and actively educate all their employees about the importance of those policies.

CORRUPTION

❖

CORRUPTION is not only about corrupt politicians and officials. South Africa is a living example of privately owned companies doing business with state criminals in order to win lucrative contracts or other commercial advantages, often in state procurement.

There is also 'javelin-throwing', a process whereby corrupt officials sign off on a lucrative tender, knowing that they will be leaving the employ of government in the near future and will transfer to the beneficiary company as either a director or senior employee.

Then there is the manipulation of the black economic empowerment (BEE) agenda, where BEE companies have been awarded a private or government contract at an agreed price (often an inflated amount to take into account various bribery payments to government officials and associates) without either having to complete a fair bidding process or having to prove their capability to fulfil the terms of the contract. Contracts infected with this form of corruption are rarely performed properly or even sometimes at all.

What happened at Transnet is a good example. To obtain a lucrative contract to supply locomotives to the state-owned ports and rail company, South China Rail reportedly undertook to pay more than £250 million (R5 billion) in bribes to Gupta-linked shell or BEE companies, yet it failed to comply with strict local-content and supplier obligations required to assist in growing the South African economy. Another example is in the Free State under Ace Magashule, by all accounts a Gupta associate; there, the failure to build 11 000 homes for those in dire need was reportedly a direct result of building contracts being awarded to BEE companies run by political cronies with no or little building experience, and would certainly have failed any transparent or fair procurement process.

Then there is the nefarious role played by consultants who engaged in negotiations and brokered deals with evidently corrupt government officials and associates. Global brand names such as SAP and McKinsey earned enormous fees and, in my view, thereby helped with the looting and diversion of scarce taxpayers' money from providing much-needed health care, education and housing in a country still weighed down by the apartheid legacy of mass unemployment, poverty and deliberate under-skilling.

Globalisation has made it easier for criminals to dissipate tainted funds to countries unconnected to the underlying crime, so that they are also drawn into the web of corruption. Without the cooperation and coordination of states, criminals are able to dodge the rule of law by relocating themselves and their stolen funds to another jurisdiction. Criminals often exploit the lack of political will in some states to fund the fight against financial crime, by choosing to locate assets in jurisdictions where regulations are weaker, regulators are underfunded or where there is less transparency around corporate ownership.

Many criminals also attempt to relocate to countries where there is no extradition agreement in place. Up until now, governments have paid lip service to curbing financial crime without actually doing so. The UK and South Africa, for example, both have strict anti-money laundering regulations but the Guptas seem to have easily managed to evade this legislation with the assistance of South African public officials and London-headquartered or -located global banks and professional enablers.

Dubai (where they have a home) is an example of the global reach of the Guptas in safeguarding their wealth and preventing their accounting to authority. So is India (their country of birth, where they also reside) and Hong Kong (through which they allegedly funnelled laundered funds and received kickbacks).

For instance, evidence presented to the Zondo Commission shows that around R52 million was moved from South Africa to

Hong Kong via Homix (a Gupta-owned company) to Morning Star International and YKA International Trading Company (Hong Kong companies). As stated in my written submissions to the Zondo Commission, some of the funds laundered in Hong Kong were used to purchase diamonds via companies such as Simoni Gems (a Hong Kong company linked to the Guptas that received funds from South African Gupta companies). These funds have not yet been repatriated to South Africa, nor have the Hong Kong authorities taken any public action against the Guptas. More than $100 million of the alleged kickbacks received by the Guptas over purchases of locomotives by Transnet were reportedly channelled through the HSBC Hong Kong accounts of their front companies Tequesta and Regiments Asia.

As I detailed in my Zondo Commission submission, the Guptas, after fleeing from South Africa in early 2018, lived in Dubai at Villa L35, Lailak Street, Emirates Hills, identifiable by the Gupta gold crest at the entrance gates and probably purchased with laundered funds. More than three years after they fled, the Guptas have still not been extradited to face trial in South Africa, nor have any monies in Dubai been repatriated to South Africa.

The Guptas are Indian by birth and have a number of family members, businesses and properties in India. They commissioned the building of the £10-million (R200-million) Shiva Dham temple in their hometown of Saharanpur, reportedly using laundered funds, and continued to haemorrhage funds at an alarming rate, including funding a wedding for two of their sons costing R427 million in June 2019. While the Indian authorities claim to have investigated the Guptas, they too have repatriated no funds to South Africa.

I further argued in my Zondo Commission submissions that the active assistance and determined cooperation of diplomats and states is critical if what is left of South Africa's stolen funds is ever to be repatriated, and the extradition of the Guptas to face trial in

South Africa is ever to occur. States must also strengthen regulations and enforce them within their jurisdictional reach to ensure that there is a real deterrent against engaging in illegal activity. It is not enough to establish legislation such as the UK's Bribery Act 2010 and South Africa's own powerful anti-corruption legislation.

I submitted that enforcement and investigative agencies (such as the Serious Fraud Office, National Crime Agency and Financial Conduct Authority in the UK, and the Directorate for Priority Crime Investigation within the South African Police Service and the NPA and the Special Investigations Unit in South Africa) need to be utilising the legislation to conduct investigations and require proper resourcing to do so. Yet in neither country has that been the case. In the UK, these agencies have not had anything resembling the resources required to combat financial crime in recent years, leading to a request in 2019 from the head of the National Crime Agency for an additional £2.7 billion in funding for that agency alone.

Banks and professional enablers should be on the frontline in combatting financial crime, and it should be a source of shame for the world's leading economies that the two groups responsible for facilitating what clearly seems like corrupt practices in foreign countries are headquartered in their jurisdictions (London, New York, Delhi and Shanghai, for instance). How can it be right that the average, honest citizen on a modest or medium income is subject to all manner of frustrating and time-consuming bureaucratic procedures and requirements to open a bank account or legitimately move money, but somehow banks wave through global crime, such as that allegedly perpetrated by the Guptas, their cronies and allies, on a gargantuan scale?

While it might seem counterintuitive to seek assistance from the very entities that, in my view, contributed to state capture and assisted corrupt persons to move stolen funds out of South Africa (HSBC, Standard Chartered, Bank of Baroda, McKinsey,

KPMG, Hogan Lovells, SAP and Bain & Co, to name a few), their involvement is crucial. Funds moved across the world today leave a digital footprint. Banks especially possess the technological and financial clout needed to force change, and that power should be harnessed to assist – not hinder or obstruct – regulators to target their limited resources.

❖

I RECOMMENDED to the Zondo Commission a series of reforms to ensure that it becomes difficult to impossible for criminals to continue to hide behind complex layers of shell companies to obscure true ownerships.

Banks and professional enablers should be required to share otherwise confidential client information between them – something that did not happen over the Zuptas. Significant advances in technology have made it easier than ever to collate, store and share data. Yet financial-crime prevention is thwarted by the failure to share information within banks and professional enablers; between banks and professional enablers; and between banks and professional enablers and states across borders.

Banks and professional enablers should be the first line of defence when it comes to corruption, and a partnership between the private and public sectors is integral to reducing financial crime. Although some sharing of information already occurs, it is paltry and ineffective, and banks should stop hiding behind client confidentiality (or the limits of current reporting systems) and work collaboratively and proactively to share useful data and intelligence on a confidential basis with regulators and enforcement agencies.

In particular, banks and professional enablers must prevent 'passporting', whereby criminals gain access to a financial institution's multinational network through a less regulated jurisdiction or product area. Banks and professional enablers should

269

not be allowed to claim ignorance of the activities of branches placed in jurisdictions in a bank's multinational operations where anti-money-laundering policies and procedures are not as rigorous, or where there are opaque banking and corporate structures.

I gave the example of the South African branch of Bank of Baroda, which was exploited by the Guptas to gain access to its global infrastructure. And when I pointed out before the Zondo Commission that the same was true of Standard Chartered for Dubai, the bank's Johannesburg office protested that it could not be held accountable for the activities of its Dubai office. My rejoinder was to advise: 'When in a hole, stop digging.' Standard Chartered, like HSBC and Bank of Baroda, is a global institution. In each bank, the looted billions were siphoned from their South African offices through their international digital pipelines to offices in Dubai and elsewhere. They cannot be allowed to get away with saying, 'Nothing to do with me, guv.' They are global institutions, culpable of facilitating the money laundering.

Banks and professional enablers should face additional sanctions at both an organisational and an individual level. Licences should be immediately stripped from banks if they consistently fail to meet anti-money-laundering standards. A 'senior manager's regime' should be introduced to ensure personal responsibility. This should include disbarment for money laundering and corruption failures; removal of permission to work for any regulated entity (such as a bank); and fines and perhaps even prison for the most serious offences. This would encourage management to take a more proactive role in combatting financial crime and corruption, especially over state procurement where taxpayers' money is at stake.

Increased protection is needed to ensure that the important and legitimate aims of the BEE programme are not undermined through corrupt manipulation by a few (such as the Guptas).

Contracts with SOEs have been awarded to BEE enterprises unable to properly fulfil those contracts, or indeed to further the aims of the BEE agenda. Therefore, special attention must be paid to better regulating and promoting the BEE programme to ensure that it delivers its intended benefits and is not malevolently manipulated.

Surely there needs to be increased transparency around whether BEE entities have a relevant track record, meet basic skills requirements and satisfactorily fulfil their contract against key performance indicators? Those that exploit the BEE initiative usually create a shell company with very few employees solely to win the contract. In other words, they pervert the admirable and necessary objectives of BEE. Much greater transparency and accountability is therefore essential.

Extradition agreements are another weak point. Some of the main culprits providing a safe haven for corrupt individuals are Dubai, Hong Kong and tax havens in the Caribbean. It is important that money laundering and other types of financial crime are extraditable offences and that the guilty are extradited.

I concluded before the Zondo Commission that making the changes needed to combat financial crime, investigate potential corruption and repatriate stolen funds will not be easy. However, the people of South Africa should never have suffered from such obscene looting and devastation. South Africa had under the Zuptas a corruption near-death experience. And that corruption has lingered on, deeply embedded at all levels of government – from ANC ministers downward to provincial, city and municipal level.

All of this must be fully eradicated if the country is ever to prosper for the many, not just the tiny few – and if the values of the freedom struggle are ever again to be realised.

Future

UNFOLDING a paper napkin while we were talking over dinner in Johannesburg in 2017, Martin Kingston, head of banking group Rothschild & Co in South Africa, and someone with a long ANC-linked pedigree, explained his take on state capture, corruption and cronyism.

'Imagine a series of icebergs,' he said to me, drawing a dozen or so of them. 'This is the largest, the Zuma/Gupta one. But there are many others floating around.'

His ominous point was that, by the end of the catastrophic Zuma decade, corruption had become ubiquitous and, like icebergs, mostly invisible. Simply to blame the Zuptas was to underestimate the extent of the disease infecting South Africa's public and business life. For instance, even late in 2020 I learnt of the 'percentage ministers', the label for those known by insiders to exact, through their relatives or closest appointees, a cut of public contracts for which they were responsible.

If there were any doubt about Martin's graphic illustration, it was revealed in 2020, during the early months of the COVID-19 pandemic, by the naked corruption around the supply of personal protective equipment (PPE) and the delivery of food supplies to starving people. Had the rot set in so deep that South Africa no longer had any sort of moral compass left?

However, South Africa was not alone in this. In England there was an uncanny symmetry between business friends of Tory ministers and the PPE and related contracts their companies were granted to combat the pandemic.

Nevertheless, as former South African trade and industry minister and influential communist Rob Davies points out in his new book,[1] corruption had 'become a significant issue before Zuma's presidency' through the phenomenon of 'tenderpreneurs' seeking inflated public procurement contracts with officials, and politicians seeking and obtaining bribes and kickbacks to grant or receive tenders. This in turn had a debilitating effect on local ANC branches, with factions vying for tenderpreneuring, or gatekeeping. He also argues that the 'extensive financialisation' that followed the global banking crisis of 2008–2009 opened opportunities for corruption because so many functions and services performed in-house in both the public and private sectors were outsourced to new companies.

Nevertheless, it is a puzzle that corrupt rulers like Zuma, Mugabe and many others throughout the world – including in the northern hemisphere – are content to allow their economies to go to the dogs. You might have thought that at the very least they would view economic success and prosperity as in their own selfish interest, not least in providing more lucrative opportunities to plunder. Instead they have a death wish for their own countries because, in today's financially integrated, globalised world, foreign-investor confidence is absolutely critical to create domestic jobs and prosperity.

❖

UNDER Nelson Mandela and Thabo Mbeki, many more jobs were created and prosperity increased, partly because South Africa ranked relatively high in international measures of attractiveness for foreign investors and 'ease of doing business'. Under Zuma, the country was downgraded to near-junk status, inequality widened, growth collapsed and unemployment and poverty soared: experts estimate that his decade in power saw the loss of a shocking 20 per cent of the country's wealth.

'Radical economic transformation' remains essential – as long as it does not amount to taxpayer theft, or 'redistribution' to only a tiny new elite, as that phrase came to mean under Zuma, and as it still means to his disciples and cronies. As the former CEO of Business Leadership South Africa, Bonang Mohale, pointedly warned in May 2019: 'We want to increase the size of the economy, otherwise we will soon be talking about the redistribution of poverty and not the redistribution of wealth.'

Moreover, the debate over 'radical economic transformation' is often conducted as if South Africa was insulated from intense global competition, when no country under today's globalisation can be. For example, *every year* there are 7.5 million new Chinese graduates and 7 million new Indian graduates, mostly in science, engineering, technology and ICT. South Africa annually produces 180 000 new graduates; this is, proportional to population size, only *half* the annual new graduate numbers of these two fast-emerging economic superpowers.

Sadly, South Africa is being undercut – on low cost, high skills and high quality – by many other countries as well. Yet the only way to prosper in today's globalised world is through investment in high skills and new technology, especially with the new industrial revolution of robotics and artificial intelligence. Some experts suggest that in successful economies, two-thirds of today's primary-school children will grow up to do jobs that currently do not exist. COVID-19 has almost certainly accelerated this process, just as it has accelerated digitalisation trends in everything from health and education to banking.

And on education, South Africa's schools have to be fixed quickly, because standards are abysmal. Although the ANC has spent more on education per capita than any other developing nation, and managed to double black school attendance from the apartheid days, black schools have consistently found themselves short of textbooks and decent facilities. This is due as much to incompetent management and corruption as it is to officials at a trade union reportedly involved in a jobs-for-cash racket and protecting bad or lazy teachers. The result: killing opportunities for black children.

Under Zuma, standards plummeted: the World Economic Forum ranked South Africa 138 out of 140 countries for the quality of its education, below desperately poor, undeveloped states such as Burundi, Benin and Mauritania. This is not so much scandalous as criminal – and the product of bad governance and corruption.

❖

NUMEROUS commentators – far better qualified and far more appropriate to offer advice than me – have pronounced on South Africa's future.[2] But a number of areas have struck me as especially important.

For all the good intentions of President Ramaphosa, South Africa's government has been gripped by a frustrating sclerosis. For example, in May 2019 I introduced to its authorities a proposal to recover looted funds from the Gupta family and their enablers, including international banks and companies, on a no-win-no-fee basis. It seemed a no-brainer. An independent litigation funder would not charge the South African Treasury any fees until and unless the recovery of assets was successful.

Senior NPA officials that we met liked the idea, but they were snowed under by more urgent imperatives and needed ministerial clearance. I spoke to several senior ministers who seemed keen, as did other well-placed individuals. But this route had never been taken before, I was told, and it was important to go through due process, especially because lawyers representing the Zumas and others were well versed in exploiting technicalities to trip up legal actions.

Everyone understood that there is always a very short window of opportunity to repatriate stolen funds before they are either spent or dissipated through shell companies and tax havens. They also understood that holding the Guptas to account would send a powerful message to other corrupt individuals, government officials and foreign companies: if you loot, there will be consequences and your gains will not be safe anywhere in the world.

Equally, everyone understood that the NPA had been debilitated during the Zuma era and that it had neither the budget nor the capacity to pursue a complex and expensive global civil litigation exercise against the Guptas. Litigation funders, as I had been briefed by the international private-sector partnership who had sought my help for introductions, are common in both the UK and US. In return for financing costly and complex civil cases, they expect a reasonable percentage of the assets recovered to represent their upfront costs and risk of non-recovery. So South African taxpayers would not pay a single rand until assets were recovered – and, even then, that would be a tiny, negotiated proportion of those recovered funds.

I explained that the specialist groups I was introducing were engaged at the time in the $3-billion claim brought by the Nigerian state against Shell, Eni and JP Morgan. It had already succeeded in repatriating $75 million to Nigerian taxpayers, with much more confidently expected. So there was a successful African precedent. We gave other examples of similar actions in the Caribbean and North Africa. But the project could only operate if the South African state, probably through the NPA, authorised the signing of court documents and other actions necessary to successfully recover the stolen money.

At time of writing this has still not happened, less because of political resistance than lack of capacity available for the presidency and ministers to deliver decisive or innovative outcomes

I experienced something similar in trying to persuade National Treasury to utilise the well-developed mechanism of export credit finance to fund capital projects such as hospitals, energy, transport and other vital infrastructure. Predominantly European countries have supplied this 'government-to-government' model of financing for years, including right across Africa, Latin America and Asia, but not so far for South Africa. Again, it seemed a no-brainer to me when I was asked to introduce the notion to ministers in mid-2019.

Suppose an infrastructure project costs €100 million (R1.8 billion). In accordance with international guidelines, the supplier country provides that capital upfront and it is repayable over ten years at euro interest rates (around three to four per cent and therefore very low by comparison with South African rates). The only string attached is that there has to be a 30 per cent business-supplier content from the country providing the funding. In South Africa's catastrophic financial predicament, the advantages are blindingly obvious: upfront funding from outside during an acute shortage inside; spending in the economy, creating local jobs and growth; two-thirds of the work done by South Africans (including BEE companies); and delivery, for example, of a much-needed hospital or new power station.

The British government, through the UK Export Finance unit in the Department of Trade, offered £3 billion (approximately R600 billion) in 2020, but found great difficulty in getting take-up from anybody in government – as I did. Meanwhile, the economy remained stuck in the doldrums and vital projects the president wanted – and indeed had established the Public-Private Growth Initiative, chaired by Roelf Meyer, to deliver – remained an aspiration only.

As I had discovered as a government minister myself, politicians and above all their civil servants love *process* – setting up task forces, producing policy papers, even introducing new legislation. But the question is, what *output*, what *delivery* results from all that governmental theatre?[3] In South Africa's case, sadly, the answer seems much too little.

SEVERAL other observations seem relevant on South Africa's system of government, which follows a similar model to Britain's, except in one crucial respect: incoming ministers appoint a bevy of their own senior civil servants, and not just a few political advisers. This has opened opportunities for corruption and cronyism, and sometimes closed off expertise and ability. Although, as I experienced, a couple of political advisers to each Cabinet minister are important to assist with delivery, the advantages of a professional and independent civil service are enormous: institutional memory, expertise and (at its best) high standards of integrity are the main ones, and South Africa's public administration is very short of all those.

The country's electoral system is also a problem. It delivers numbers of MPs for each party directly proportional to votes cast, which is a big plus. But a big negative is that those MPs are only accountable to their *party* and not to their *voters*. The ANC's leadership determines who is on the party list and, critically, in what order: the higher up the list, the better the chance of being elected. The merit of constituency-based electoral systems is that MPs have to be accountable to their voters as well and can ultimately be dismissed by them, which provides an important counterweight to party elites, especially corrupt ones. Under Britain's system, MPs are directly elected by their constituencies and that requires local accountability. But it is not proportional, so governments with a majority of MPs are habitually formed on less than half the national vote: a big negative. Maybe South Africa could adopt something like Germany's additional member system, which has a combination of directly elected constituency MPs and ones from their party lists.

Across the world, the fusion of state and party has proved a recipe for corruption. The Leninist model of the party taking power, allegedly on behalf of the people, has in practice proved a poisoned chalice and almost without exception a formula for authoritarianism and corruption. The countries of the former Soviet Union are obvious examples, as are Nicaragua, Zimbabwe, Kenya, Zambia and Angola. Cyril Rampahosa has been hemmed in by Zuma allies, especially party secretary-general Ace Magashule, who was charged with corruption and fraud in 2020, and was suspended in May 2021. The president's ability to appoint ministers on merit and probity, and to govern in the best interests of the country, continues to be constrained by the influential remnants of Zuma acolytes at the top of the ANC – and through it into government.

On the other hand, from my experience in the UK Labour Party, it is important that leaders are accountable to grassroots members so that they remain true to party values and manifestoes. I was part of a generation of Labour activists who, under Tony Benn's leadership, won hard-fought battles in the late 1970s and early 1980s to introduce democratic reforms. Labour leaders and MPs had become too remote from local members and too disdainful of party policies. Empowering members to directly elect the party leader by one-member-one-vote, allowing constituency parties to reselect or reject their local MP between general elections, and granting party members a greater say over policy-making – these were all progressive reforms to ensure Labour ministers did not become state apparatchiks but missionaries for greater social justice and equality.

But fusing party functionaries with the civil service removes an important countervailing power to elitism and therefore corruption. In Zimbabwe, under Robert Mugabe and his successor, Emmerson Mnangagwa, the ruling ZANU-PF became welded to the state, mobilising the army and the security services to protect itself, to subvert democracy and the rule of law, and to loot the country. Jacob Zuma embarked upon the same strategy in South

Africa, and his disciples have ever since battled to maintain that legacy, using their party positions to manoeuvre for state power.

Which also raises the role played by the SACP. With its relatively large membership and disproportionate numbers of ANC MPs and ministers, the SACP also has questions to answer about its culpability in both South Africa's and the ANC's degeneration under Jacob Zuma. It backed his capture of power in 2007 and continued to stick by him until 2017, when it switched to supporting Cyril Ramaphosa. But, as the only communist party across the world to be part of a government in a parliamentary democracy, it has yet to reconcile offering an independent position with sharing responsibility for office and standing for good governance.

❖

THE elephant in the room is why liberation movements, on obtaining power, so often become corrupted – for that happened consistently from Kenya to Zimbabwe, from Angola to Mozambique. And it's not just throughout the African continent, but also in Latin America – look, for instance, at the once inspirational Sandinistas and once heroic Daniel Ortega in Nicaragua.

Ronnie Kasrils tackles this troubling question in his book *A Simple Man*, citing an article, written in 1991 by Rivonia trialist and SACP member Rusty Bernstein, titled 'The corridors to corruption'.[4] Bernstein analysed the shift in Eastern European and African nations from revolutionary fervour to institutionalised corruption. He also talked of factors he described as being 'in embryo in our own South African liberation movement'. That was three years before the ANC obtained power.

Bernstein wrote about 'the subtle process by which the foretaste of power that corrupts seems to be creeping upon us unnoticed. We ignore the warning signs at our peril. Unless we can

280

identify and eliminate the factors which have corrupted good honest leaders and organisations elsewhere we could well repeat the experience of their decline and fall.' Kasrils argues that Bernstein analysed 'the metamorphosis from comrade to minister', of how the experience of taking power could lead revolutionary activists to downgrade their integrity and morality. They could quickly become enveloped by the new lifestyle of the ministerial car and chauffeur, the ministerial residence, the advisers, the bodyguards. Then there is the diplomatic round of champagne and smoked salmon. All of this could so easily prompt a (maybe unconscious) slide into a quite different character for even the most dedicated of liberation activists.

Bernstein's was a salutary analysis of the governing parties of Eastern European communist states becoming alienated from their grassroots and popular support, their leaders insulated by a corrupt lifestyle and authoritarian practices, all of which led to their ignominious collapse, one after another, in 1989.

I don't accept that power automatically or inevitably corrupts; it didn't do so to Nelson Mandela or Julius Nyerere. But the trappings and pressures of power tend to insulate former leaders and activists from their base, and to encourage maintenance of the status quo even when change is urgently needed. That phenomenon in newly independent African states was made worse by the way the former colonial powers resisted majority rule until the last minute, and in some cases sabotaged it on transition – like the Portuguese as they pulled out of Angola's capital, Luanda, pouring concrete into lift shafts.

This is absolutely no excuse for the ANC's slide into corruption, but colonialism and its offspring, apartheid, have a lot to answer for, for resisting majority rule and democracy instead of preparing for it. Democracy is not easy to establish; it has taken centuries of struggle in Britain, and is still far from complete. Colonial powers should all along have been building the basis for a new democratic political dispensation and preparing its foundations, including elementary things such as generous pensions for those losing office so they are not tempted to cling on. But of course colonialism's mandate was the very opposite: to grab power, to keep it, to self-enrich and to plunder.

On winning power, the ANC tried to clean up the rotten apartheid networks of bribery and kickbacks from the state, including the Bantustan governments, in addition to the problem of white entrepreneurs dangling bribes in front of politicians to acquire business footholds.

It is also important to acknowledge that the dominant global economic agenda of neoliberalism and hyperglobalisation opened opportunities for predatory individuals and forces. And they were able to exploit a genuinely motivated policy of BEE to corruptly snatch wealth and resources for themselves and their cronies in the exercise that became known as 'state capture', which even had the effrontery to appropriate the leftist term 'counter-revolutionary' to manipulate gullible opinion against critics of Zuma and his corrupt cronies. It was like turning truth on its head, which was exactly what Bell Pottinger specialised in.

None of that excuses anybody in the ANC from taking the bait, but it does provide a context for ego and ambition triumphing over what was bred into the ANC by its collective leadership during the Tambo-Mandela era – serving the people, not oneself.

❖

AMONG the many emails I received after exposing the international dimension to Zupta state capture were those from 'jaundiced whites', many blaming anti-apartheid activists (sometimes abusively, especially on Twitter) for helping secure the transformation to democracy. It was as if *we* were responsible for the spread of corrupt and dysfunctional government.

Such people may grudgingly have accepted the Mandela presidency but never accepted the consequences, namely, that their grotesquely privileged existence had to end and that, frankly, they were lucky to get off so lightly. Yet, as the Zuma presidency became mired in scandal, they barely concealed their smirks, proclaiming 'I told you so', overlooking their support for apartheid, and the affluence they had enjoyed at the expense of mass misery. Others hectored me over the terrible murders of white farmers, spoiling their case, however, by consistently aligning themselves with Donald Trump and the US alt-right. Was their objective seriously to invite broader support or to feed conspiracy theorists of the global white right as they retreated into their own white laagers?

They also refused to acknowledge the corruption at the heart of the apartheid state. As Hennie van Vuuren argues compellingly in his book *Apartheid, Guns and Money*, 'There was rampant money laundering through supposedly reputable international banks by the state-owned arms company, Armscor ... The current struggle against [Zuma-inspired] corruption in South Africa is undermined by a basic lack of appreciation of the nature of that corruption and the criminal networks that facilitate it – namely, that they are continuities of a profoundly corrupt system that predates the first democratic election.'[5]

❖

THEN there is the role of trade unions – vital in any genuinely free and democratic society, and which in South Africa played an important role in the freedom struggle.

As a lifelong trade unionist, I have been on both sides of the negotiating table, sometimes bargaining on behalf of union members or lobbying for their cause, sometimes representing government as a Cabinet minister. Before I was an MP, I spent 14 years as a research officer helping Britain's Communication Workers Union in tough negotiations, brinkmanship and the occasional strike, when we had to take a stand and defend our members' interests through confrontation rather than cooperation.

But it seems to me that many of South Africa's union leaders are not addressing key issues. They can see how the National Treasury was bled dry through corruption and patronage – and that was before the COVID-19 whiplash. In the 2020 South African public-sector workers' wage dispute, the unions insisted on sticking to a 2018 agreement based on growth expectations for the economy that had meanwhile fallen through the floor. Yet when the finance minister stood firm, Cosatu even talked of 'an act of provocation' akin to 'a declaration of war', and others rejected what they called an attempt to resolve the crisis of capitalism at the expense of public-service workers. But neither addressed the root causes of the problem: a country on the brink of bankruptcy. The South African economy had grown disastrously slowly in recent years, even before the pandemic, hitting tax revenues hard and setting government borrowing on a rising path.

And slow or negative growth makes South Africa's struggle to bring its public finances into balance almost impossible. Higher public debt due to a bigger budget deficit makes potential business investors nervous, causing firms to postpone expansion plans and to hesitate before hiring new workers. So potential jobs fail to materialise and millions of people have to suffer lousy living standards from which they are aching to escape. The better life that the ANC has promised them for decades remains a distant and doubtful prospect, always over the horizon no matter how hard they strive to reach it.

If trade unions don't face up to this they will haemorrhage members, as Britain's experience shows. The Labour government faced a shock fourfold jump in the world oil price in 1974, triggering soaring inflation rates worldwide and forcing it to scurry to the

International Monetary Fund for a loan bailout on tough terms.

The trade unions responded with public-sector strikes and the notorious 'winter of discontent' in 1978–1979, when rubbish rotted in the streets and essential services were paralysed. I well recall at the time as a union research officer and left-wing party activist feeling betrayed by my own Labour government. But the culmination of that confrontation was not the shift to the left I wanted. It was the election of a right-wing government led by Margaret Thatcher, a neoliberal crash programme of huge cuts, decimation of mining and manufacturing, appalling rises in poverty and record levels of post-war unemployment – and trade-union membership plummeting to *under half* its 1979 peak.

Both the trade unions and the country paid a heavy price for clinging to an outdated adversarial industrial-relations system characterised by conflict and mutual suspicion. And South Africa is heading the same way which, as sure as night follows day, will see a collapse in its trade-union membership as well as economic stagnation.

Both countries would be better served by following the German example, where robust cooperation between unions and employers is routine, and no one calls it betrayal. And German union representatives are not industrial pacifists. Far from being 'soft', they are hard-headed and tough. At the height of the 2008–2009 global financial crisis they negotiated earnings freezes or even pay cuts in return for commitments to maintain jobs. Such flexibility can be a boost to a company facing lost orders and cash-flow problems as recession takes hold, and the German economy and German workers weathered that global crisis much better than did Britain's.

The German model of industrial democracy or codetermination has never become the norm for British bosses. The German results speak for themselves: much higher living standards, much greater export success, much stronger manufacturing, world-class training and skills, better social cohesion – and stronger trade unions too.[6]

Forty years ago Britain's unions represented 50 per cent of the UK workforce. Since then they have lost over half their members and two-thirds of their workplace representatives. The union share of the workforce is now 21 per cent and still falling remorselessly, with a miserly 13 per cent in the private sector. Yet Britain's unions have never really faced up to their shrinking support. Blaming globalisation or capitalism or government or greedy bosses will not revive their fortunes or deliver the kind of deals that working people want from unions. South Africa's unions follow the UK example at their peril.

❖

COMPARED with other countries liberated from colonialism, and despite all that has betrayed his legacy, Mandela's ANC generation bequeathed a series of crucial, powerful countervailing forces to elitism, inequality and corruption.

There is hope from a vibrant civil society, forged originally during the anti-apartheid struggle, and resurrected both to challenge any attempt by the ruling ANC to undermine democratic structures and processes, and to demand a renewed leadership in harmony with the Mandela vision. It has embraced a broad coalition of radical activists, trade unionists, human-rights campaigners, feminists, churches and progressive business leaders. Its residual strength is in stark contrast to other African nations, notably Zimbabwe.

Again in contrast to similarly liberated countries, whether in Africa or Latin America, there is a vigorously independent media: outspoken talk radio stations; respected and fearless investigative online publications such as *Daily Maverick* and *BizNews*; and good newspapers such as *Business Day, Mail & Guardian* and *City Press*.

And although cronyism has produced lazy and incompetent public officialdom, large numbers of public servants still work hard, resist corruption and political manipulation, and strive for excellence. Although there may not be enough of them, they provide a platform for a new political leadership to build upon.

The South African judiciary has powers envied by most other democracies, and the Constitutional Court can (and *does*) annul statutes of Parliament that are deemed to contravene the country's Bill of Rights and has not been shy to rule against the president. The country can be very proud of – and grateful for – the strength of its rule of law and the independence of its judiciary.

The country has a solid framework of law, financial regulation and corporate governance, with a relatively wealthy and resilient economy. South Africa also has an influential business sector that anchors the society in an important way and contributes not only to the GDP but to its cultural and voluntary sectors as well. There is also great business entrepreneurialism at the top, though a deeper entrepreneurial culture needs actively to be supported and promoted among small businesses and in the less formal parts of the economy.

But the question for all corporate leaders is not only whether they will actively join the struggle against corruption (from which a minority have benefited) but, equally important, whether they will encourage fundamental economic transformation. It is not possible to do the first credibly without also doing the second. There needs to be a discussion between government, business, the unions and civil society on how best to achieve both aims. Ownership should certainly be spread much more deeply into the workforce so that the number of stakeholders in the economy is expanded exponentially. Focusing on board-level and BEE initiatives alone has not spread wealth and ownership widely enough (and the concentration of ownership in a few hands remains a huge problem in Britain and most other countries too). Equally, risk-takers and entrepreneurs deserve to be rewarded because they create jobs and prosperity.

As part of this project, the South African state needs to be transformed as well. There are around 900 SOEs – most of them inefficient, many bankrupt and leeches on the taxpayer, who should be funding other things such as better education, health and housing. But a neoliberal, small state is not the answer either in the modern age – if it ever was. In the most successful economies the state plays a vital role not simply to provide high-quality public services but to encourage economic growth, in part by actively promoting innovation. A smarter, interventionist, risk-taking state is therefore the answer.[7]

My iPhone's smart technologies were not invented by Apple: the internet, GPS, touch-screen display and Siri voice-activated facility all originated from American state-funded research-and-development programmes. But a private, risk-taking entrepreneurial company such as Apple was needed to bring them to the market in a way that the state could never have done. As John Maynard Keynes wrote in 1926: 'The important thing for government is not to do things which individuals are doing already, and to do them a little better or a little worse; but to do those things which at present are not done at all.'

To succeed, the left (including the ANC whose better elements are on the left) needs to redefine its stance on the state, not least as a credible alternative to the neoliberal 'small state', which will otherwise continue to sweep the board.

But in order to retain taxpayer support, the state needs to be efficient, effective, honest and responsive to public demand, not bloated, hopeless, corrupt and indifferent to citizens' needs – as the South African state has become. It simply isn't sustainable for 70 per cent of tax revenues to go on funding public-sector wages and servicing the national debt. South Africa's citizens, black and white, will not tolerate continued inflation-busting pay rises for public-sector workers while the state's productivity and delivery collapses and private-sector workers suffer real wage declines.

❖

IN democracies, all ruling parties need to face the threat of losing to be kept true. And the opposition, in the form of the Democratic Alliance (DA) and the EFF, inflicted defeats in 2016 on the Zuma-led ANC, especially at city and municipal government level. Worry about losing support in the 2019 national elections was a factor in the switch away from Zuma to Cyril Ramaphosa at Nasrec in December 2017, the ANC's then chief whip, Jackson Mthembu, once a Zuma supporter, told me afterwards.

Admittedly, the DA lost its way once Ramaphosa became president in early 2018, and its neoliberal economic agenda will never answer South Africa's needs or win majority support. Aside from its flawed and confused leadership and lack of clarity about what it really stands for, the DA's economic policy will ultimately prove to be an epitaph unless it presents something credible to voters.

Julius Malema's EFF are deeply damaged populists, their leaders exposed for alleged corrupt dealings, and the party's anti-white, anti-coloured, anti-Indian version of 'Africanism' is so far away from Mandela's non-racial vision (or Sobukwe's or Biko's) that it will never be trusted to run the country. The EFF's menacing attacks on journalists are symptomatic of an ugly totalitarianism. Notwithstanding its pro-poor/anti-elite rhetoric, the EFF is on the right of the left-right spectrum.

There is fertile soil for the emergence of a capable opposition if it rejects the DA's neoliberal economics and the EFF's populist opportunism. For unless the ANC reinvents itself, it will die and it will deserve to do so, even if that takes a while yet – or at least until it is challenged by a credible opposition. And the ANC may

well limp on in office with declining support on a dwindling electoral turnout as voters try to get on with their lives despite bad
governance and the absence of a credible alternative. But unless
it genuinely renews – the hardest thing for any party in power, as
I experienced as a Cabinet minister before Labour became too
complacent and we lost in 2010 – the party is on borrowed time.

❖

NEVERTHELESS, it is important not to forget the progress
South Africa has made from the evil days of apartheid. When
Siya Kolisi captained the Springboks to become 2019 Rugby
World Cup winners, he buried Danie Craven's infamous pledge
during our STST campaign half a century earlier: 'There will be
a black Springbok over my dead body.'

Archbishop Desmond Tutu has always been grounded and
candid in his optimism, and blunt about the failures that followed
the extraordinary Mandela era. But he said after the joyous 2019
Rugby World Cup triumph: 'We are a special country, and an extraordinary people. On days such as this we understand that when
we pull together the sky is the limit. When we believe in ourselves,
we can achieve our dreams.'

Two years earlier, in December 2017, Mandela's widow, Graça
Machel, said that South Africans should stop agonising about how
the country Mandela created had 'slipped through their hands'.
Instead, they should remember his famous words: 'It is in your
hands to make of the world a better place for all.'

Let's hope she is right, because it may be that the anti-apartheid
struggle spawned exceptional figures thrown up in exceptional circumstances. But whenever I return to South Africa, I am entranced
and drawn to return again. Despite the corruption and crony-
damaged dysfunctional public utilities, the country remains an
inspiration: marvellous to visit and joyously transformed from the

evil days of apartheid when I left Pretoria as a teenager in 1966.

The people are mostly warm, courteous and hospitable, and since 1994 have treated me generously. Although other 'public enemies' have long supplanted and downgraded me, I have no illusions that some still hate me ... But I refuse to be a hater myself.

My journey from my Pretoria boyhood has provided many other insights.

I have learnt that if you try to do *too much*, you'll end up doing *too little*, that if you try to do *everything*, you'll end up doing *nothing*. Better to focus on concrete objectives and not to get carried away with grand designs, ideological rhetoric or the supercilious purism of the armchair critic. Instead, as Alan Paton once counselled me, try to be an *all-or-something* person, not an *all-or-nothing* person.

And, as a senior activist once advised me with wisdom and acumen when I was just 20: 'There are too many people in politics mainly motivated for the position, the status, the profile, sometimes even the income. Try always to *do something*, never simply to *be someone*.'

But stick to your principles – even if you have to be pragmatic about achieving them. I tried to do that as a government minister, whatever the many pressures to duck and weave, to evade and avoid, while navigating all the stresses and media firestorms – but it is for others to judge whether I managed that or not.

And always try to make a difference for the better, however small, whoever you are, whenever it is, bearing in mind what the late John le Carré said: 'The fact that you can only do a little is no excuse for doing nothing.' Or as Nelson Mandela expressed it: 'What counts in life is not the mere fact that we have lived. It is what difference we have made to the lives of others.'

South Africans of all colours often ask me despairingly, 'What can I do when we have so many bad politicians and lazy or incompetent public servants?' My reply is to sympathise but gently to correct them by saying that there *are* good politicians despite the bad ones, the gangsters and the chancers. There *are* many dedicated, honest and able public servants, and that everyone can try to be a good teacher, or a good nurse, or a good businessperson, or a good parent, or a good sales assistant, or a good waiter – in short, to do their best whatever they do in life, because, aggregated, that will change things over time.

In teaching leadership and conflict resolution since 2017, first at Wits Business School then at GIBS, I have been struck by the numbers of vibrant, bright students – the majority young black citizens, including hugely talented women – who have the potential to be future leaders of the country, in whatever roles they can play. The question to be fought for is whether the country will allow them and so many others to express that full potential.

But meanwhile I commend to you what my dad told me in 1965 as I sat next to him in the passenger seat of our VW minibus while he drove: 'If change was easy it would have happened a long time ago. Stick there for the long haul.'

We were returning home to Pretoria at the time, and his advice encouraged me both to remain active in politics for six decades and to keep trying to make a difference.

In retrospect, my Pretoria boyhood was formative, cementing values, deepening commitment, moulding character and inserting steel. Despite the harassment, despite the hanging trauma, despite the jailing and banning, despite life under Special Branch siege, those were halcyon days of wonderful parents and close siblings, witnessing and experiencing comradeship, bravery, selflessness, sacrifice, duty, excitement, passion: the best of humanity – and of course, the outdoor life of sport, fun and play in the sun.

I look back on those Pretoria days less as ones of darkness and threat, more of inspiration from special people during a special time.

Notes

Boyhood

1   See Walter Hain, *Apennine War Diary: An Artist's Sketch Book 1944–1945* (Epsom: Brewalda Books, 2015).

Arrest

1   Gordon Winter, *Inside BOSS* (London: Penguin, 1981).

Hanging

1   Randolph Vigne, *Liberals Against Apartheid: A History of the Liberal Party of South Africa, 1953–68* (London: Macmillan Press, 1997).

2   For their story, see my *Ad & Wal: Values, Duty and Sacrifice in Apartheid South Africa* (London: Biteback, 2014).

Exile

1   See Peter Hain and André Odendaal, *Pitch Battles: Sport, Racism and Resistance* (London: Rowman & Littlefield; Johannesburg: Jonathan Ball, 2021).

Militancy

1   For an account, see Peter Hain, *Don't Play with Apartheid* (London: Allen & Unwin, 1971).

2   For a detailed Anti-Apartheid Movement Archives dossier of these mostly illegal operations presented to South Africa's Truth and Reconciliation Commission in November 1997, see www.aamarchives.org/archive/trc-evidence.html and www.aamarchives.org/archive/history/1980s/gov24-memorandum-to-the-home-secretary.html.

Victory

1   See his book on the campaign: Stuart Harris, *Political Football* (Melbourne: Gold Star Publications, 1972).

2   For an account of the campaign, see Larry Writer, *Pitched Battle: In the Frontline of the 1971 Springbok Tour of Australia* (Melbourne: Scribe, 2016).

3   See Trevor Richards, *Dancing on Our Bones: New Zealand, South Africa, Rugby and Racism* (Wellington: Bridget Williams Books, 1999).

4   For a short video of the protest: www.youtube.com/watch?v=ejV2BQpkd8g.

Revenge

1   See Peter Hain, *Political Trials in Britain* (London: Allen Lane, 1984), Chapter 7; Robert Hazell, *Conspiracy and Civil Liberties* (London: Bell, 1974); and Robert Spicer, *Conspiracy* (London: Lawrence and Wishart, 1981).

2   For an account of the case, see Derek Humphry (ed), *The Cricket Conspiracy* (London: National Council for Civil Liberties, 1973).

Thief

1   Kamil tells his buccaneering story in *The Diamond Underworld* (London: Allen Lane, 1979), though he is quixotically Delphic regarding my case.

2   Wyatt's visit took place a week after these allegations surfaced. Four months later Thorpe resigned, and in 1979 was tried and acquitted of conspiracy to murder Scott. His three co-defendants did, however, admit to a conspiracy.

3   See my book *A Putney Plot?* (Nottingham: Spokesman, 1987).

4   Confirmed by, among others, Barrie Penrose and Roger Courtiour, *The Pencourt File* (London: Secker & Warburg, 1978).

5   See, especially, Stephen Dorril and Robin Ramsay, *Smear!* (London: Fourth Estate, 1991); see also Philip Murray, 'South African Intelligence, The Wilson Plot and Post-Imperial Trauma', in Patrick Major and Christopher R Moran (eds), *Spooked: Britain, Empire and Intelligence since 1945* (Newcastle: Cambridge Scholars, 2009).

6   See Peter Wright, *Spycatcher* (Sydney: Heinemann, 1987).

7   Chapman Pincher, *Inside Story* (London: Sidgwick & Jackson, 1978). For confirmation that elements in MI5 and the CIA sought to discredit Wilson and bring down the Labour government, see David Leigh, *The Wilson Plot* (New York: Pantheon Books, 1988).

8   See Hennie van Vuuren, *Apartheid, Guns and Money* (London: Hurst & Co; Johannesburg: Jacana, 2017).

9   From my contemporaneous note of the conversation.

Secret Missions

1   For his account of this episode, see Donald Woods, *Asking for Trouble* (London: Victor Gollancz, 1980). The copy he gave me is inscribed: 'To Peter whom I met on the road to Damascus.'

2   For an insider account by my co-author of these developments, see Hain and Odendaal, *Pitch Battles*.

3   See Hain and Odendaal, *Pitch Battles*.

4   See Robert Harvey, *The Fall of Apartheid* (London: Macmillan, 2003); and the film *Endgame* (2009).

5   For the full background, see Hain and Odendaal, *Pitch Battles*.

6   See my biography: *Mandela: His Essential Life* (London: Rowman & Littlefield, 2018).

Returnings

1   *Mike Terry, An Extraordinary Man* (Sheffield, 2009, private publication); and www.aamarchives.org.

Betrayal

1   Having been driven out of South Africa by one of the British Anti-Apartheid Movement's most successful campaigns, Barclays returned after 1994.

2   It should be noted that Hogan Lovells consistently denied these accusations. The SRA refused to take action and the South African Law Society of the Northern Provinces ruled that the firm's South African office did not commit professional misconduct.

3 Pieter-Louis Myburgh, *Gangster State: Unravelling Ace Magashule's Web of Capture* (Cape Town: Penguin, 2019).

Future

1 Rob Davies, *Towards a New Deal: A Political Economy of the Times of my Life* (Johannesburg: Jonathan Ball, 2021).

2 Including Richard Calland, Somadoda Fikeni, Steven Friedman, Mark Gevisser, William Mervin Gumede, Adam Habib, Justice Malala, Aubrey Matshiqi, Moeletsi Mbeki, Njabulo Ndebele, Lovelyn Nwadeyi and Max du Preez.

3 See my memoir *Outside In* (London: Biteback, 2012), especially Chapter 9, 'Ministers and Mandarins'.

4 Ronnie Kasrils, *A Simple Man: Kasrils and the Zuma Enigma* (Johannesburg: Jacana, 2017).

5 Van Vuuren, *Apartheid, Guns and Money.*

6 See, for example, John Kampfner, *Why the Germans Do it Better* (London: Atlantic Books, 2020).

7 See my *Back to the Future of Socialism* (Bristol: Policy Press, 2015); and Mariana Mazzucato, *The Entrepreneurial State: Debunking Private vs Public Sector Myths* (London: Anthem Press, 2013).

Main sources

Hain, Peter. *Don't Play with Apartheid* (London: Allen & Unwin, 1971).
— *Political Trials in Britain* (London: Allen Lane, 1984).
— *A Putney Plot?* (Nottingham: Spokesman, 1987).
— *Outside In* (London: Biteback, 2012).
— *Ad & Wal: Values, Duty and Sacrifice in Apartheid South Africa* (London: Biteback, 2014).
— *Mandela: His Essential Life* (London: Rowman & Littlefield, 2018).
Hain, Peter and André Odendaal. *Pitch Battles: Sport, Racism and Resistance* (London: Rowman & Littlefield; Johannesburg: Jonathan Ball, 2021).
Hain, Walter. *Apennine War Diary: An Artist's Sketch Book 1944–1945* (Epsom: Brewalda Books, 2015).
Humphry, Derek (ed). *The Cricket Conspiracy* (London: National Council for Civil Liberties, 1973).
Myburgh, Pieter-Louis. *Gangster State: Unravelling Ace Magashule's Web of Capture* (Cape Town: Penguin, 2019).
Richards, Trevor. *Dancing on Our Bones: New Zealand, South Africa, Rugby and Racism.* (Wellington: Bridget Williams Books, 1999).
Winter, Gordon. *Inside BOSS* (London: Penguin, 1981).
Woods, Donald. *Asking for Trouble* (London: Victor Gollancz, 1980).
Writer, Larry. *Pitched Battle: In the Frontline of the 1971 Springbok Tour of Australia* (Melbourne: Scribe, 2016).

Index